Principles in Practice

The Principles in Practice imprint offers teachers concrete illustrations of effective classroom practices based in NCTE research briefs and policy statements. Each book discusses the research on a specific topic, links the research to an NCTE brief or policy statement, and then demonstrates how those principles come alive in practice: by showcasing actual classroom practices that demonstrate the policies in action; by talking about research in practical, teacher-friendly language; and by offering teachers possibilities for rethinking their own practices in light of the ideas presented in the books. Books within the imprint are grouped in strands, each strand focused on a significant topic of interest.

Adolescent Literacy Strand

Adolescent Literacy at Risk? The Impact of Standards (2009) Rebecca Bowers Sipe
Adolescents and Digital Literacies: Learning Alongside Our Students (2010) Sara Kajder
Adolescent Literacy and the Teaching of Reading: Lessons for Teachers of Literature (2010) Deborah Appleman
Rethinking the "Adolescent" in Adolescent Literacy (2017) Sophia Tatiana Sarigianides, Robert Petrone, and Mark A. Lewis
Restorative Justice in the English Language Arts Classroom (2019) Maisha T. Winn, Hannah Graham, and Rita Renjitham Alfred

Writing in Today's Classrooms Strand

Writing in the Dialogical Classroom: Students and Teachers Responding to the Texts of Their Lives (2011) Bob Fecho
Becoming Writers in the Elementary Classroom: Visions and Decisions (2011) Katie Van Sluys
Writing Instruction in the Culturally Relevant Classroom (2011) Maisha T. Winn and Latrise P. Johnson
Writing Can Change Everything: Middle Level Kids Writing Themselves into the World (2020) Shelbie Witte, editor
Growing Writers: Principles for High School Writers and Their Teachers (2021) Anne Elrod Whitney
Cultivating Young Multilingual Writers: Nurturing Voices and Stories in and beyond the Classroom Walls (2023) Tracey T. Flores and María E. Fránquiz

Literacy Assessment Strand

Our Better Judgment: Teacher Leadership for Writing Assessment (2012) Chris W. Gallagher and Eric D. Turley
Beyond Standardized Truth: Improving Teaching and Learning through Inquiry-Based Reading Assessment (2012) Scott Filkins
Reading Assessment: Artful Teachers, Successful Students (2013) Diane Stephens, editor
Going Public with Assessment: A Community Practice Approach (2018) Kathryn Mitchell Pierce and Rosario Ordoñez-Jasis

Literacies of the Disciplines Strand

Entering the Conversations: Practicing Literacy in the Disciplines (2014) Patricia Lambert Stock, Trace Schillinger, and Andrew Stock
Real-World Literacies: Disciplinary Teaching in the High School Classroom (2014) Heather Lattimer

Doing and Making Authentic Literacies (2014) Linda Denstaedt, Laura Jane Roop, and Stephen Best

Reading in Today's Classrooms Strand

Connected Reading: Teaching Adolescent Readers in a Digital World (2015) Kristen Hawley Turner and Troy Hicks
Digital Reading: What's Essential in Grades 3–8 (2015) William L. Bass II and Franki Sibberson
Teaching Reading with YA Literature: Complex Texts, Complex Lives (2016) Jennifer Buehler

Teaching English Language Learners Strand

Beyond "Teaching to the Test": Rethinking Accountability and Assessment for English Language Learners (2017) Betsy Gilliland and Shannon Pella
Community Literacies en Confianza: *Learning from Bilingual After-School Programs* (2017) Steven Alvarez
Understanding Language: Supporting ELL Students in Responsive ELA Classrooms (2017) Melinda J. McBee Orzulak
Writing across Culture and Language: Inclusive Strategies for Working with ELL Writers in the ELA Classroom (2017) Christina Ortmeier-Hooper

Students' Rights to Read and Write Strand

Adventurous Thinking: Fostering Students' Rights to Read and Write in Secondary ELA Classrooms (2019) Mollie V. Blackburn, editor
In the Pursuit of Justice: Students' Rights to Read and Write in Elementary School (2020) Mariana Souto-Manning, editor
Already Readers and Writers: Honoring Students' Rights to Read and Write in the Middle Grade Classroom (2020) Jennifer Ochoa, editor

Children's and YA Literature Strand

Challenging Traditional Classroom Spaces with YA Literature: Students in Community as Course Co-Designers (2022) Ricki Ginsberg
Restorying Young Adult Literature: Expanding Students' Perspectives with Digital Texts (2023) James Joshua Coleman, Autumn A. Griffin, and Ebony Elizabeth Thomas
Deepening Student Engagement with Diverse Picturebooks: Powerful Classroom Practices for Elementary Teachers (2023) Angie Zapata

Technology in the Classroom Strand

Reimagining Literacies in the Digital Age: Multimodal Strategies to Teach with Technology (2022) Pauline S. Schmidt and Matthew J. Kruger-Ross
Literacies Before Technologies: Making Digital Tools Matter for Middle Grades Learners (2023) Troy Hicks and Jill Runstrom

Deepening Student Engagement with Diverse Picturebooks

Powerful Classroom Practices for Elementary Teachers

Angie Zapata
University of Missouri

National Council of Teachers of English

340 N. Neil St., Suite #104, Champaign, Illinois 61820
www.ncte.org

Staff Editor: Cynthia Gomez
Imprint Editor: Cathy Fleischer
Interior Design: Victoria Pohlmann
Cover Design: Pat Mayer
Cover Images: Angie Zapata

©2023 by the National Council of Teachers of English.

All rights reserved. No part of this publication may be reproduced or transmitted in any form or by any means, electronic or mechanical, including photocopy, or any information storage and retrieval system, without permission from the copyright holder. Printed in the United States of America.

It is the policy of NCTE in its journals and other publications to provide a forum for the open discussion of ideas concerning the content and the teaching of English and the language arts. Publicity accorded to any particular point of view does not imply endorsement by the Executive Committee, the Board of Directors, or the membership at large, except in announcements of policy, where such endorsement is clearly specified.

NCTE provides equal employment opportunity (EEO) to all staff members and applicants for employment without regard to race, color, religion, sex, national origin, age, physical, mental or perceived handicap/disability, sexual orientation including gender identity or expression, ancestry, genetic information, marital status, military status, unfavorable discharge from military service, pregnancy, citizenship status, personal appearance, matriculation or political affiliation, or any other protected status under applicable federal, state, and local laws.

Every effort has been made to provide current URLs and email addresses, but because of the rapidly changing nature of the web, some sites and addresses may no longer be accessible.

Library of Congress Control Number: 2023934387

Dear Reader,

As a former high school teacher, I remember the frustration I felt when the gap between Research (and that is how I always thought of it: Research with a capital R) and my own practice seemed too wide to ever cross. So many research studies were easy to ignore, in part because they were so distant from my practice and in part because I had no one to help me see how that research would make sense in my everyday practice.

That gap informs the thinking behind this book imprint. Designed for busy teachers, Principles in Practice publishes books that look carefully at NCTE's research reports and policy statements and puts those policies to the test in actual classrooms. The goal: to familiarize teachers with important teaching issues, the research behind those issues, and potential resources, and—most of all—make the research and policies come alive for teacher-readers.

This book is part of the strand that focuses on Children's and YA Literature. Each book in this strand highlights a different way to think about this topic—whether you're a classroom teacher or an English educator—and is organized in a similar way: immersing you first in the research principles surrounding teaching children's and YA literature (as laid out in the NCTE position statement *Preparing Teachers with Knowledge of Children's and Young Adult Literature*) and then taking you into actual classrooms to see how the principles play out. Each book closes with a teacher-friendly annotated bibliography to offer you even more resources.

Good teaching is connected to strong research. We hope these books help you continue the good teaching that you're doing, think hard about ways to adapt and adjust your practice, and grow even stronger and more confident in the vital work you do with kids every day.

Best of luck,

Cathy Fleischer
Imprint Editor

Contents

Acknowledgments xiii

Preparing Teachers with Knowledge of Children's and Young Adult Literature xv

Chapter 1 . . . . Shifting Our Classroom Literature Landscape 1

                    Interrogating Our Positionalities: Investing in Our Growth as Teachers of Diverse Literature 8

                    A Brief History: Sustained Calls for the Radical Inclusion of Diverse Literature 10

                    Understanding and Enacting a Critical Literature Response Framework 14

                          Classroom Conditions for Enacting a Critical Literature Response Framework 15

                          Classroom Commitments for Enacting a Critical Literature Response Framework 17

                    Make It Yours 22

Chapter 2 . . . . Toward a Critical Literature Response Framework 25

                    Unpacking Our Positionalities 27

                    Getting to Know Mariposa Street Elementary School 29

                    Classroom Practices to Support a Critical Literature Response Framework 31

                          Foundational Classroom Practices Underlying a Critical Literature Response Framework 32

                          Digging Deeper into Powerful Critical Literature Response Classroom Practices 33

                    Enlivening a Critical Literature Response Framework: Starting Your Journey 46

                    Professional Resources to Support a Critical Literature Response Framework in the Classroom 47

                          Social Media 47

	Publishing Houses	50
	Resources for Text Selection	52
	Professional Reading	52
	National Book Awards	55
Chapter 3	Becoming Critical Picture Readers	57
	Entering Lottie's First-Grade Classroom	59
	Enlivening a Critical Literature Response in an Early Childhood Classroom	60
	Classroom Approach 1: Valuing Young Children as Knowing and Capable	61
	Classroom Approach 2: Supporting an Expansive View of Early Reading	63
	Focused Literature Exploration: What Makes Family?	64
	Launching Book Floods and Picture Reading with Picturebooks	65
	Sharing Literary Arrows	66
	Conferring with Readers during Book Flood	67
	Whole-Group Share	68
	Critical Encounters with Picturebooks	70
	Critical Encounter 1: Interrogating Skin Shade through Visual Thinking Strategies	70
	Critical Encounter 2: Inferring Critical Meaning from Illustration	74
	Critical Encounter 3: A Teacher's Reflections toward Change	78
	What Critical Encounters Can Teach Us	80
	Tips to Support Critical Encounters in Literature with Young Children	80
Chapter 4	Talking to, with, and across Wide and Varied Picturebook Collections	83
	Entering Kara's Fourth-Grade Classroom	86
	Enlivening a Critical Literature Response Framework in an Elementary Classroom	88
	Classroom Approach 1: Eliciting More In-Depth Talk from Readers	88
	Classroom Approach 2: Growing Vocabulary to Discuss Complex Issues	90

Contents

                Focused Literature Exploration: Border-Crossing Experiences
                in the United States 92

                Preparing and Launching Wide and Varied Picturebook
                Collections 93

                     Interpreting and Interrogating Motifs and Symbols in
                     Illustrations. 96

                   Musical Pairings 97

                   Amplifying Students' Everyday Connections across
                   Literature and Their Lives 98

                Critical Encounters with Picturebooks 102

                   Critical Encounter 1: Questioning Themes of Meritocracy
                   through Picturebooks. 102

                   Critical Encounter 2: Reading Power in Illustration 105

                   Critical Encounter 3: Challenging Misconceptions of
                   Blackness. 107

                What Critical Encounters Can Teach Us 108

                   Tips to Support Critical Encounters in Literature with
                   Young Children. 109

Chapter 5. . . . . Inviting Multilingual and Multimodal Literature Response . . . 111

                Entering Whitney's Fifth-Grade Classroom 114

                   Getting the "Long Conversation" Started as Readers
                   and Writers 114

                Enlivening Critical Literature Response in an Upper-Elementary
                Classroom. 117

                   Classroom Approach 1: Supporting an Expansive View
                   of Language. 118

                   Classroom Approach 2: Exploring Relationships between
                   Language and Identity 119

                Focused Literature Exploration: Linguistically Diverse
                Picturebooks as Mentor Texts. 121

                Launching Multilingual and Multimodal Literature Response . 122

                   Reading Voices, Reading Identities, Resisting Assumptions
                   about Language and Identity. 122

                   Language Maps and Lists: Documenting Our Linguistic
                   Toolkits 124

                   Language and Identity Self-Portraits 126

                Critical Encounters with Picturebooks 128

                   Critical Encounter 1: Rethinking Our Reading of Language
                   Differences 128

        Critical Encounter 2: Helping Students Deconstruct
        Assumptions 131

        Critical Encounter 3: Making Claims into Your Language
        and Identity 132

    What Critical Encounters Can Teach Us 134

        Tips to Support Critical Encounters in Literature with
        Young Children 134

Chapter 6 . . . . Launching a Critical Literature Response Framework in
    Your Classroom 137

    Collaboration and Outreach: Building Your Critical Literature
    Response Collaborative 141

    Questions Revealed 144

    Let's Do This! 147

Annotated Bibliography 149

Notes 155

References 157

Index 161

Author 167

And we jumped
        and we ran
            and we played
                    and the whole wide wide world felt like it belonged to us.

And some days we scraped our knees. But there was always an older kid nearby who'd say **It's gonna be all right** and might even tell us stories about being our age, about stitches and broken arms.

And if someone said **Boys don't cry**, some big boy always said **Oh yeah?** and had a story about the time he cried and cried until our eyes grew wide. Our hurt knees forgotten.

There was always some new kind of fun. We built forts out of enormous boxes then admired what we made together.

                                    We said **You sure can draw**
                                      And **You sure can build**
                                    And **You sure can jump**
                                    And **You sure can sing.**
                                            and we meant it.

    —Excerpt from *The World Belonged to Us* (2022) by Jacqueline Woodson, illustrated by Leo Espinosa

Acknowledgments

This book is written for educators who hold the spirit of children in their hearts, who enter new experiences with wonder and awe, curiosity, and joy. This book is written for children who feel like they belong to the world and the whole wide world belongs to them. When we feel like we belong to the world and the whole wide world belongs to us in the ways Jacqueline Woodson reminds us in the excerpt from her poem that opens this book, then we carry the desire to care and to make for a better world at the forefront of our work, and we understand the significance of better representation in the literature we share with children.

This book is the culmination of a yearlong collaborative inquiry research project focused on how teachers are sharing picturebooks that portray a diversity of racial, linguistic, ethnic, and community experiences. During this tumultuous season in education that currently witnesses a surge of book bans and censorship, the narrowing of curricular mandates and adopted materials, and the burden of worry imposed by a small but vocal, powerful few who live in fear of difference, my energy and passion for diversity in children's picturebooks has been sustained by the mighty number of children, families, teachers, librarians, and other education professionals who continue to embrace the power of reading pictures and words. May this book be another tool you carry with you on your journey toward anti-oppressive education. May it help you feel invigorated with fresh approaches and energized with a rejuvenated spirit as an educator and picturebook curator for children's reading lives.

My editor and the NCTE book production team exercised tremendous patience as they awaited this publication. Through a global pandemic and global racial justice movements; falling in love and getting married; selling, buying, and moving into a new home; undergoing two major surgeries; dealing with the loss of beloved pets; and surviving the demands of being a first-time primary investigator for two multisite grants (all of which happened in the same two years), somehow this book got written. Cathy Fleischer—thank you for your reading and rereading of chapter after chapter, providing feedback and care. My family and I will never forget your kindness and guidance as a book editor for this first-time book author.

Here in Missouri, I have the good fortune of a tremendous personal-professional support network. I am grateful to my literacy colleagues Rob Petrone and Mike Metz, who encouraged me to keep writing. The voices of my current and previous doctoral student research partners and coauthors stayed with me as I wrote, including those of Professors Selena Van Horn and Monica Kleekamp and soon-to-be-professor Adrianna Ybarra González. I want to acknowledge my research partnerships with Professors Sarah Reid and Mary Adu-Gyamfi, whose work and contributions to the data collection, archive, and analysis have made this book possible. They endured the yearlong process of a multisite research project with me and received my worrywart questions about photos and artifacts (and they still take my calls!). The data featured in this book are possible only because of their work on the project. Thank you, Mary and Sarah, for reminding me about the importance of entering research with laughter, love, and humility.

Thank you to my lifelong teacher partners Nancy Valdez-Gainer, Corinna Bliss Green, Misha Fugit, Daryl Moss, and now the Picturebook Collective that has evolved into something very real right here in Missouri! Their willingness to share their practice, let me learn from them and think alongside them, has fed my teacher and researcher soul and led me to Whitney, who led me to Kara, and soon after, to Lottie, all of whom you will know intimately after reading this book. Whitney, Lottie, and Kara—your excellence as educators breathes life into this book; thank you for allowing me to learn with and from you.

To my family—my mother, my father, and my sisters, Marisa and Ethel, and their children, who remind me every day that our family stories matter. And Galen—there's not a pirate story in this book, but here you will find a pirate ship and pirate treasure. See? 🏴‍☠️ 💰. Thank you for standing next to me on this voyage, for reminding me to take one thing at a time, especially during such an unbelievable first three years together. Eres el amor de mi vida, te amo.

Preparing Teachers with Knowledge of Children's and Young Adult Literature

This statement, formerly known as **Preparing Teachers with Knowledge of Children's and Adolescent Literature**, *was updated in July 2018 with the new title,* **Preparing Teachers with Knowledge of Children's and Young Adult Literature.**

Originally created by NCTE Children's Literature Assembly (CLA), 2004, revised July 2018

OVERVIEW

Purpose: Given increased calls for diversity in the English language arts curriculum and growing awareness of the need for young people to see themselves in the books they read, NCTE has commissioned an updated statement on preparing teachers with knowledge of children's and young adult literature.

Key Message: Research shows that when students are given the chance to read books that respect the questions, challenges, and emotions of childhood and adolescence, they read with greater interest and investment (Buehler, 2016; Mueller, 2001). Research also shows that teachers who are readers themselves do a better job of engaging their students in reading (Morrison, Jacobs, & Swinyard, 1999). Thus, teacher educators must support preservice teachers as they build rich and deep knowledge of children's and young adult literature over the course of their certification programs. Then teachers must invest in their own continued growth, learning, and development as children's and young adult literature advocates throughout their professional lives.

Context: A committee of English educators has updated NCTE's 2004 statement *Preparing Teachers with Knowledge of Children's and Adolescent Literature* by calling teachers at all stages of their careers to cultivate knowledge of books for young people, be readers of these books themselves, affirm diversity in book selection, and teach children's and young adult literature in ways that honor the books' literary quality as well as their potential to spark personal and social transformation.

STATEMENT

Evidence indicates that teachers' knowledge of children's and young adult literature is inconsistent and uneven from community to community, school to school, and classroom to classroom. Preservice teachers do not read any more than the general population (McKool & Gespass, 2009). Many of today's teachers have never taken a class in children's and young adult literature, and some states have eliminated the requirement for a dedicated course in children's and/or young adult literature for teaching certification. A growing number of schools no longer employ a librarian, who may be the only professional in the building who has formal training in children's and young adult literature, collection development, and matching young readers with books. Without librarians, the burden for reading advisory and material selection falls to classroom teachers, who often lack the training needed to perform these tasks.

Therefore, teacher education programs have the opportunity—and the responsibility—to

- *introduce* preservice teachers to books for children and teens;
- *develop* preservice teachers' understanding of the inherent value of these books for both general reading and classroom use;
- *raise* preservice teachers' awareness of the power of these books to affirm lived experience, create empathy, catalyze conversations, and respect the questions, challenges, and emotions of childhood and adolescence;
- *call* preservice teachers to embrace the roles of reading advocate and book matchmaker alongside their work as implementers of curriculum;
- *inspire* preservice teachers to commit to reading these books throughout their professional lives;
- *cultivate* in preservice teachers a commitment to teaching these books in ways that honor their literary quality as well as their potential to spark personal and social transformation;
- *build* preservice teachers' capacity for continued growth, learning, and development as advocates of children's and young adult literature.

As an organization, NCTE compels teachers at all stages of their careers to invest in books for young people—as readers of those books and as advocates for their worth in the classroom.

Recommendations

NCTE recommends that teacher educators and teachers commit to the following four principles in the service of increasing their ability to teach and advocate for children's and young adult literature.

1. Know the literature.

Preservice teachers should cultivate book knowledge throughout various methods courses and across their entire teacher preparation program, regardless of state certification requirements. They should develop broad and sustained knowledge of quality books in the fields of children's and young adult literature, including fiction, nonfiction, and multimodal texts.

At the same time, they should build knowledge of resources—including review journals, websites and blogs, social media discussions, book awards, and author appearances at local libraries and bookstores—that can provide them with information about quality new books and their potential for classroom use and reading advisory.

They should also invest in relationships with librarians and organizations such as NCTE and ALAN (Assembly on Literature for Adolescents of NCTE) that can help them build capacity to discuss and recommend books, evaluate literature, remain current, and discover new ways to teach children's and young adult literature effectively.

2. Be readers.

Teachers who are engaged readers do a better job of engaging students as readers. According to Morrison, Jacobs, and Swinyard (1999), "perhaps the most influential teacher behavior to influence students' literacy development is personal reading, both in and out of school" (p. 81). Teachers should commit to leading literate lives and becoming connected to reading communities—whether in person or through social media—that support them as readers and literacy professionals. Teachers should understand the value of different modes and platforms for reading (Garcia & O'Donnell-Allen, 2015) and build their capacity to read with a critical, discerning eye (Newkirk, 2011).

3. Affirm diversity and exercise critical literacy.

In alignment with NCTE's Resolution on the Need for Diverse Children's and Young Adult Books (2015), NCTE challenges teachers and teacher educators to assume a transformative activist stance (Stetsenko, 2016) that supports a future of equality for all youth by engaging students with diverse books, which offer readers what scholar Rudine Sims Bishop (1990) calls windows, mirrors, and sliding glass doors. It is essential that youth have access to books in which they can see themselves and engage with the lives of others (see, for example, platforms created by the current and former National Ambassadors for Young People's Literature, including Jacqueline Woodson, Gene Luen Yang, and Walter Dean Myers). NCTE believes that books help readers transform their lives and expand their visions of the world.

Nevertheless, there is a dearth of diverse books for youth in the United States as seen in yearly statistics about trends in multicultural children's book publishing prepared by the Cooperative Children's Book Center (CCBC) of the School of Education at the University of Wisconsin-Madison. The #WeNeedDiverseBooks and #ReadInColor social media campaigns have illuminated the paucity of diverse books in the marketplace. Although the CCBC recently observed that children's picture books feature an increased number of characters with "brown skin . . . of unspecified race or ethnicity, with no visible culturally specific markers in either the story or the art," the CCBC questions whether books with racially ambiguous characters provide actual windows, mirrors, and sliding doors for today's readers (Horning, Lindgren, Schliesman, & Tyner, 2018). NCTE joins the CCBC in urging educators to not only advocate for more authentically diverse children's and young adult books from US publishers, but also to support authors, illustrators, publishers, and booksellers whose work represents multiple perspectives and cultural diversity in the lives of all children.

In addition to being advocates and supporters of diverse literature for youth, educators who assume a transformative activist stance must build their capacities for discernment and critical evaluation so they are prepared to choose children's and YA books wisely and strategically from the books available to them. Simply because a book features diverse characters does not mean that the book endorses equality and/or cultural understanding (Apol, Sakuma, Reynolds, & Rop, 2003; Dávila, 2012). For example, some popular works of contemporary, "multicultural" realistic fiction privilege the assumption that all residents of the United States should embrace dominant mainstream culture (e.g., *My Name is Yoon* [Recorvitis, 2003]; *One Green Apple* [Bunting, 2006]). Some of these books reinforce assimilation social narratives (Yoon, Simpson, & Haag, 2010) and/or endorse monocultural language and identity (Ghiso & Campano, 2013). Educators and students should collectively cultivate critical literacy practices to critique the social narratives that are endorsed by the books they select (Leland, Lewison, & Harste, 2012; Morrell, 2007) and talk back to the literature (Enciso, 1997).

Educators who affirm diversity and exercise critical literacy as part of a transformative activist stance recognize that they are always learning and expanding their capacities for transformation. They are open to guiding difficult discussions about inequality with students and are willing to tolerate the possibilities of "wobbling" while they explore uncharted territories with students (e.g., Fecho, 2005; Garcia & O'Donnell-Allen, 2015). They recognize that children's books are political (Nodelman, 2008; Stephens, 1992) and are the artifacts of the authors', illustrators', and/or publishers' views of the world (Willis & Harris, 2003) and/or US history (Thomas, Reese, & Horning, 2016). Moreover, these educators follow national conversations via media and blogs about diverse books, especially related to issues of power and representation (e.g., Reading While White; American Indians in Children's Books).

4. Use appropriate pedagogy.

Teaching children's and young adult literature is about more than getting students to fall in love with reading. Preservice teachers also need to learn appropriate and effective strategies for helping students find books that will engage them as readers and as participants in critical, significant conversations about their lives (NCTE, 2006; Tschida, Ryan, & Ticknor, 2014). This requires a deep knowledge of excellent books and the willingness to carefully curate a classroom library that provides appropriate choices for all students (Crisp, Knezek, Quinn, Bingham, Girardeau, & Starks, 2016; NCTE, 2017). Preservice teachers also need to know evidence-based strategies for supporting student knowledge of literary crafting—that is, how authors develop characters, construct plots, and employ other literary elements to create an exemplary work. Examining literary craft does not mean that the focus is on dissecting a book's structure or meaning. Rather, teachers should be skilled at helping students develop a common language for determining what makes a book excellent literature. Finally, teachers need to know how to advocate for the freedom and autonomy to create classrooms that support research-based pedagogical strategies for teaching children's and young adult literature (Mathis et al., 2014; NCTE Children's Literature Assembly, 2004).

WORKS CITED

Apol, L., Sakuma, A., Reynolds, T. M., & Rop, S. K. (2003). "When can we make paper cranes?" Examining pre-service teachers' resistance to critical readings of historical fiction. *Journal of Literacy Research, 34,* 429–464.

Buehler, J. (2016). *Teaching reading with YA literature: Complex texts, complex lives.* Urbana, IL: NCTE.

Bunting, E. (2006). *One green apple.* New York, NY: Houghton Mifflin.

Crisp, T., Knezek, S. M., Quinn, M., Bingham, G., Girardeau, K., and Starks, F. (2016). "What's on our bookshelves? The diversity of children's literature in early childhood classroom libraries." *Journal of Children's Literature 42*(2), 29–42.

Dávila, D. (2012). In search of the ideal reader for children's non-fiction books about el Día de Los Muertos. *Journal of Children's Literature, 38*(1), 16–26.

Enciso, P. (1997). Negotiating the meaning of difference: Talking back to multicultural literature. In T. Rogers & A. Soter (Eds.), *Reading across cultures* (pp. 13–41). New York, NY: Teachers College Press.

Fecho, B. (2001). "Why are you doing this?" Acknowledging and transcending threat in a critical inquiry classroom. *Research in the Teaching of English, 36*(1), 9–37.

Garcia, A., & O'Donnell-Allen, C. (2015). *Pose, wobble, flow: A culturally proactive approach to literacy instruction.* New York, NY: Teachers College Press.

Ghiso, M., & Campano, G. (2013). Ideologies of language and identity in U.S. children's literature. *Bookbird, 51*(3), 47–55.

Horning, K., Lindgren, M., Schliesman, M., & Tyner, M. (2018). A few observations: Literature in 2017. *CCBC Choices 2018*. Madison, WI: Cooperative Children's Book Center. Retrieved from: http://ccbc.education.wisc.edu/books/choiceintro18.asp[1]

Leland, C., Lewison, M., & Harste, J. (2012). *Teaching children's literature: It's critical*. New York, NY: Routledge.

Mathis, J. B., Aziz, S., Crisp, T., Graff, J. M., Kesler, T., Liang, L. A., Sekeres, D. C., & Wilfong, L. (2014). Teaching children's literature in the 21st century. *Journal of Children's Literature, 39*(1), 56–61.

McKool, S. S., & Gespass, S. (2009). Does Johnny's reading teacher love to read? How teachers' personal reading habits affect instructional practices. *Literacy Research and Instruction, 48*(3), 264–276.

Morrell, E. (2007). *Critical literacy and urban youth: Pedagogies of access, dissent, and liberation*. New York, NY: Routledge.

Morrison, T. G., Jacobs, J. S., & Swinyard, W. R. (1999). Do teachers who read personally use recommended literacy practices in their classrooms? *Literacy Research and Instruction, 38*(2), 81–100.

Moss, B., & Young, T. A. (2010). *Creating lifelong readers through independent reading*. Newark, DE: International Reading Association.

Mueller, P. N. (2001). *Lifers: Learning from at-risk adolescents*. Portsmouth, NH: Heinemann.

National Council of Teachers of English. (2006). *Resolution on preparing and certifying teachers with knowledge of children's and adolescent literature*. Urbana, IL: NCTE.

National Council of Teachers of English. (2015). *Resolution on the need for diverse books*. Urbana, IL: NCTE.

National Council of Teachers of English. (2017). *Statement on classroom libraries*. Urbana, IL: NCTE.

NCTE Children's Literature Assembly. (2004). *Preparing teachers with knowledge of children's and adolescent literature*. Urbana, IL: NCTE.

Newkirk, T. (2011). *The art of slow reading: Six time-honored practices for engagement*. Portsmouth, NH: Heinemann.

Nodelman, P. (2008). *The hidden adult*. Baltimore: The Johns Hopkins University Press.

Recorvitis, H. (2003). *My name is Yoon*. New York, NY: Farrar, Straus and Giroux.

Sims Bishop, R. (1990). Mirrors, windows, and sliding glass doors. *Perspectives, 1*(3), ix–xi.

Stephens, J. (1992). *Language and ideology in children's fiction*. New York, NY: Longman.

Stetsenko, A. (2016). *The transformative mind: Expanding Vygotsky's approach to development and education*. New York, NY: Cambridge University Press.

Thomas, E., Reese, D., & Horning, K. (2016). Much ado about *A fine dessert*: The cultural politics of representing slavery in children's literature. *Journal of Children's Literature, 42*(2), 6–17.

Tschida, C., Ryan, C., & Ticknor, R. (2014). Building on windows and mirrors: Encouraging the disruption of "single stories" through children's literature. *Journal of Children's Literature, 40*(1), 28–39.

Willis, A., & Harris, V. (1997). Preparing preservice teachers to teach multicultural literature. In J. Flood, S. Brice Heath, & D. Lapp (Eds.), *Handbook of research on teaching literacy through the communicative and visual arts* (pp. 460–469). New York, NY: Macmillan Library Reference USA.

Yoon, B., Simpson, A., & Haag, C. (2010). Assimilation ideology: Critically examining underlying messages in multicultural literature. *Journal of Adolescent & Adult Literacy, 54*(2), 109–118.

STATEMENT AUTHORS

This document was revised by an NCTE working committee comprising the following:

    Jennifer Buehler, chair – Saint Louis University, St. Louis, MO

    Denise Dávila – The University of Texas at Austin

    Amy McClure – Ohio Wesleyan University, Delaware, OH

    Donalyn Miller – Author and Consultant, Colleyville, TX

This position statement may be printed, copied, and disseminated without permission from NCTE.

Shifting Our Classroom Literature Landscape

Chapter One

I have a distinct memory as a beginning teacher in Texas working with twenty-six first graders in a fully bilingual classroom, a memory to which I attribute an enduring passion for and commitment to finding great books to place in young children's hands. When I first began teaching in 1997, the bilingual program was new to the school and curricular materials had yet to be purchased. Determined to flood the room with stories and songs, I checked out as many books from the library as I could, only to find my chalkboard railing dressed in picturebooks written primarily in English. I reconciled my disappointment by telling myself that these books would have to do given my limited resources. That was the beginning of an emerging tension that resides within me to this day, almost three decades later. What books might be just right to launch our youngest children's reading and writing lives? How should representation of students' lives, languages, and literacies factor into the selection of texts? Where can I find those books? And how do I share these books with children so that they amplify the too often unheard voices in the classroom? I have learned over time that the tension between satisfaction with the literature collection we *have* and the literature collection we *know our students deserve* for a robust reading and writing life is one many of us negotiate as teachers, librarians, and caregivers of early childhood and elementary school-aged children.

Soon enough as a beginning teacher, I uncovered translated titles and found myself sharing picturebooks like *Abran paso a los patitos* (1997), a translation of Robert

McClosky's *Make Way for Ducklings* (1941), and *Un día de nieve* [*Snowy Day*] (1991) by Ezra Jack Keats during our read-aloud time. Although translations of English titles offered us narratives to read in Spanish and in English, over time I realized students also needed books that reflected more familiar experiences. As much as we loved *Un día de nieve*, as immigrants and children of immigrant families from the temperate climates of Mexico, Perú, Cuba, Colombia, Ecuador, Puerto Rico, and other Central and South American countries living in South Texas, no one in our classroom (including me!) had ever seen snow. Eventually our basal readers in Spanish arrived, but the collection merely offered us more translations. We marched forward nonetheless and leaned on the limited and unfamiliar portrayals in the basal readers for our language arts learning. I was happy to have literature written in Spanish to share with children, but I knew that students deserved stories in their classroom that better reflected their everyday realities and knowing.

As I continued teaching well into the next decade, I was introduced to an incredible body of bilingual picturebook authors and illustrators. The illustrated songbooks of José-Luis Orozco found their way into my hands, and my teaching life changed forever. I'll never forget sharing *De Colores and Other Latin-American Folk Songs for Children* (1999), an anthology of popular songs in Spanish brilliantly performed by Orozco and exquisitely illustrated by Elisa Kleven. I was immediately transformed by the way print came to life as we listened to the audiocassette of his performance, and I was so impressed with how quickly the children became picture readers, spending time carefully inspecting Kleven's intricate drawings. Our literacy lives also thrived as we read and performed the written songs and rhymes curated by Lulu Delacre in her illustrated collection titled *Arroz con leche: Popular Songs and Rhymes from Latin America* (1992). Students sang these familiar songs with tremendous energy during shared reading. They swayed as they sang, hooking arms as they carefully kept their big eyes on each other and on the enlarged print I wrote out and my mother illustrated (see Figure 1.1). Through this experience, I found myself reconnecting to my bilingual childhood, printing the lyrics to these familiar songs on oversized charts and bringing them home to share with my mother, who would sing them with me and then illustrate them.

It was then, as an early career teacher holding up students' stories and songs in picturebook and shared-reading formats, that I realized how the texts we put in front of our young readers matter and, more specifically, how the songs and stories we share in the classroom matter (Fox & Short, 2003). I began to see the elementary classroom as a vibrant constellation

> **Inviting Teacher Reflection**
>
> As you examine the literature collection your students access daily, reflect on the following:
>
> - Whose stories are represented?
> - Whose stories are missing?
> - What communities are represented among the authors? Illustrators?
> - Do the authors and illustrators identify as members of the communities they are depicting?

FIGURE 1.1. Crafting my own linguistically diverse texts based on familiar songs for bilingual literacy instruction, with my mom as illustrator.

where letters and sounds, song, and story, family and community, representation and authenticity of students' languages and histories matter. Through stories that students can identify with, I have repeatedly experienced the teaching of reading as more than just "leveling up" and word calling, but also as a transformative literacy encounter that builds lifelong readers and writers who understand the power of stories, especially their own.

As a teacher, I continued to grow my knowledge of authors and illustrators I could share with students. I followed up on conversations with librarians, bookstore owners, and others interested in bringing more culturally and linguistically specific literature to young people. In my pursuits, I was introduced to the art and picturebooks of Carmen Lomas Garza, whose picturebooks were essential for my teaching of memoir to third and fourth graders (and later to preservice teachers). Each carefully illustrated panel painting the pages of her books, such as *In My Family / En mi familia* (1996) and *Family Pictures / Cuadros de familia* (2005), offers richly detailed visual compositions for students to inspect and savor and emulate. Garza's books mentored us through personal explorations of family stories and launched many a young writer into crafting a narrative, both in print and through art.

It was in this season that I also learned about the pivotal work of author Alma Flor Ada. Her book *A Magical Encounter: Latino Children's Literature in the Classroom* provided me with a deeper understanding of the rich history of the collection I found myself building for students. As Ada (2003) explains,

> Children and youth should have access to the best of their culture and the universal human culture. To be meaningful, their education needs to include the best of what has been created specifically for them, and high-quality literature, rich and diverse, needs to have a central place in the education of children and youth. (p. xiii)

Building this literature collection early in my career became an essential part of my life as a language and literacy teacher of beginning readers and writers. I had cultivated a deep passion for literature as I learned from and with young children and their immigrant families, and Ada's work ignited the proverbial flames. The fire I have for children's picturebooks had been set and has been burning brightly ever since.

As I began teaching third- and fourth-grade designated English as a Second Language (ESL) classes in Austin, Texas, I found a steady increase in titles that offered the representation I was seeking. The emerging works of Yuyi Morales, Raúl Colón, Duncan Tonatiuh, Eric Velasquez, and Monica Brown became the beating pulse of our language and literacy lives. Their early publications, vibrant with the beautiful portrayals of Latinx communities, breathed life into our classroom reading and writing community and through example taught us how the details of our own lives were worth animating in the classroom and holding still on paper. Producing stories and pursuing inquiries that reflected daily life commanded our language arts learning.

National and regional book award committees I participated in also introduced me to emerging Latinx authors and illustrators and sharpened my critical lens when selecting picturebooks. I particularly looked to the Tomás Rivera and Pura Belpré book awards for authentic portrayals of Mexican American and other Latinx communities in children's literature. The annual Texas Book Festival in Austin brought me up close and personal with favorite illustrators like Yuyi Morales and her sister Magaly Morales. From students and the talents of authors and illustrators I followed, I could not stop learning about the power of culturally specific literature. And soon I found myself not only obtaining my master's degree, but eventually finishing my dissertation at the University of Texas to better understand how bilingual picturebooks such as *Dear Primo: A Letter to My Cousin* (2010) by Duncan Tonatiuh, *Marisol McDonald Doesn't Match* (2011) by Monica Brown, and *Little Night* (2007) by Yuyi Morales could support language and literacy learning among young children of Latinx heritage.

Now, as part of my work as a language and literacy researcher and teacher educator, I not only follow international and national book awards, like the American Library Association (ALA) Youth Media Awards, but I also attend conferences like the National Council of Teachers of English (NCTE) Annual Convention, read relevant research and books on issues of children's literature, and engage in collaborative research with teachers interested in sharing picturebooks with diverse representation with their students. In the last few years, social media (through platforms such as blogs, webinars, and social networking accounts—see the annotated bibliography at the end of this book) focused on literature for children and youth have provided lively and generative spaces for learning. For example, alongside her team of graduate students during her tenure at Penn State, Ebony Elizabeth Thomas launched Humanizing Stories (@healingstories), which offers a robust ongoing and annual list of children's and YA literature, media, and comic favorites. Laura Jimenez's (@booktoss) scholarship and social media work not only affirm our shared moral and ethical commitment to demanding better representation in texts, but also teach us *how* to develop a lens to do so. Debbie Reese's (@debreese) work on the *American Indians in Children's Literature* blog and her activism on X (formerly Twitter) have similarly taken us through the process of challenging our own assumptions about representation of Native communities in literature for children and youth and developing a keen awareness of children's literature about diverse communities written by authors and illustrators who also identify as members of the group depicted in their books. As I do my best to read the work of so many, I have realized I have so much more to learn, and that humility and a listening ear are essential to the work of sharing diverse picturebooks with young children. In the chapters ahead, you will read more about some of the humbling experiences I have had as I engage in this work.

Among the most important voices in the field of children's literature that we, as educators and researchers, have been smart enough to attend to is that of Rudine Sims Bishop (1990). Her metaphor of mirrors, windows, and sliding glass doors has been taken up by so many of us to highlight the transformative power of diverse literature in the hands of children and youth. She notes how books offer windows of experiences into worlds that may be real or imagined, familiar or new, and how those books can also be sliding glass doors through which readers can use their imaginations to cross the threshold into the author's crafted world. Under the right lighting conditions, Bishop explains, a window can also be a mirror that reflects potentially transformative experiences through which we can see our own lives and understandings as part of the broader human experience. As Bishop explains, "Reading, then, becomes a means of self-affirmation, and readers often seek their mirrors in books" (p. x). More recently, Debbie Reese (2018) has extended the metaphor to include a curtain when talking or writing about Native stories. In doing so, she highlights the way

> [N]ative communities resisted historical oppression and continue to preserve our culture by cultivating our ways in private spaces—behind the curtain. While Native people share some of our ways publicly in the present day, there is a great deal that we continue to protect from outsiders.

Furthermore, it conveys the importance of how #OwnVoices knows what belongs within the community and what knowledge can be shared outside of our communities. (p. 390)

Experiencing diverse picturebooks as mirrors, windows, and/or sliding glass doors and acknowledging the hidden histories that communities hide behind curtains requires that we stretch our knowledge of picturebooks to extend beyond the powerful and talented collective of old favorites that dominate collections. We must recognize the limitations of status quo literature collections of Eurocentric texts that promote white supremacy. By diverse picturebooks, I specifically mean books with writing and illustrations that work together to center marginalized groups of all kinds, including but not limited to those marginalized for reasons of gender, sexuality, neurodiversity, mental health, or disability (Thomas, 2016). We must enthusiastically widen the scope of our awareness and learning to include portrayals of Indigeneity, diverse ethnicities, and People of Color, as well as picturebooks that offer representations beyond those of cisgendered, heteronormative, standardized English-only worlds, and be mindful of portrayals of dis/abled communities. To grow our knowledge and to hold ourselves accountable to the works of underrepresented communities, we must seek out and lift the voices that have too long been ignored on our elementary classroom bookshelves.

Unfortunately, for so many young children, because the literature collections they access in schools are overwhelming representative of white, heteronormative, middle-class, and English-only speaking experiences, reading can be a damaging experience. As children from nondominant communities read books that do not reflect how they are in the world, and are read to from books that consistently hold up experiences and languages other than their own, too many miss out on the opportunity to identify as readers, connect with literature, and build their personal language and literacy lives in schools. Imagine reading only books that reinforce the message that your life experiences are not worthy of writing about or that your stories do not merit being shared with the class. Imagine never seeing the roundness of your Brown face in the books read in your classroom or hearing your family's ways with words as poetic or powerful prose. Or if your stories are shared, they are part of some multicultural celebration to be discussed only briefly once or twice a year, exoticized as something to be received as divergent from the everyday. Consuming a narrow literary diet is not healthy, and peppering literature collections with diverse texts as seasoning is not any better.

We must shift the literature landscape in young children's classrooms toward a greater diversity of representation to begin to undo the long history of denying all children a fuller reading and writing life.

My own experiences as a daughter of immigrant parents in the United States, together with those of the children and families I have shared time with and the amazing literature I have learned from, are challenging me to remain attuned to the critical work of advocating for better representation of diverse communities in children's books and for those who write and illustrate them. By critical, I mean that with young children, we can interrogate and resist the power structures reflected in literature and literature instruction that repeatedly identifies communities as deficient and marginalizes their voices and experiences as insignificant (Luke, 2013; Vasquez et al., 2019). Flooding our classrooms with diverse picturebooks is not enough; we must also be critically oriented as we select and share this transformative literature in the classroom.

In my almost thirty years in language and literacy education, I have had a front row seat to the gradual developments in the field of diverse literature and am inspired and motivated by the advocacy among teachers and scholars moving the work along. The stories in our classrooms are changing, slowly, and there are still so many more stories to be told. As I remain expectant and hopeful for what is to come, I am also left with this question:

As the stories in our classrooms are changing, how are we changing the way we teach stories?

This book explores the question of "how" around diverse literature: *how* might we share diverse picturebooks with young children? It is a question we must commit to pairing with the broader conversation around diverse literature in order to critically anchor this work in young children's classroom language and literacy learning. Drawing on the NCTE position statement *Preparing Teachers with Knowledge of Children's and Young Adult Literature*, as well as on the work of a teacher collective committed to better representation in picturebooks, this book urges you to both reimagine your picturebook collection and rethink literature instruction as essential, critical work for both literacy development and a broader sense of citizenry among young children. For more than a decade, in both Texas and the Midwest, I have been part of a picturebook collective, a group of educators interested in learning more about literature-based instruction with racially, linguistically, and ethnically diverse picturebooks. Since early 2018, a group of experienced elementary teachers in the Midwest and I have gathered after school to learn more about picturebooks, and we continue to do so today. Through intimate looks at three different elementary teachers participating in this recent collective as they develop and refine their instruction with diverse picturebook collections, you will

> **Inviting Teacher Reflection**
>
> As you examine your literature-based instruction, reflect on the following:
>
> - How do you typically share picturebooks with children?
> - Do you share all picturebooks in the same way? If not, in what ways do your approaches vary?
> - Consider the ways in which you might share diverse picturebooks differently than picturebooks that feature animals as protagonists.

gain insight into how sharing diverse picturebooks can enliven and awaken a critical look at representation in both illustrated and written narratives for young children. Teachers familiar with this work will find this book to be a resource to reinvigorate the commitments and practices they have already developed. If sharing diverse picturebooks with young children is new to you, this book provides entry points for beginning this work in your own classroom and developing a sense of the field at large. Sharing diverse picturebooks in the elementary classroom creates needed opportunities for young children to develop a critical awareness of text in rigorous and engaging ways, and this book is designed to help you do so.

Interrogating Our Positionalities: Investing in Our Growth as Teachers of Diverse Literature

If you have long been a reader and teacher of diverse picturebooks, then you have probably already experienced the transformative potential of this literature and understand its significance for young readers' language and literacy lives, as well as for their identities. In addition to our personal experiences, we can draw on the number of recent calls to end curriculum violence (Jones, 2020) and on advocacy for radical inclusion in the pursuit of educational equity to reflect on and redesign our literature instruction for young children. In her discussion on ending curriculum violence for the online education magazine *Teaching Tolerance*, Stephanie P. Jones (2020) recently explained:

> In order to reclaim our schools as sites of real learning and safety rather than suffering and racial trauma, it is necessary to help prepare teachers to critically examine what curriculum violence looks like within their discipline. Both prospective and current practitioners should continue to frame teaching as a reflective and reflexive practice by asking important questions of themselves and their curricula. Teachers should have continued support for professional development that is antiracist at its core and includes narratives of joy and resistance. (para. 23)

Despite the cycles of banning books and censorship that we have experienced over many decades (and more recently observe a resurgence of), the radical inclusion of diverse portrayals in literature will continue, and more examples of teaching with diverse literature in early and elementary classrooms will remain needed. As the majority of teachers of young children remain white, middle-class women who might not necessarily identify with or have experiences with the communities represented among the children and families in their classroom, and as the number of Teachers of Color like me seek ways to advocate for the experiences of People of Color in curricula, taking time to uncover and interrogate one's bias in teaching becomes even more important.

This book is designed to help teachers navigate this call for reflective and reflexive practice and poses questions throughout to encourage a critical, anti-oppressive/antiracist stance, one that centers the lives and languages of People of Color and decenters the dominant cisgender, white, middle-class, heteronormative experience too often reified in picturebooks. As research has repeatedly taught us, given the persistence of educational disparities by race, ethnicity, and class, we must ensure that our classroom instruction has the potential to bring us closer to equity in schools and society (Yoon & Templeton, 2022). I believe teaching young children to examine and respond to diverse representations in children's picturebooks has the power to begin to do so.

The NCTE position statement *Preparing Teachers with Knowledge of Children's and Young Adult Literature* (available online and at the beginning of this book) similarly asks that we take time to cultivate our own knowledge of the field, to be aware of the content and teaching resources available to us and invest in relationships with networks that can develop our literature instruction. This book not only provides resources to familiarize you with the literature but also nudges you to reflect on how your identity and beliefs play a role in your decision making and instruction in the classroom.

My own positionality does not exempt me from constant self-reflection. I recognize my privilege as a cisgender, lighter-skinned, fully bilingual Latina who is nondisabled and holds a higher education degree. I have also experienced how quickly those privileges dissipate when someone brings assumptions about my personhood based on reading my name on paper before meeting me in person, learning I am a daughter of immigrants, or seeing only limitation in my Brown skin or how my family's language permeates my talk. Those experiences, research, and reflection have taught me that flooding our rooms with the transformative titles of diverse picturebooks is merely one aspect of our work as teachers. We must be aware of the way our own histories, identities, and beliefs shape our selection of books for children, bias us toward some stories more than others, and politicize our teaching. Although this book is focused primarily on the "how" of teaching with diverse literature, it does not ignore how our identities and beliefs shape that work. Throughout this book, you will find invitations to interrogate your own biases and learn from three elementary classroom teachers as they reflect on their beliefs in practice during critical literature encounters in the classroom.

A Brief History: Sustained Calls for the Radical Inclusion of Diverse Literature

If you have picked up this book, you are probably already aware of or perhaps curious about the role of diverse literature in the hands of young children in schools. Although this topic has more recently been politicized as either an issue of censorship or political liberalism, the demand for better representation and diversity in literature is not new. This book builds on the extensive history of debate about diverse literature to rethink and revise our own literature instruction. I provide a concise overview of this history in what follows next.

We have a long history of sharing texts with children to guide them as readers. From hornbooks to McGuffey Readers, basal readers to ebooks, finding "books" for children to read and to teach children to read has long been our work as educators. My colleagues LaGarrett King and Jonda McNair have helped me understand how the field of children's literature (apart from publications such as W. E. B. Du Bois's magazine, *Brownies' Book*, for example) has a long history of furthering racial stereotypes through the texts we have shared with children (Zapata et al., 2019), as children's literature has always mirrored the racial context of its era.

In 1965, eleven years after segregation was outlawed in schools by the US Supreme Court, Nancy Larrick highlighted the disproportionate number of white characters in children's picturebooks. In her article "The All-White World of Children's Books," she explored the question, "Why are they always white children?" Through her analysis of children's books published at the time, Larrick illustrated how not all children, particularly Children of Color, were seeing their lives, their stories, on the pages of books. In the wake of desegregation and multicultural movements in education, calls for and commitments to seeing the faces of diverse families in literature were made by many in the field, particularly book publishers. Decades later, however, Walter Dean Myers (1986), acclaimed young adult and children's author, expressed frustration, lamenting the continued absence of Black experiences in children's literature and the failed attempts by the field to commit to better representation in these texts. He noted how budget cuts and changing politics were to blame for the stagnant movement. Twenty-eight years later, in another *New York Times* article, Myers (2014) found himself still asking, "Where are the people of color in children's books?"

Indeed, where *are* the People of Color in children's books? Year after year, the Cooperative Children's

Teacher Professional Resource: About *Brownies' Book*

In 1919, writer, scholar, and activist W. E. B. Du Bois recognized the need for young African Americans to see themselves and their concerns reflected in print. Use this QR code to learn more about the magazine he founded.

Book Center (CCBC) at the University of Wisconsin–Madison School of Education similarly finds that the overwhelming majority of books published for children reflects Larrick's and Myers's assessments. A collaborative of established literature scholars (Huyck & Dahlen, 2019) found that despite there being a slight but steady increase in the number of books published by and about People of Color, recent children's literature publications continue to demand further scrutiny. Examining the CCBC's 2018 multicultural publishing statistics focused on representations of American Indian/First Nation, Latinx, African/African American, and Asian Pacific Islander/Asian Pacific American peoples, David Huyck and Sarah Park Dahlen (2019) offer us a more nuanced look at the data through an infographic (see Figure 1.2). They explain:

> One important distinction between the 2015 and 2018 infographics is that we made a deliberate decision to crack a section of the children's mirrors (Rudine Sims Bishop, "Mirrors, Windows, and Sliding Glass Doors," 1990) to indicate what Debbie Reese calls "funhouse mirrors" and Ebony Elizabeth Thomas calls "distorted funhouse mirrors of the self." Children's literature continues to misrepresent underrepresented communities, and we wanted this infographic to show not just the low quantity of existing literature, but also the inaccuracy and uneven quality of some of those books. (para. 6)

FIGURE 1.2. A visual representation of diversity in children's books, 2018.

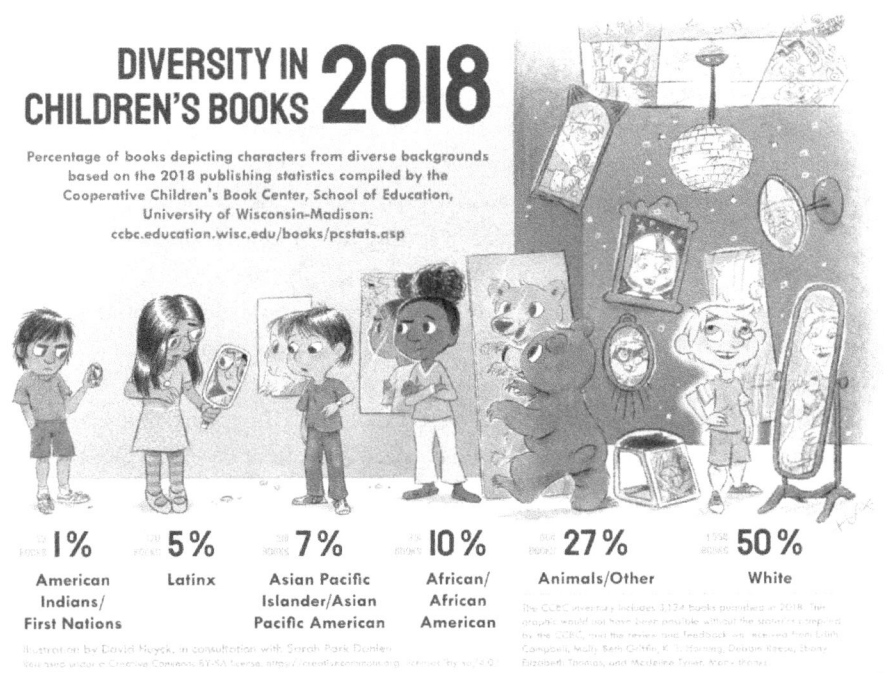

Unfortunately, as the infographic illustrates, the literature being published as we progress through this 2020 decade too often reinforces stereotypes and tropes of diverse communities and their histories. Calls for diverse literature that reflect authentic experiences of the communities portrayed cannot cease. We must look beyond isolated narratives and seek better representation of the lived nuances of our students' everyday realities.

Myers, and more recently his son, award-winning children's and YA author Christopher Myers, who similarly posted a commentary on the dismal state of diverse representation in children's literature (Myers, 2014), have not been alone in calling attention to the consistent findings of the CCBC. Through social media and other networked venues, the movement for better representation in literature has moved into a public sphere that has made the conversation more accessible to educators, librarians, families, and other interested stakeholders in the lives of young children. In the wake of COVID-19 and social distancing protocols, this digital network of children's literature enthusiasts has been a lifeline for continued professional learning. A second-grade teacher in a rural US community or a kindergarten teacher in Southeast Asia can now follow and be in conversation with favorite authors, illustrators, other educators, and advocates of diverse literature. Interested followers can feel connected to the growing conversations and link to valuable resources. Through this digitally networked community, I personally have been incredibly inspired and informed by the classroom teachers who shape the conversation and move the field forward. Noteworthy are teacher-led social media initiatives like #DisruptTexts and Build Your Stack, as well as national literacy organization position statements that provide us with research summaries and guidance to take the work to our classrooms and communities (see the end of Chapter 2 and the annotated bibliography for resources).

Through #DisruptTexts, for example, Tricia Ebarvia, Lorena Germán, Kimberly N. Parker, and Julia E. Torres have launched a nationwide conversation to challenge the pervasive presence of a dominant literary canon that holds up the same titles and authors in the classroom year after year, leaving little room for the new, more relevant titles for children and youth. Primarily through the hashtag #DisruptTexts on social media, they have invited us all to reconsider our own beliefs about and practices with literature. Those online conversations are later gathered and published at the #DisruptTexts website. Similarly, NCTE launched Build Your Stack, a national initiative focused exclusively on helping teachers build their book knowledge and their classroom libraries. Through literature-focused sessions at the NCTE Annual Convention, booklists, recommendations curated by NCTE members (teachers, librarians, administrators, and researchers), and professional learning experiences across the country, Build Your Stack is committed to making sure the right books find their way into readers' hands.

The International Literacy Association (ILA) has also focused on providing leadership on the topic of literature for children and youth through a collection of research-based position statements, white papers, research advisories, literacy leadership briefs, and reports reflecting ILA's perspective on current topics and trends for language and literacy education. In 2018, ILA published their brief on diverse literature and how it can transform literacy learning (Zapata et al., 2018). Like NCTE's, the ILA position statement centers the importance of the critical selection of and instruction with diverse literature. These and so many of the social media initiatives and research-based calls that continue to shape the movement, policies, and practices for better representation in literature have become important resources as they provide helpful syntheses and rationales to support our learning and instruction with diverse literature.

Among the more influential movements directly impacting the need for change is a growing collective of educators, librarians, publishers, authors, illustrators, and scholars identifying as the "Diversity Jedi." Through their research, teaching, books, social media activism, and talks, the Jedis have openly challenged the status quo of dominant deficit portrayals of marginalized communities in literature and have critiqued the notable absence of diversity in children's literature. Their regular calls for better representation in children's literature have provoked and inspired the field. Although those resistant to their message have characterized the Jedis' work as censorship, it is not. Instead, their calls are urging us to reconsider the sharing of literature that does not meet a standard of authenticity. As we enter heated and vital debates around diverse children's literature, any contention on the matter can point us to areas of needed development and exploration and impel us to listen, learn, and develop expertise as we take on the work of selecting and teaching with diverse literature. The work of the Diversity Jedi has become an important and essential resource for all of us.

In sum, although the calls for and the discussions about diverse literature now include more accessible venues, the shift toward better representation of diverse communities remains slow, and many of the portrayals published continue to be concerning. There has been powerful advocacy and research moving the field forward, but the call for rethinking the way we teach with diverse literature remains urgent. To address this need, this book builds on the powerful metaphor of books as windows, mirrors, and sliding glass doors (Bishop, 1990) and the efforts of so many others to demand (1) better representation of marginalized communities in picturebooks *and* (2) that we do better in our classroom teaching of these texts. Specifically, I share how early childhood/elementary school teachers and their students can attend to the complexities of exploring family, colorism, immigration, and linguistic diversity, as well as their intersections, as presented in children's picturebooks.

Understanding and Enacting a Critical Literature Response Framework

To recap, not only does critical literature selection and access matter, but so does literature instruction. How we share diverse literature with young children is the heart of a transformative literature experience. The questions of how and in what ways have become more important to me as I see the call for diversity in literature begin to transform classroom literature bookshelves. The power of the books resides not only in the written and illustrated portrayals but *also* in the ways teachers and students are sharing them together. This book, guided by the NCTE position statement's emphasis on directly impacting classroom practice, offers a Critical Literature Response Framework as an entry point for launching new practices with diverse picturebooks.

A Critical Literature Response Framework can best be described as a set of literature-based classroom practices that can enhance children's developing awareness and exploration of the history, joy, and vibrancy of marginalized experiences through a critical lens. To truly enact the framework, these four components are essential:

 Conditions for Enacting a Critical Literature Response Framework

 Commitments for Enacting a Critical Literature Response Framework

 Classroom Practices for Enacting a Critical Literature Response Framework

 Collaboration and Outreach for Enacting a Critical Literature Response Framework

In Chapter 2, I provide an evidence base for the framework and details about the underlying classroom practices that inform it (specifically, book floods, picture reading, wide and varied picturebook collections, and multilingual/multimodal literature response). The chapters that follow, the heart of this book, take you into actual classrooms where teachers are enacting the framework through diverse picturebook instruction. To amplify the power of these classroom practices, I emphasize how classroom discussions truly thrive under particular classroom conditions, deepen with specific kinds of teacher commitments, and flourish through teacher collaboration and outreach.

In the rest of this chapter, I unpack the idea of classroom conditions and teacher commitments, explaining their relationship to a Critical Literature Response Framework. And I conclude the book with more about the importance of collaboration and outreach.

Classroom Conditions for Enacting a Critical Literature Response Framework

It's important to note that a Critical Literature Response Framework thrives in classrooms (see Figure 1.3) where literature can (1) evoke aesthetic response, (2) invite critical interrogation, and (3) impel public action or praxis.

FIGURE 1.3. Classroom conditions for enacting a Critical Literature Response Framework.

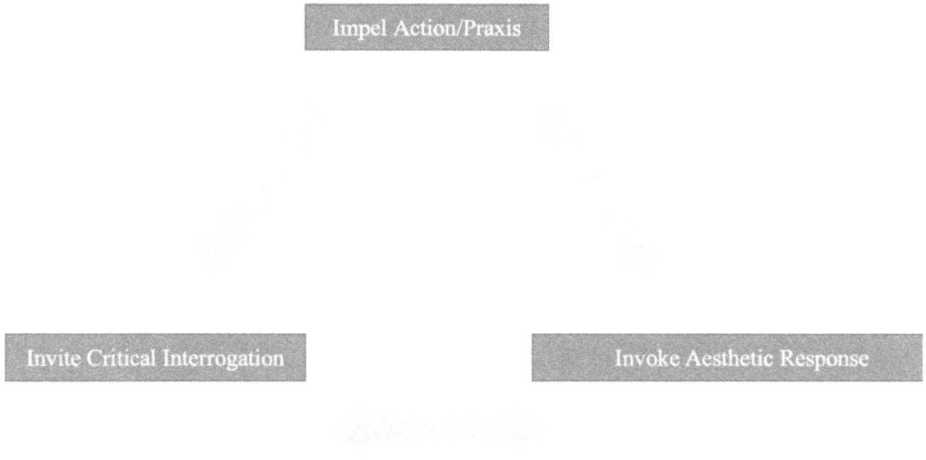

- Impel Action/Praxis
- Invite Critical Interrogation
- Invoke Aesthetic Response

Evoke Aesthetic Response

Conceptualizing the picturebook as sociopolitical art asks us to slow down to take in the messages provoked by an aesthetic reading. While reading *aesthetically*, a reader is focused on the very personal experience of reading for pleasure (Rosenblatt, 1995). Much like we would step into a museum and breathe in the experience to reflect, revisit, and consider art's meaning in our lives, entering a picturebook for the first time can evoke a complex constellation of responses. In this case, the teacher is the curator, serving as a guide for readers' initial meanderings through the print and illustrated narratives (Eeds & Peterson, 1991) and receiving students' aesthetic readings of the text. Art has long documented popular culture and social movements, working as historical artifacts that reflect a specific era. Diverse picturebooks can similarly document the sociocultural turns and political movements unfolding before us. It makes sense that to establish a context in which readers respond to diverse picturebooks critically, the books must be received as sociopolitical art first and foremost and that students' inaugural encounters with these texts be aesthetic and focused on their personal responses

> **Teacher Professional Resource: Shared Read with Colleague**
>
> For more on picturebooks as sociopolitical art, use this QR code.
>
>

(Zapata, 2022). Too often in adopted commercial curricula, literature is framed as something we "use" rather than as sociopolitical art we respond to. Perhaps you too have encountered statements such as, "I used that book to teach a main idea" or "How can I use that book to teach setting?" If we understand reading as a transaction between text and reader, then understanding books only as a tool to "use" decenters the poem that is produced between reader and text and focuses only on what the reader does with the text. Therefore, you will find that for a Critical Literature Response Framework, I lean on language such as "contexts for sharing" books rather than "how to use" the literature.[2]

Invite Critical Interrogation

After having the opportunity to steep in the storyworld of a picturebook, readers can take up invitations to critically interrogate the written and illustrated narrative. Foundational to a Critical Literature Response Framework are spaces where teachers sit side by side as fellow readers of these texts to model critical reading of print and illustration for our students. Providing examples and opportunities for young readers to inspect, identify, and interrogate power in diverse literature establishes invaluable conditions for a transformative experience in reading. I use the word *conditions* (and not *strategies*) intentionally here because supporting a Critical Literature Response Framework can cut across all reading experiences, not just the reading of diverse picturebooks. By nurturing conditions in which reading demands that we ask, for example, "From whose perspective is this written? Whose voice is missing? What messages are advocated for? Which are silenced?," reading critically becomes a normalized lens through which to read and respond to *all* texts.

Impel Action/Praxis

Certainly, the work of growing critical readers is aimed toward nurturing a sense of social justice that impels students into action through literacy. Helping children develop the lifelong tools needed to deconstruct text contributes to their capacity to make informed decisions on their own when faced with injustice or deficit thinking in literature, as well as in life. A Critical Literature Response Framework can support children in coming to their own conclusions when navigating multiple perspectives across an array of texts, a practice that allows children to make up their own minds as to where they stand on any issue and then act accordingly. More than an exploration of text, critical reading impacts the way readers move through the world and how they share that learning to effect change with humility and a commitment to making a better world. For example, children who explore the diversity of language differences available in a collection might find themselves interested in inventorying the different languages and language varieties in their classrooms or schools and find ways to amplify the rich voices of their community through text and audio productions they make available in their school library. Or, at the individual level, children who read about different skin shades may find themselves affirmed and seen when discovering their faces mirrored in picturebooks.

Classroom Commitments for Enacting a Critical Literature Response Framework

Not only do the classroom conditions matter for enacting a Critical Literature Response Framework, but so do our commitments as literature educators. The Critical Literature Response Framework provides a theoretical and research-based foundation for the instructional practices featured in this book and deepens instruction when situated in the following commitments as critical curators of literature: (1) teachers' critical stance, (2) literature-based instruction, and (3) critical encounters with text. As I offer a brief discussion of each commitment, I situate them as research based and as tied to the principles presented in the NCTE position statement.

Commitment 1: Developing a Critical Stance as the Teacher

As advocates for diverse literature in the hands of young children, we have a moral and ethical imperative to ensure that we are situating our sharing of diverse literature in ways that bring children closer to a transformative reading experience. Given our work as teachers guiding young children as they develop critical lenses for reading picturebooks, it makes sense that we too have done the work of reading, learning, and orienting toward a critical lens. In other words, to thoughtfully enact a Critical Literature Response Framework with integrity, we must know the literature and exercise a critical perspective by expanding our ideas about what counts as literature and developing an anti-oppressive approach. I lean on Rodríguez and Swalwell's (2021) argument that there is no such thing as a neutral approach to teaching because every choice in text, approach, and material is grounded in a deeper ideology, whether or not we are aware of it. An anti-oppressive philosophy centers social justice-oriented approaches to teaching and requires that we develop a critical consciousness that engages us in reflection that challenges racism and anti-Blackness. Through reflection we can revise and refine our practice as we uncover the way our own biases and assumptions and broader cultural worldview impact the way we teach with children's literature.

As the NCTE position statement declares, "Educators who affirm diversity and exercise critical literacy as part of a transformative activist stance recognize that they are always learning and expanding their capacities for transformation" (p. xv). An emphasis on *critical* here suggests that teachers who subscribe to a "transformative activist stance . . . build their capacities for discernment and critical evaluation so they are prepared to choose children's and YA books wisely and strategically from the books available to them" (p. xvii). Helping young children discern and learn from (or challenge) the narratives portrayed in diverse picturebooks means we must commit to our role as critical curators of picturebooks, embrace an anti-oppressive approach to education, and invest in revisioning our work as helping children not only to decode print and image but also to interrogate the texts before them. Our prowess as critical literacy educators can begin to come to fruition only when we dedicate our professional learning in this way. When we make a lifetime commitment to reading and working through essays, books, podcasts, and other texts focused on topics of race, ethnicity, bias, xenophobia, and other relevant issues, and engage in discussions with our colleagues about the impact of our beliefs and positionalities on our teaching, we commit to a journey that can ultimately only enhance the Critical Literature Response Framework experiences of our students.

In addition, we must develop our expertise as readers and stewards of texts and pursue additional resources to support our ongoing growth as critical literature educators. Entangled with the work of supporting young readers' critical reading is learning about authors, illustrators, publishers, booksellers, and the ongoing social media conversations about diverse children's books that exist outside of the immediate collections we access. Moving beyond the titles available in our local bookroom or the shelves of our libraries demands that we be both creative and critical in seeking books to turn to for building collections. While booklists of diverse picturebooks abound, alongside our students we must learn to thoughtfully cull from these lists, to critique the written and illustrated narratives identified in those lists and ultimately be able to produce our own preferred list in collaboration with others. At the end of Chapter 2 and in the annotated bibliography of relevant resources, I offer a rich list of resources to help you launch this aspect of your journey with your colleagues so that you can begin to "know the literature," as the NCTE position statement calls us to do.

Commitment 2: Practicing Literature-Based Instruction

A Critical Literature Response Framework classroom is grounded in thoughtful literature-based instruction. By literature-based instruction, I refer to instruction that gives children access to high-quality texts and in which the teacher actively integrates literature for learning and teaching. Although this commitment may sound redundant, in the wake of state and district mandates that nudge us more and more toward scripted, isolated phonics curricula, children's access to literature has been reduced to preselected read-alouds with very tight objectives; sadly, in these curricula, putting authentic texts in children's hands for learning to read and write is considered only an enrichment experience. When literature for children and youth is a core component of language and literacy instruction, you have a literature-based classroom. Teaching language arts in the context of the narratives, illustrations, colors, print, design, literary genres, and all of the features that picturebooks afford provides meaningful context for children learning to read and write. As so many schools are returning to mandated isolated reading and writing instruction, a literature-based classroom can be considered radical. However, what might it mean to teach comprehension and vocabulary as part of—rather than separate from—the work of being a critical literature response reader? How might repeated, critical reading of diverse picturebooks through different lenses support emerging readers? Rather than see the work of learning to read and reading to learn as mutually exclusive endeavors, how might the critical reading of diverse picturebooks enhance both simultaneously? As the NCTE position statement urges:

> Teaching children's and young adult literature is about more than getting students to fall in love with reading. . . . [T]eachers also need to learn appropriate and effective strategies for helping students find books that will engage them as readers and as participants in critical, significant conversations about their lives. (p. xviii)

Indeed, literature-based instruction means that we guide students as they move toward becoming independent readers able to read critically to determine the quality of a text (or absence thereof).

In the chapters that follow, you'll learn from children and their teachers engaged in literature-based practices that produced invaluable openings for critical reading. From the careful selection of diverse picturebooks to supporting children as "picture readers," these three classrooms were able to critically interrogate literature. Through collaborative literature response discussions, readers made intertextual connections across an array of texts, identified personal mentor texts for writing, and leaned on shared touchstone texts for making meaning. Repeated reading of the picturebooks for different purposes made these practices possible, because it is only through constantly getting their hands on books that children get to know an illustrator, identify with a character, and unpack themes and narratives. In the classroom chapters, you'll note how I highlight repeated reading of diverse picturebooks among young children and their teachers as an essential practice, illustrating the Critical Literature Response Framework's "appropriate use of pedagogy" that the NCTE position statement calls for.

A commitment to literature-based instruction values picturebooks as multimodal texts that demand more than the reading of print narratives and answering a list of comprehension questions that traditional instruction approaches engage in. As the NCTE position statement explains, we educators must "understand the value of different modes and platforms for reading" (p. xvii). Our invitations to respond to literature, therefore, must not only capitalize on the affordances of reading print narratives in picturebooks, but also emphasize how color, size, or perspective contribute to the broader narrative of a book, which, in turn, invites children to experience the synergy of reading all these features together. Another way to capitalize on the multimodal aspects of critical literature response is the response invitations themselves. In concert with collaborative meaning-making discussions, students must have opportunities to respond to literature through a variety of multimodal formats. Writing, making, drawing, and embodiment of responses are just a few of the ways we can create new and enhanced pathways for students to make meaning from the narratives they encounter in diverse picturebooks. Understanding the impact of the materiality of literature response, from inspecting the paper jacket covers to acting out a character's motives with our bodies, can only enhance a critical literature response classroom. This also includes invitations to young children to lean on digital technologies as part of literature response, including creating podcasts, movies, digital posters, and other digital literacies.

Commitment 3: Valuing Critical Encounters with Text

Practicing a Critical Literature Response Framework in the early childhood and elementary classroom is a commitment to not only centering young children's negotiations with diverse picturebooks but also decentering our exclusive position as expert and authority. The emphasis here on decentering our position does not suggest that we take a backseat to the reading, but instead asks that we be open to the critical encounters that emerge as young children navigate their own and others' experiences of picturebooks. I characterize critical encounters with literature (DeNicolo & Fránquiz, 2006; Reid et al., 2022) as those moments when a text elicits a response that urges deeper discussion into justice-oriented issues or interrogation of power, or that produces a potentially transformative moment that changes someone's previously held beliefs. These are the moments, microbursts of collective meaning making, that are ultimately the heart of a Critical Literature Response Framework, because these moments produce fissures in book talk that can ultimately make for a better world (Bomer & Bomer, 2001). This means that to practice a Critical Literature Response Framework, we must work on being comfortable with being uncomfortable. We must be okay with not always knowing "the answer" in the moment a critical encounter unfolds.

The NCTE position statement offers encouragement on this matter:

> Educators who affirm diversity and exercise critical literacy as part of a transformative activist stance recognize that they are always learning and expanding their capacities for transformation. They are open to guiding difficult discussions about inequality with students and are willing to tolerate the possibilities of "wobbling" while they explore uncharted territories with students (e.g., Fecho, 2005; Garcia & O'Donnell-Allen, 2015). (p. xvii)

The "wobbling" the statement mentions calls on both our students' and our own flexibility to negotiate moments of tension with the themes explored, to hold back on forcing connections to topics that students are not inviting us into, and to follow up with those same discussions when the moment presents itself. It's the kind of flexibility in teaching that cannot always be planned for but can instead be thoughtfully improvised to dig deep into complex topics. In the classroom chapters that follow, we'll hear from teachers as they "read the room" and share their decision making to move (or not) into the critical encounters that emerge. Teachers whose classroom experiences are explored in this book share what they were thinking and what they did when faced with critical encounters and how they might or might not have done things differently upon reflection.

The courage to step into discomfort alongside your students and to not make decisions about your instruction out of fear but rather out of a commitment to making a better world (Bomer & Bomer, 2001) and to everyday advocacy (Fleischer & Garcia, 2020) must be grounded in humility. Our humility acknowledges that we may not always know precisely how we feel or how to respond to texts in the moment, but that we *are* devoted to reflection that informs the next actionable steps. Our humility makes us okay with experiences and learning that challenge our preconceived ideas. Our humility quells our fears of "messing up" and recognizes that we will probably make mistakes along the way. Our humility reminds us that we are not "saving" or "empowering" students but offering a platform for young children to develop their own agency and thoughts. Ultimately, our humility as educators nurtures a community of readers who feel confident in recognizing and resisting injustice.

These commitments, when nested in the classroom conditions for enacting a Critical Literature Response Framework (see Figure 1.4), don't stand alone as solutions to inequity in the classroom. They are presented here individually to provide transparency about their meaning. By doing so, however, I do not mean to suggest that they should be enacted independently in the classroom. Quite the opposite; it is in the act of living out these principles as a dynamic ensemble that a pedagogy of instruction comes to life WITH diverse picturebooks and WITH children's responses to the texts. Many of these principles have already been carefully studied as viable approaches to critical literacy classrooms. What this book does is highlight what is possible when we bring these research-based practices together in critically oriented, anti-oppressive literature-based classrooms.

FIGURE 1.4. Conditions and commitments for a Critical Literature Response Framework.

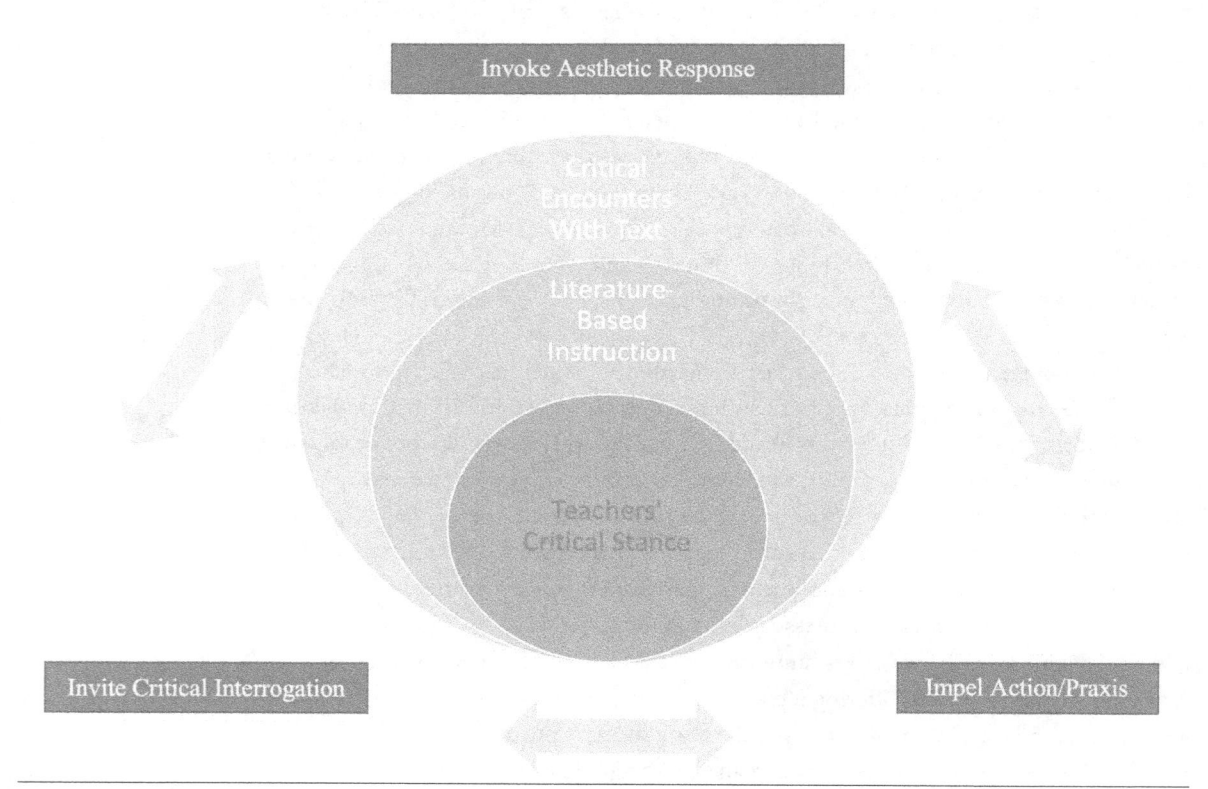

- Invoke Aesthetic Response
- Critical Encounters With Text
- Literature-Based Instruction
- Teachers' Critical Stance
- Invite Critical Interrogation
- Impel Action/Praxis

Make It Yours

These classroom conditions and commitments are not about providing a set of prescribed approaches but about helping you to nurture a classroom context in which you and your students can experience diverse children's picturebooks in transformative ways. These conditions and commitments offer a pathway to rethink and reimagine what is possible when teaching with diverse lit. Yet I recognize that many questions remain as you consider enacting this work in your own classroom, questions such as:

So what might this work look like in my own classroom if I'm still working on unpacking my own beliefs and positionality? I don't want to cause more harm, even if I have good intentions.

How do I navigate this work in the context of state policies and a district-adopted curriculum that demand I teach reading and writing out of context?

How do I amplify the marginalized voices in my classroom *and* offer windows and sliding glass doors into worlds that are different from my students' own?

In the chapters focused on Lottie's first-grade classroom, Kara's fourth-grade classroom, and Whitney's fifth-grade classroom, you will get to know and hear from the teachers as they share how they navigated many of these questions in ways that met the needs and possibilities of their learning communities and where they were in their own journeys. I lean on their work to say that the answers are within you and your students as a classroom community. The work must be tailored to meet the possibilities and demands within your own classroom. Moreover, we must recognize that we teachers grow into these practices as we negotiate our beliefs and uncover our own biases. As each day unfolds and as we encounter experiences and texts that open our minds, our practices can evolve. What I can say is that what enhances a Critical Literature Response Framework is that we remain vigilant in our growing awareness, exercise humility, and put in the work each day in ways that directly inform our next steps.

As you move through the chapters focused on the work in three elementary classrooms, I encourage you to reflect on your own approach to the practices featured in a Critical Literature Response Framework and to consider what they might look like for you and your students. I also invite you to reflect on your own racial, linguistic, and educational biases you might be bringing to the work. Teaching is a political act; every day, we bring our own beliefs about how the world should be and what our children should know to the work of teaching language and literacy. Enacting a Critical Literature Response Framework demands that we address our own biases and make commitments to ourselves and our students to confront them. In each classroom chapter, you are invited to stop and reflect on a critical encounter and hear from the teachers as they speak to their own struggles and negotiations as they engaged in this work. The teachers featured here are not perfect, nor do they claim to be. Instead, they are educators who recognize the limits of their own knowledge and are committed to learning and doing better.

Chapter 2 provides even more insight into Lottie's, Kara's, and Whitney's teaching practices. I will juxtapose introductions to these teachers and their developing ideological work alongside an overview of instructional practices that compose a Critical Literature Response Framework, as well as an extensive list of resources to supplement your learning and planning. Among the most salient instructional practices, I focus on engaging in book floods, valuing picture reading, sharing wide and varied literature collections, and inviting multilingual and multimodal literature response.

Chapters 3 through 5 animate a Critical Literature Response Framework through classroom examples. These chapters highlight classroom implementations of curricula that integrate diverse literature explorations of immigration, families, and language study. Through vignettes, related research, curriculum overviews, and, more importantly, an up close look at teachers and students at work, I showcase how the classroom conditions, commitments, and practices of a Critical Literature Response Framework can be lived out. Chapter 3 homes in on the role of visual literacy through reading pictures as a form of multimodal response. Chapter 4 defines the role of a wide and varied picturebook collection in exploring nuanced representation in literature. Chapter 5 amplifies how multimodal and multilingual literature response can enhance and extend students' critical reading.

In the final chapter, I look across all three classroom literature explorations to highlight the dynamism of a Critical Literature Response Framework when sharing diverse literature with young children. I also invite you to consider the power of collaboration and outreach as part of the work of embracing a Critical Literature Response Framework. Together, the chapters illustrate how we can make new discussions possible and create openings for teachers and students to enter critical encounters that are ultimately transformative.

I've designed this book to support your own work as a classroom curator of diverse picturebooks. Experienced teachers with a long history of doing this work will, I hope, encounter new literature instruction ideas to pursue, new titles, new authors, and invitations to continue doing the work of unpacking your own implicit bias and beliefs. For those new to the work and unsure about the role of diverse picturebooks in your classroom, welcome. May this book give you the courage and foundational knowledge to move forward in your efforts to build your students' language and literacy lives and fulfill your commitments to making the world a better place.

Children's Literature Cited

Brown, M. (2011). *Marisol McDonald doesn't match / Marisol McDonald no combina* (S. Palacios, Illus). Library Ideas.
Delacre, L. (1992) *Arroz con leche: Popular songs and rhymes from Latin America*. Scholastic.
Garza, C. L. (1996). *In my family / En mi familia*. Children's Book Press and Lee & Low Books.
Garza, C. L. (2005). *Family pictures / Cuadros de familia*. Children's Book Press.
Keats, E. J. (1991). *Un día de nieve* [*Snowy Day*]. Puffin Books.
McCloskey, R. (1941). *Abran paso a los patitos*. Penguin.
Morales, Y. (2007). *Little night / Nochecita*. Square Fish.
Orozco, J. L. (1999). *De colores and other Latin-American folk songs for children* (E. Kleven, Illus.). Puffin Books.
Tonatiuh, D. (2010). *Dear primo: A letter to my cousin*. Abrams.

Toward a Critical Literature Response Framework

Chapter Two

There's something about watching someone else move through an experience that helps us reflect on our own. I know, for example, that as much as I enjoy trying out a new recipe to see what results, I also really like watching my mother float through the kitchen while talking me through her recipes. Watching her work with ingredients and troubleshoot and refine a recipe when she over- or underestimates in some way gives me so much insight into an activity I too often see as magical and impossible. Nothing beats learning from watching, reflecting, and trying again when cooking.

I would argue the same for learning to teach in new ways—nothing beats learning from watching, reflecting, and trying again when teaching. I'm taking time here to briefly introduce you to three teachers I have learned from, to invite you to similarly observe and learn from them. I invite you to step into the work of expanding your own worldviews and classroom practices through close descriptions and interpretations of these teachers' practices with children's picturebooks within a Critical Literature Response Framework. Lottie, Kara, and Whitney are each in a different place in their critical social educator journey, and each has varying degrees of teaching experience that many of us will identify with. Here and in Chapters 3 through 5, I highlight the classroom literature practices they use to make room for the brilliance of the children they serve, particularly those whose histories and knowledge are too often buried in a narrow curriculum.

Lottie, Kara, and Whitney and I came together with other interested educators, doctoral students, and preservice teachers because of our shared commitment to literature-based literacy instruction and our commitment to better representation in the literature. As a picturebook collective, we gathered multiple times a semester over five years to explore new titles, authors, and illustrators; to build community with one another in ways that contribute to our personal well-being; and to share concerns, excitement, and ideas focused on diversity in children's literature.

Lottie, Kara, and Whitney have each personalized a Critical Literature Response Framework to invite their students into reading, as I hope you will. They enact this framework with students who bring a vast of array of knowledge and resources, including a first grader reading the Harry Potter books; a most discerning fifth-grade reader who is just coming into decoding print; newcomer children of immigrant parents from across the globe, bringing forty-seven different languages into the classroom; and students who have never ventured beyond the borders of their neighborhood. Lottie, Kara, and Whitney would not call themselves expert literature educators by any means (even though I would!), yet they recognize how far they have come in their beliefs and practices over the last five years and how far they would like to go. I follow their journeys in this book because I believe their learning and teaching can provide guidance for other educators who, like them, often find themselves trying to learn alongside children and stories that reflect experiences and understandings that are very different from their own.

What these teachers share is a deep passion for picturebooks as an important platform for creating openings into critical encounters with text and for supporting their students' growing literacy lives. They share an even deeper commitment to ensuring that students equip themselves with the tools needed to challenge xenophobia, racism, and linguistic bias. Our commitment to the ways diversity in children's picturebooks can support students' reading demanded that we get our hands on published picturebooks (both old and new), follow favorite authors and illustrators and experts on social media, and keep up with the ongoing conversations about diverse picturebooks. These efforts kept us moving forward until we realized we had to dig deeper, to recognize the importance of critically selecting and sharing diverse picturebooks with children if we wanted to decenter the predominantly white, able-bodied, male narratives perpetuated in the books currently most available to children. Uncovering one great book nudged us to find others to complement, extend, or challenge the narratives children were reading. We found ourselves needing to confront our own discomfort around talking about whiteness, race, language, and identity. Experiencing how quickly children took up the opportunities to enter conversations about racism, language bias, and justice affirmed how important these efforts were.

I characterize these teachers' classroom settings as literature-based classrooms, where literature serves not only as the primary vehicle for language and literature learning, but also as an essential platform for other content areas. Reading literature was always nested in a meaningful context in these classrooms, and reading literature with diverse representation even more so. These three teachers also share the belief that all students have the capacity to engage in critical discussions. As you will see in each of their classroom chapters, these teachers believe that no matter the "reading level" ascribed to a student, no matter the language designation given, no matter their race or ethnicity, no matter what their IEP indicated or what faith they practiced at home, each of their students was a reader able to engage in critical literature discussions. Whether through whole-class read-alouds, partner shares, independent writing, or small-group discussion, each teacher offered an array of participation structures and literacy modalities so that every child could contribute to the discussion.

Unpacking Our Positionalities

Lottie, Kara, and Whitney all identify as white, middle-class, able-bodied, cisgender women who teach young children who bring to the classroom both their culturally, linguistically, racially, and ethnically specific histories and unique ways of knowing, ways that are different from those of these teachers. Together, these three amazing educators reflect the dominant teaching demographic of school-based educators of young children in the United States. I do want to be transparent and share the tension I experience in featuring the voices of three white teachers in this book. Given that I feel a deep commitment to amplifying the experiences of Black and Brown communities in literature education and research, why highlight these three white teachers? We have long relied on Black and Brown women to do the work of advocating for equity in education; now more than ever we seek white teachers as allies to also create openings for critical literacy in the classroom through anti-oppressive approaches. In the Midwest community where I currently work, these are the educators I encounter, and their commitments and desires and journeys to do better for their students have informed my learning as well. I also feel fortunate that through our picturebook collective, we get to highlight how white educators can step into these ways of teaching with humility and care, particularly when in conversation with other Women of Color educators. I am thankful to have met and formed relationships with three teachers so willing to do the work and to allow me to learn by their side in order to share our journey with you.

If you are a white, middle-class woman who identifies as cisgender and able-bodied, you will perhaps feel familiar with some aspects of these teachers' experiences. If you are not, I hope their experiences will invite you to reflect on how your own identity impacts your teaching and your students' learning experiences. I, for example, identify as Latina and bilingual. These and other aspects of my identity feel more pronounced to me when I interact with these intrepid teachers. We each walk through

> **Inviting Teacher Reflection: Defining Your Positionality and Limits of Knowledge**
>
> As you consider your own beliefs and practices around literature, reflect on the following:
>
> How do you identify yourself? How might you characterize your identity?
>
> In what ways do your gender, race, ethnicity, and linguistic identity and abilities shape the way you live and teach in your classroom?
>
> What implicit bias lives within you?
>
> What privileges do you acknowledge in your life? What privileges are absent?
>
> In what ways do you see implicit bias impacting your decision making in the classroom?
>
> What readings are you engaged with to help you do this work? Who are you in conversation with as you do this work?

the world differently, but they accept me as I share how my experiences can be racialized in ways that theirs are not. Whether it's being told to "go back home," or being told *before hearing me speak* that I can get help with my English, or too often being confused with the only other Latina professor in my department, I acknowledge how these and so many of my racialized experiences absolutely inform the way I move in the world.

However you do or do not identify with these three teachers, I take time here to briefly attend to their and my identities to emphasize the significance of unpacking our positionalities when teaching within a Critical Literature Response Framework. I do this to nudge teachers who identify as white to similarly reflect and to be in conversation with others in your professional learning community, including People of Color, so that together you can expand your perspectives and understandings by hearing about experiences that are very different from your own. Again, especially because this book centers on the practices of teaching children's literature through critical literature response, we cannot ignore the significance of how our beliefs and identities impact the way we select and share literature and the ways we enact this framework in the classroom.

Where we all might identify with these teachers is in sharing a commitment to developing critical literacy orientations (including the personal internal negotiations with critical literacies) and in teaching children who bring unique sociocultural histories that are different from our own. Even those of us who share similar racial or linguistic identities with our students can locate the unique intersections of identity that make us each distinct. For example, I may be bilingual, like many families of Latinx communities, but I also note the different varieties of Spanish and English we speak, the different countries of heritage, as well as the different racial and economic circumstances that shape our lives. Lottie, Kara, and Whitney may all identify as white, like many of their young students, yet they also encounter the different rural experiences and language variances that shape their students' lives and that are different from their own. Pinpointing the sites of both unique histories and universal experiences you share with your students can only enhance the way you teach children's picturebooks and is the first step toward recognizing the way privilege does and does not affect your classroom life.

I also believe that we can all appreciate insights into these teachers' negotiations with a Critical Literature Response Framework. In this book, you will encounter both the moments when rich discussion about critical issues emerged among the children as well as the missed moments for digging deeper that we uncovered upon review and reflection of our teaching. Despite the best of our intentions in enacting a Critical Literature Response Framework and our commitment to doing no harm, it is highly likely that you will miss the mark at times, just as we did. Through the classroom and teacher insights I share in Chapters 3 through 5, you will see some of our most significant takeaways. We found that this work takes time and thought and reflection toward change (Adu-Gyamfi et al., 2021). We also found that doing this work requires tremendous humility to acknowledge that the ways we ask questions or select texts reflect our positionalities, and that we can all at times be complicit in centering whiteness or privilege even though we aim to resist those very things. I am so grateful for the openness and humility these three teachers exercised by allowing me into their classrooms, which in turn allows me to foreground the complexity surrounding the work of a Critical Literature Response Framework, as well as provide helpful case studies for others to learn from.

Getting to Know Mariposa Street Elementary School

It's easy to fall in love with Mariposa Street School upon walking through the red front door. As a public elementary school that serves kindergarten through fifth-grade students, the school always has a busy hum to it. The first time I walked the halls of Mariposa Street School, I could not ignore the incredible artwork that covered the walls. Children's self-portraits, colorful mosaics, complex visual scientific representations, and so much more flooded the senses. And, as a school with a long history of teachers who share a commitment to arts-based integration in their instruction, the visual and multimodal experiences the children were having was undeniable. Unfortunately, by the time I finished my work with the teachers for this book, the effects of narrow science-of-reading mandates and the teaching of skills in isolation as an exclusive practice were evident. Like so many teachers, Lottie, Kara, and Whitney were navigating these pressures to meet the expectations of their district administration alongside their dedication to arts-based integration, as well as other commitments to what they understand as essential to teaching children. For many of you currently teaching, this tension might be familiar. Even as I wrote this book, the sociopolitical climate was so fluid in response to "learning loss" rhetoric (Bomer, 2021) and book ban movements (Kissel, 2023) that I have no doubt the demands on teachers will continue to evolve and change in ways that will directly impact what and how we teach literature. The classroom work featured in this book worked in concert with the state standards, district mandates, and school expectations. What I argue here is that a Critical Literature Response Framework not only complements most curriculum objectives but also exceeds the demands of many mandated teaching and learning standards. The focused literature explorations and the discussions of picturebooks that these teachers enact daily meet the demands of any rigorous language and literacy curriculum.

Like so many schools, the vibrancy of the Mariposa Street School community is deeply shaped by the teachers, students, and families who walk through those red doors every day. Recognized as the second oldest elementary school in a rural suburban community in the heart of the Midwest, Mariposa Street School is located in a university town that boasts an emerging international community residing within a predominantly white, midwestern space. We describe the area as "rural suburban" given that our community is nestled deep in the heart of farming country, yet, as a small college town, we have the amenities of a suburban area. This context produces a rich juxtaposition of students who bring global histories, a wide range of socioeconomic experiences, and language diversity, as well as rural and urban experiences. Exploring a Critical Literature Response Framework with this diverse student body of young children produces a unique set of classroom experiences for the children and their teachers. Sitting next to children of farmers are children of immigrant families from Pakistan and El Salvador, children who identify as Christian and some as Muslim. The classrooms featured here are predominantly white and English speaking, but the richness of the racial, linguistic, and ethnic complexity within such a generic description became more pronounced as students engaged in discussions of picturebooks reflecting more than the typically white, English-speaking, heteronormative experience. Sharing the picturebook stories in the classroom encouraged the children to share their own. Sharing stories that were written in different languages moved children to share their own. Sharing stories about different families prompted children to share their own. What working with these teachers taught me is this: when we change the stories we share in the classroom, we must also change the way we share those stories. What results is the emergence of the stories that too often remain buried behind limited literature collections and limited interpretations of language and literacies.

Changing the stories we share and changing the ways we share those stories changes what is possible for our children in their language and literacy classrooms for the better.

Classroom Practices to Support a Critical Literature Response Framework

So, if we change the stories in our classrooms, how can we change the way we share and teach with those stories? We know that supporting readers in elementary classrooms demands that we keep in mind all kinds of readers and writers, including those just emerging in their concepts of print, beginning in their reading of books, or reading independently in more complex texts. The reading response practices shared below are reimagined in so many different ways in Lottie's, Kara's, and Whitney's classrooms, as are the writing practices. Writing includes not just putting pencil to paper but also "making" with a wide array of tools, designing with digital technology, and composing with bodies. Reading includes not only decoding print but also reading images, making meaning from sound, and inferring across multiple media. Doing this work demands that you take up and support a more expansive view of literacy. By engaging a wide array of literacies in the classroom, more opportunities for children to respond to literature emerge for our students to take up and make their own.

Entering Lottie's, Kara's, and Whitney's classrooms in the chapters that follow, you'll encounter many language and literacy teaching practices. I want to briefly overview a few foundational practices first and then dig deeper into four of the more important literature-based approaches implemented in these three classrooms. If you have been teaching for a while, some of these may seem like old hat, but I encourage you to think about new ways you might enact the practices in your classroom. If you are new to teaching young children in the language arts, you might want to start small and develop these practices as they make sense to you. Either way, I hope these descriptions encourage you to continue to be in conversation with your colleagues and watchful of your students, and that you explore how the practices are and are not enacted in your classroom. Consider why they are or aren't as you explore the similarities and differences between what you do and the practices described here. And finally, open yourself

Inviting Teacher Reflection

As you consider your own beliefs and practices around literature, reflect on the following:

How do you define literacy?

What kinds of literacies are supported in your classroom?

What tools, materials, meaning making, and composing practices do you model?

In what ways might you stretch the way you teach language and literacy in your classroom as more than a paper-and-pencil learning opportunity?

Professional Resources for Learning More about Literature Response

As you consider your own beliefs and practices around literature, reflect on the following:

- *Comprehension through Conversation: The Power of Purposeful Talk in the Reading Workshop* (2006) by Maria Nichols

- *What a Character! Character Study as a Guide to Literary Meaning Making in Grades K–8* (2005) edited by Nancy Roser and Miriam G. Martinez

- *Teaching Children's Literature: It's Critical!* (2023) by Christine H. Leland and Mitzi Lewison

to making some of these practices your own in ways that serve your journey toward launching a Critical Literature Response Framework in your classroom.

Foundational Classroom Practices Underlying a Critical Literature Response Framework

Alongside engaging children in talk about text, we can support and extend that talk through writing, drawing, making, and so much more. Some of the foundational ways the teachers at Mariposa Street School do this is through the following:

- *Reader-Response Notebooks:* The opportunity to write, draw, and doodle on paper can offer students a focused space to begin to document and grow their personal responses to literature. Feedback is critical here, whether oral or written; taking time to receive student thinking in the notebook provides an additional audience to develop their thinking. The advantage of collecting these responses in one place like a notebook is that students can interpret their responses to stories and reflect on their development as readers over time.

- *Language Charts:* Publicly documenting classroom talk and ideas produced during shared read-aloud events is powerful practice. More than a worksheet or an anchor chart that students complete before the discussion, a language chart (Roser et al., 1992) truly is an authentic record of the emerging themes and discoveries the children make as they discuss literature. These charts focus on big ideas, slowly grow over the course of literature explorations, and can zero in on particular concepts such as character development, themes, or even writer's craft. As a classroom teacher, I wrote down the children's thoughts during instruction or invited students to jot their thinking on sticky notes that were then added to the chart. When discussions were particularly rich, I took time after school to collect their thinking and synthesize it on the same chart to refine along with the children the next day.

- *Arts-Based Integration Approaches*: Thoughtfully integrating arts (e.g., drama, song, drawing) as part of reading-response work is essential in every classroom. Literacy instruction that threads together content and skills across music, visual arts, dance, and theater is more than learning with arts activities added on as an extra. Impactful arts integration rests on a foundation of thoughtfully planned learning goals. Teachers address a scope and sequence, keep in mind state or national standards for arts and other curricular areas, and are often supported by partnerships with community and regional arts organizations. Quality arts instruction builds on students' existing knowledge and skills. To learn more about arts integration, check out The Kennedy Center Arts Integration Resources via this QR code.

If any of these practices feels unfamiliar or new, I invite you to inventory the myriad ways you already do (and don't!) launch literature response in your classroom using the questions featured in the following invitation to reflection. Afterward, consider exploring some of the resources noted above to support your work.

Digging Deeper into Powerful Critical Literature Response Classroom Practices

Now that you have a wider sense of what you are and are not already doing in your classroom to support a Critical Literature Response Framework, I highlight four practices from Mariposa Street School—book floods, building wide and varied collections, visual thinking strategies, and multimodal and multilingual literature response (see Figure 2.1)—that were essential to each of the featured classrooms. Independently, each of these practices can do great things for young readers when they are common practice in the classroom. But together and in the context of the commitments and conditions of a Critical Literature Response Framework, we found that children were able to carve out productive spaces to enjoy, inspect, interrogate, and learn from the literature for transformative discussion.

> **Inviting Teacher Reflection**
>
> As you consider your own beliefs and practices around literature, reflect on the following:
>
> What are the literature response invitations in your classroom?
>
> How do you support different pathways for students to respond?
>
> What materials and resources do you make available in your classroom for children to use to respond to literature?
>
> In what language and language varieties do your students respond?
>
> How often do you model different literature response possibilities?

FIGURE 2.1. Literature-based practices that enliven a Critical Literature Response Framework.

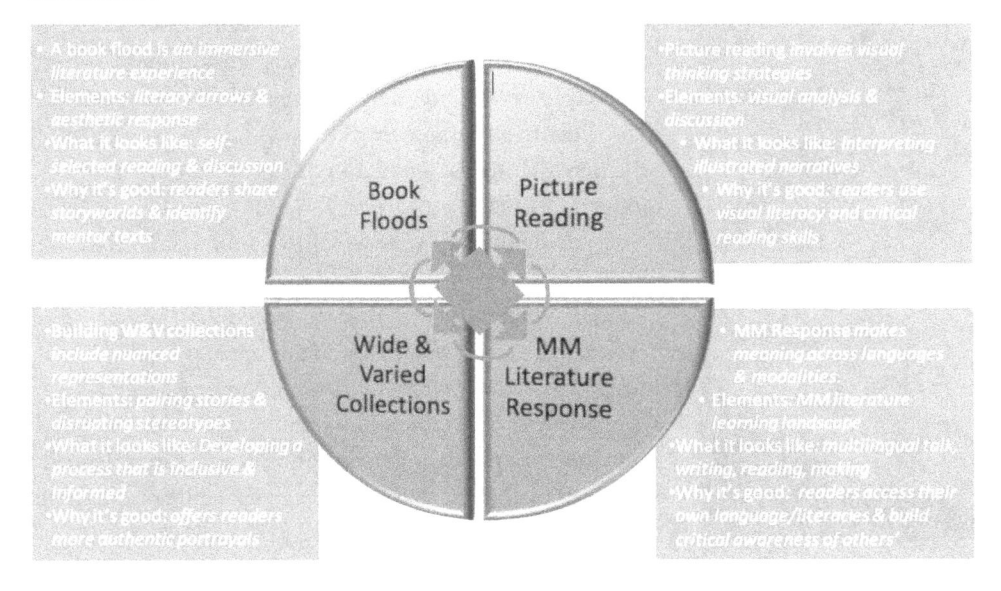

- A book flood is *an immersive literature experience*
- Elements: *literary arrows & aesthetic response*
- What it looks like: *self-selected reading & discussion*
- Why it's good: *readers share storyworlds & identify mentor texts*

Book Floods

- Picture reading *involves visual thinking strategies*
- Elements: *visual analysis & discussion*
- What it looks like: *interpreting illustrated narratives*
- Why it's good: *readers use visual literacy and critical reading skills*

Picture Reading

- Building W&V collections *include nuanced representations*
- Elements: *pairing stories & disrupting stereotypes*
- What it looks like: *Developing a process that is inclusive & informed*
- Why it's good: *offers readers more authentic portrayals*

Wide & Varied Collections

- MM Response *makes meaning across languages & modalities*
- Elements: *MM literature learning landscape*
- What it looks like: *multilingual talk, writing, reading, making*
- Why it's good: *readers access their own language/literacies & build critical awareness of others*

MM Literature Response

Practice 1: Book Flood

Flooding the classroom with picturebooks. I typically describe a book flood as time to "steep" in the literature. By immersing young readers in a pool of literature, they will enjoy the benefits of dipping into and swimming in stories. A book flood is essentially a deluge of thoughtfully selected books made accessible to the students. I emphasize *access* here as the essential component—through book floods, children access literature collections daily. We know from research that more time with eyes on print has positive outcomes for readers and that opportunities to read for pleasure can contribute to students' overall positive attachment to reading (Duke, 2000). We also know that a book flood must coincide with great instruction to fulfill this potential, a lifeguard and coach of sorts for readers as they navigate new story waters. With access to a vast number of books and thoughtful guidance, we can significantly affect the way students identify as readers and the reading habits they grow. In the book floods I suggest, we are also supporting young children's access to stories that are both similar to and different from their own.

To support a Critical Literature Response Framework, young readers are immersed in a diversity of stories that provide mirrors and windows and sliding glass doors. Consider what it might mean to clear space in the curriculum for students to explore and read self-selected books about People of Color both for pleasure and for inquiry within a wide and varied collection. What is possible when representation of historically absent communities is a part of children's everyday literature encounters? How might children recognize the different language varieties in their own lives as they read linguistically diverse texts? It makes sense that access and opportunity to read stories and pictures that reflect different lives, languages, and literacies has the potential to foster a generative space for students' questions, connections, and discussion of the rich diversity of living and being in the world (see Figure 2.2).

FIGURE 2.2. Inviting children to immerse themselves in a book flood through self-selection and literary arrows.

Using literary arrows. What I find unique about a book flood approach, at least in the ways I have observed teachers implement it, is that teachers don't always prescribe a narrow focus as students enter the collection. Instead, they offer what my mentor Nancy Roser calls "literary arrows," literature invitations that help students cut their own pathway through their reading experiences. For example, rather than limit your repertoire of questions to story grammar elements (*Who is the main character?*

What is the setting?), also invite students into explorations of character (*As you explore this collection, take note of how you are similar to and different from the character*) or theme (*We've been talking about power, so as you explore this collection, take note of how power is expressed in both the written and the illustrated stories. Be prepared to talk about your noticings*). These kinds of literary invitations provide initial guidance into a book flood while also leaving room for readers' own discoveries and aesthetic responses. These literary arrows also provide a shared entry point for discussion to build on over time (see Figure 2.3).

Centering aesthetic responses. I want to emphasize that such an approach for a book flood truly centers reading aesthetically *first*—identifying favorite authors and illustrators, connecting with characters, feeling challenged by unfamiliar narratives, or questioning the way plots are resolved. This more open approach to reading, one that allows students' initial experiences with new titles to be personal, can seem radical for some, particularly in a climate of scripted curricula that dictate reading objectives narrowly. But what I've observed in so many classrooms, including my own, is that this repeated opportunity to freely familiarize yourself with titles, authors, illustrators, and beloved characters becomes an important reading ritual, one that makes it easier for children to craft text-to-text connections and comparisons, unpack themes and patterns, and more freely share their stories from home (see Figure 2.4).

Repeated reading. Repeated engagement with the same book (a book they have self-selected) can help children know that text very well, so much so that they elect to lean on that picturebook as a mentor text for writing or drawing and as a touchstone text for making sense of a social justice issue. I cannot emphasize enough how repeated opportunities to enter a book flood and read picturebooks are essential to a Critical Literature Response Framework. With time to read and respond to a number of picturebooks in a personal way guided by literary arrows, students have a full repertoire of characters, issues, and responses to lean on for learning. But proceed with caution: Repeated reading of text is powerful when students feel motivated and engaged by the narrative and characters. Under different conditions, the repeated reading will fall flat.

FIGURE 2.3. Flooding the room with critically curated collections.

FIGURE 2.4. Centering aesthetic experiences: Making time for children's personal responses to picturebooks.

These ways of navigating literature are certainly ones we can relate to as adult readers. If you've ever participated in a book club, how often do you ask one another, "Who is the main character? What is the setting? What is the main idea of the text?" Probably seldom or never. In the everyday ways you and I (experienced readers) talk about books, we'll address the story grammar elements in the context of our personal responses to text. More often, we talk about the parts of our self-selected book that moved us, surprised us, or confused us rather than list the problem and solution of the story. Just the other day, my husband and I were talking about *A Tree Grows in Brooklyn* by Betty Smith (1992). We didn't find ourselves quizzing each other on the main characters or trying to identify the main idea. Instead, we explored the coming-of-age themes and reflected on our childhoods, and we found ourselves naming characters and exploring other story elements to do so. I do not want to suggest that we *not explicitly* teach story grammar elements like character and setting to young children. Instead, we can *also* teach those elements in the context of students' authentic experiences with text rather than treat those elements solely as isolated objectives. Young children can dig deeper into the role of those elements in story when given repeated opportunities to know literature intimately, and a book flood affords such opportunities.

In the classroom chapters you'll encounter here, book floods were ongoing practices connected to both open-ended (everyday) and focused or closed (for units of study) explorations. I highlight the focused book floods, although I think many of the practices you'll observe are relevant for both open-ended and focused book floods. For example, when inquiring into civil rights, Lottie flooded her first-grade classroom with picturebook narratives of both familiar and hidden civil rights histories. She also worked to ensure that there were titles connecting the justice issues of the 1950–1960 civil rights era to those of today, helping to make the topics relevant to the children (you'll read about this closed book flood in Chapter 3). Children had repeated opportunities to select from the book flood, with many self-selecting different texts each time and some self-selecting the same text.

Practice 2: Building Wide and Varied Collections

Diversifying representation and perspectives when selecting picturebooks. In the work of flooding your room with a wide and varied collection, it's important to provide texts that vary in structure, genre, and representation across both authorship and portrayals. Complementing literature explorations with varied texts creates opportunities for children to read and make meaning across those texts. To build wide and varied collections, global children's literature scholar Kathy Short (2011) suggests pairing texts to build bridges across global cultures in ways that go beyond a tourist perspective of reading about diverse communities, a practice that allows only superficial understandings of the communities represented. Pairing texts in ways that put different picturebooks in conversation with one another became an important practice in the classrooms presented here, allowing students to observe, reflect on, and reconsider experiences portrayed. When we have wide collections that reflect a broad and varied approach to representation, the work of pairing texts for discussion becomes easier.

The most valuable benefit of putting different texts in conversation with one another is that children have access to diverse representations of communities and histories. Rather than perpetuate a stereotype or hold up a singular narrative about a particular community, we can provide children access to an array of realistic and authentic portrayals. What might it mean for children to read across a diversity of people and experiences through a more robust collection? What might it mean for children to read across a diversity of #OwnVoices authors and illustrators (discussed further below)? To illustrate, within a focused book flood about immigration in her fourth-grade classroom, Kara included *Dreamers* by Yuyi Morales (2018), *My Shoes and I* by René Colato Laínez (2019), *Pancho Rabbit and the Coyote: A Migrant's Tale* by Duncan Tonatiuh (2013), and *Two White Rabbits* by Jairo Buitrago and Rafael Yockteng (2015). Putting these books in conversation with one another can begin to bring awareness to the realities of different immigration experiences as they relate to differences in economic privilege and access, diversity of border-crossing terrains, family, and affectual realities including love, happiness, and joy. *Cultivating Genius* (2020) and *Unearthing Joy* (2023) author Gholdy Muhammed similarly invites us to curate collections that pair antiracist themes with Black joy. In doing so, she is calling on us as literature educators to make sure that we are not perpetuating narratives of trauma and pain as the only Black experiences featured in our literature collections.

To further highlight the subtle and not so subtle differences within represented communities and to provide a range of perspectives on an issue, we might further complexify our collections with books that extend concepts presented in one collection. For a closed book flood on immigration in her fourth-grade class, for example, Kara not only shared stories of Latinx border-crossing experiences but also integrated picturebooks with portrayals of refugee experiences from countries around the globe. Through her careful questioning and guidance in pairing texts from this collection (which you will read more about in Chapter 4.), Kara's students explored the differences between voluntary and involuntary immigration, the implications of economic status on immigration, and the role of family in immigration. Students also explored the differences between immigration and refugee experiences. For some students these were personal inquiries, and for others the collection grew awareness of the journey so many make to build new lives and how those border-crossing experiences can vary.

Picturebook selection: What should I consider? As you and your colleagues build wide and varied collections, consider these ways to further refine your selection processes. As teachers we tend to stick to our most familiar and favorite titles when selecting books. We also tend to rely on what we have available on our shelves or in the book room and are often guided by the curriculum texts we are provided. Does this sound familiar? It does to me. I remember that process from my days in the classroom. Convenience and access can dominate our text selection process, which is a reflection of how busy the teaching work life can be and how limited our resources are. How can we challenge ourselves to redefine a text selection process that truly serves our commitment to change the stories in our classroom?

I'd like to suggest here that we completely redefine and expand our process to consider more than "adding" isolated texts for Martin Luther King Jr. Day or heritage months to the collections we already have. To sincerely rebuild our collections, we should first assess the collections we already have, cull the strong texts and weed out those that are problematic and overrepresented, and start from there. The Lee & Low website features a blog post by a teacher named Veronica (2017) who offers a helpful place to begin this process through a classroom library assessment that analyzes how culturally responsive your collection is:

> We need to think critically about how these books reflect the diversity of our students, their backgrounds, and the communities in which we live while exposing them to new ideas and concepts. *Does your classroom library contain books that include main characters of color or with disabilities? Do your books featuring people of color only focus on issues of race, prejudice, or discrimination? Do they go beyond ethnic heritage months? Do they only focus on cultural traditions and foods?* (para. 2)

Specifically, Veronica (2017) offers a questionnaire that guides you through a process of assessing and transforming your classroom bookshelves. I particularly appreciate the nudge to think about representation of People of Color in literature beyond issues of race, prejudice, and discrimination. How are our children seeing their everyday selves in stories? Are they seeing themselves only in stories where they are always in conflict with others or needing to be saved?

Veronica (2017) also suggests entering this initial process with your students. In her blog post, she features the work of classroom teacher Jessica Lifshitz (2016), describing how she and her students analyzed their classroom collection to assess for cultural responsiveness. Together, teacher and students carefully made observations, noting the over- and underrepresentation of different communities. For our youngest children, just the invitation to "notice" whose voices are present and whose aren't in a collection is such a great place to begin. Asking ourselves and our students to critically interrogate texts in this way is a powerful entry point for selecting picturebooks for the classroom. At the end of this chapter, you will find direct links to the questionnaires and blog posts, resources that can certainly launch you directly into redefining your text selection process to enhance critical literature response in the classroom.

After reviewing those resources and getting started, you and your colleagues can continue to design a process informed by your continuous learning. For example, experts in the field have recently nudged us to further expand the kinds of questions we ask when selecting texts. To illustrate, Zetta Elliot (2016), award-winning author and independent publisher, asks that we also consider representation of publishers beyond the larger, established houses. Doing so helps us get to know and explore independent book publishers led by People of Color that tend to be overlooked in collections for children. Many are calling us to weigh the representation of #OwnVoices authors and illustrators. #OwnVoices is a movement in the field of children's and YA literature that calls for texts authored and illustrated by those who identify as members of the communities they are depicting in their books. The argument is that a member and insider of the community can craft narratives depicting unique sociocultural nuances and experiences with more authority than can an outsider, thereby creating more authentic portrayals. Selecting #OwnVoices texts also helps to keep in check the kinds of cultural appropriation that can produce stereotypical and harmful narratives. Assessing your collection for the authors' personal connections to the community they portray is a powerful step in building a collection with better representation. But I would also caution against stopping there. Just because a text claims #OwnVoices authorship does not mean the text is not problematic. In lieu of #OwnVoices, many are now talking about the author's cultural location and different ways of having deep experiences within a culture. We must take time to look into the author's experiences and research related to the book in author's notes and on their websites. That is why I'm suggesting you develop a process that keeps in mind not only the author's identity and cultural location but also other considerations such as the publishing house, regional and national book awards, and the advice of other teachers, researchers, authors, and illustrators doing the work.

If we skip the process of reassessing our collections and just add books with diverse representation in stand-alone bins, we isolate and limit the kinds of transformative reading experiences that are possible for our young readers. Doing so also contributes to the notion of "diverse texts" as ethnic additives or adjuncts that are merely tangential to the curriculum rather than essential and foundational texts for learning. In sum, the question for all of us is this: How can we rework and grow the collections we already have in ways that infuse better representation of marginalized communities often invisible in our stacks, across the entire bookshelf? How can we avoid simply adding a few bins of "diverse" picturebooks to what we already have?

Teacher Professional Resource

Learn more about the meaning, history, and cautions of #OwnVoices by reading the We Need Diverse Books statement on #OwnVoices literature:

> **Inviting Teacher Reflection**
>
> As you consider your own beliefs and practices around literature, reflect on the following:
>
> How do you usually select books for your classroom collections?
>
> Are the families, experiences, and voices of the children in your classroom represented? How does your collection also provide access to stories other than their own?
>
> Upon review of your collection,
>
> - Whose voices and experiences and histories are primarily represented?
> - Whose are noticeably absent?
> - Do you notice representation of award-winning authors, illustrators, and titles focused on better representation?
> - Are #OwnVoices authors and illustrators represented in your collection, and if so, are their stories challenging stereotypes of their community? Are the illustrations and language portrayals nuanced?
> - In addition to larger publishing houses, how are your collections supporting independent publishers?
>
> If you are unsure how to answer these questions, how can you and your colleagues begin to review the resources in this chapter to help develop your practice of selecting picturebooks with better representation in your collections?

When you think about developing a text selection process, it can look intimidating and almost impossible to keep up with! What I've learned, though, is that (in addition to embracing the work as a journey) the best way to stay on top of a sound selection process is to (1) schedule appointments with yourself to assess your collections; (2) continue these conversations with colleagues over time (remember, this is learning in progress), (3) learn from the experts (people doing the work), and (4) keep reading. I offer a robust list of resources at the end of this chapter and an annotated bibliography at the end of this book to help you and your colleagues begin to build your professional library (real and virtual) of resources, reflect on your positionality, grow your knowledge of the field, refine your selection process, rebuild your collections, and critically share texts. My lists are far from complete and would benefit from being paired with similar lists, but they are a place to begin. Again, although this book focuses primarily on sharing with children picturebooks with better representation, we must keep so much more in mind. I highly encourage you to spend a significant amount of time exploring what a text selection process means for you and making frequent appointments with your team over time to reflect on the status of your collections, as well as on the processes you are engaged in for growing those collections.

Practice 3: Scaffolding Picture Reading

Guiding students' reading of illustrations. Despite long appreciating the value of reading picturebooks, after spending time in these three teachers' classrooms, I am even more convinced that taking the time for picture reading (illustrations and images) adds profound and needed depth to critical literature discussions with young children. What research has taught us about picturebooks is that they (like all formats composed of multiple modalities such as print, color, sound, movement, etc.) are composed of many narratives. Reading a picturebook demands that we read both the print and the illustrated narrative *together* to make sense of the whole (see Figure 2.5). As renowned picturebook researcher Larry Sipe (2011) explains, it is in the synergy between the picture and

FIGURE 2.5. First-grade picture readers interpreting illustrations about civil rights.

the word that we come to know a picturebook's true essence. When teaching young children to read, we've historically placed greater emphasis on the print narrative and treated the illustrated narrative as an "extra." What might it mean to hold up illustrations as essential text from which to make meaning? What new insights and learning are possible when we do this?

If you've ever read a picturebook by Yuyi Morales, you'll know exactly what I mean. Each of her books is meant to be read multiple times, if not for the pictures alone. Her use of artesanía hues and motifs set the stage for exploration and appreciation of her Mexican heritage. The details in skin shade and the shape of her characters' faces and eyes portray the beauty and luminosity of Brown bodies. To ignore these visual aspects by focusing just on words on a page or basic story grammar is to ignore the artful, sociopolitical, and very personal themes available in Morales's picturebooks.

In the description of Lottie's first-grade classroom in Chapter 3, you will read how she and her students valued "picture reading" and being a "picture reader" as essential parts of the broader work of reading. I would be remiss to not also add that it was not uncommon to hear Kara or Whitney identify their upper-elementary students as picture readers and for students to clearly understand what that meant.

Whitney often asked her fifth graders to go be picture readers and to be ready to share what they'd uncovered. In the classrooms you will read about in Chapters 3 through 5, teachers guided students through the work of reading color and line as essential elements of the narrative with questions such as *How does color matter for the narrative here? What is the use of red on this page communicating? Who is foregrounded and centered on the page? What might that mean?* Teaching children to read the grammar of visual design such as color, line, perspective, shape, and other essential elements of art can only enhance the potential meanings and learning to be uncovered in a picturebook, including how to read power and interrogate marginalized experiences in visual form.

There is already significant research that sheds light on the importance of picture reading and visual literacy more broadly (see Figure 2.6). In my own research, I've noted how nonlinguistic texts (e.g., wordless picturebooks, photographs, etc.) provide an important scaffold for negotiating content, including the more complex issues and histories often presented in diverse picturebooks (Zapata et al., 2017; Zapata, 2022). Research has made clear how visual literacies provide needed additional means for meaning making and discussion in the classroom (Callow, 2008; Cowan & Albers, 2006; Pantaleo, 2013).

One way to support picture readers and their visual literacies is through visual thinking strategies (VTS) (Yenawine, 2013). VTS build on students' visual literacies and are flexible enough to be modified to interpret complex visual content (Cappello & Walker, 2016), including the art in diverse picturebooks. VTS are framed by a strategically sequenced questioning protocol designed to develop students' close observational skills and analysis of the text (Yenawine, 2013). As shown in Table 2.1 and described more fully in the classroom chapters, teachers pose focused questions during each step of the VTS protocol. Although teachers' questions can be characterized as having three distinct steps (initial visual analysis, structural analysis, extended analysis), I adapted the VTS protocol (see Zapata et al., 2017) to also support students' affectual and embodied responses to the visuals.

Teacher Professional Resource

To teach and learn more about the elements of visual design with your students and colleagues, I recommend reading the following:

- *Picture This: How Pictures Work* (2016) by Molly Bang
- *In Pictures and in Words* (2010) by Katie Wood Ray
- *Draw!* (2014) by Raúl Colón

FIGURE 2.6. First graders using their visual literacy skills to interpret metaphorical differences between light and dark.

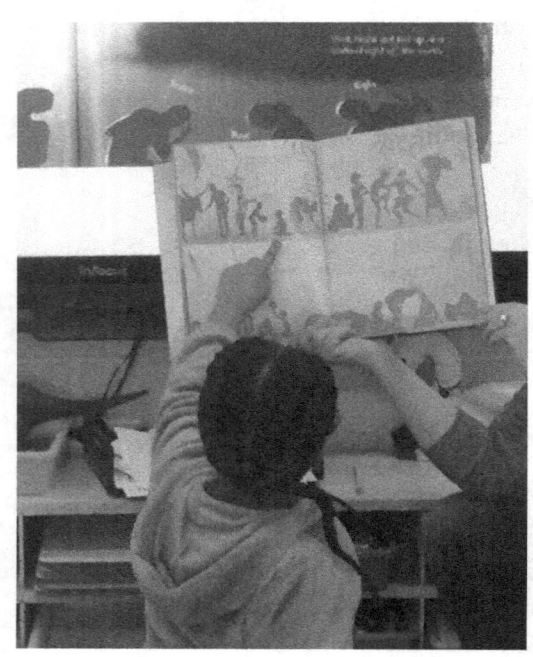

TABLE 2.1. Adapted Visual Thinking Strategies Protocol

Steps in Visual Thinking Strategies	Examples of Questions
Initial visual analysis	**What's going on in this picture?** What do you see? Who or what is the main focus? What colors are most vivid? What do you see in the foreground and what is hiding in the background? Where does your eye go first?
Structural analysis (Serafini, 2015)	**What do you see that makes you say that?** Why would the illustrator have drawn it like that? Why do the colors matter? What visual features, themes, recurring images do you see? How do the visual features provide understanding?
Extended analysis	**What more can you find?** What details did you not see the first time? What do you think is not shown in the picture? What perspective is the author taking? How is that impacting the image? Where would you be if you were in the picture? Tell me more.
Aesthetic response	**How does this image make you feel?** What emotions arise as you take in this image? What does your heart say in response to this? What is your body doing as you read this image? How does that feel?

VTS offer readers guidance to navigate so many meanings presented in an image. The VTS questions posed are open enough that multiple responses are possible but specific enough to provide focus. Notice that the first question does not ask students to share what they see but rather to share *what is going on* in the picture (Zapata et al., 2017).

The latter point, as my friend and visual literacy scholar Marva Cappello Goldstein reminds me, asks students to infer meaning and a potential narrative rather than to simply list visuals observed. A VTS approach to picturebooks affords occasions for students to explore visual meanings and themes in books representing a diversity of experiences.

Practice 4: Multilingual and Multimodal Literature Response

Making meaning of literature across modalities, languages, and language varieties.
Often, when I ask teachers what literature response looks like in classrooms, they share images of children answering prompted questions about story elements on worksheets, or students discussing their favorite parts of the story. In the classrooms you will read about here, you will see that young children are invited to respond to literature quite differently, as they are immersed in multiple modalities, or ways of making meaning, and have access to their different ways with words, or languages and language varieties, as needed. In the classrooms you will get to know here, you will observe children

recording poems as podcasts alongside painting self-portraits as literature response. You will learn from children using their bodies to interpret characters' actions. You will hear children exploring their different languages and language varieties to respond to literature. You will see children float all of this work on a "sea of talk," as James Britton (1970) teaches us, to respond to literature in the context of a Critical Literature Response Framework. I use the term *multilingual and multimodal* here to best capture this fluid movement across languages, language varieties, modalities, and meanings to respond to literature.

Specifically, I use the term *multilingual* to refer to the fluidity with which we shuttle across our ways with words to communicate. Growing up as a daughter of immigrant parents from Perú in Houston, Texas, for example, it was not uncommon to hear me say, "Hey, y'all, dondé esta mi pillow?" In my talk, I would bring together Spanish and different varieties of English, including Southern English. I still do, to be honest, and happily do so across a variety of contexts, not just at home. I'm a proud Texan, so I still like to use *y'all*, and I can't imagine removing Spanish from my talk, so I still find myself meshing my languages even as I currently live in the Midwest. I acknowledge that mixing languages is often frowned upon as a "crutch" to avoid learning to speak "proper" English and that many have viewed this practice in deficit ways that can mark how the speaker is received by others. What research (Martínez, 2010) has illustrated, however, is that this dynamic use of language is cognitively complex, systematic, and a valid and viable way to support language and literacy development among young children. We're learning from the research on translanguaging and translingual literacies (e.g., García & Kleifgen, 2020) that a classroom culture in which bi- and multilingual speakers navigate the social and cognitive demands of schooling through strategic use of their languages is a rich context for young children's language and literacy learning, as well as for their identities as bi- and multilingual people.

By multimodal literacies, I simply refer to literacies that involve two or more modes to make meaning. Reading a picture book, for example, is a multimodal literacy because the print and the image both contribute to the overall telling of the story but do so through different modes, including written language, still image, and spatial design. When we read a picturebook's words, lines, colors, layout, visual perspective, fonts, formats, materiality . . . all of it matters in order to make meaning. Supporting children's multimodal literacy learning from an early age helps to prepare them as critical readers of picturebooks and also develops a foundation to navigate the deluge of multimodal texts they will encounter in their future, including digital media such as photographs, memes, GIFs, video, and podcasts. When children understand that reading and making meaning is more than decoding print, they can more readily appreciate and employ the everyday multimodal literacies in their lives.

Providing children with multilingual and multimodal pathways to respond to literature in the classroom is an issue of equity, as well as of creative and intellectual opportunity. Invitations to respond to picturebooks in ways that extend beyond paper and pencil in Standardized English afford children access to all the ways they make meaning, not just to one. When talking about putting all of our ways with words to work, my friend and language education scholar Ramón Martínez once described it to me like this: *If we have a toolkit full of different tools, why teach someone they can only use one, and why would you pick it for them? If our linguistic toolkit is composed of different languages and language varieties, why would we limit our children to just one?* I would argue the same is true for literature response: why would we limit our children to just paper and pencil, and only to Standardized English, when there are so many tools available to them? Now, certainly, there is a place for providing guidance and mentorship for tool selection and use, but what I am suggesting is that we provide that guidance and mentorship with a diverse array of tools, not just a select few.

As a matter of equity, multimodal and multilingual literature invitations help students develop the ability to respond to ways of working with text beyond the dominant ones, such as responding to questions on paper or to linear questions during discussion. Multimodal and multilingual response opportunities afford new openings to participate in literature discussion more fully, particularly for our students who bring languages and literacies that are different from the ones we privilege in schools. As an issue of creativity and intellectual demand, responding to literature across modalities and ways with words provides all students an opportunity to think bigger and develop fluency and dexterity with a diverse array of tools. The intellectual demand is greater when we are asked to work hard to problem-solve and to consider which tools might best serve the messages we aim to convey, rather than to simply replicate a standardized form. Thinking and making across a diverse array of tools in response to literature demands imagination and thinking outside of the box. Under these conditions, new possibilities emerge, fresh ideas are explored, and transformative moments can unfold around literature.

What we also know from the research on both multimodal and multilingual literacies more broadly is that when children can access and leverage their own languages and literacies, there is a positive impact on their identities, not only as readers and writers but also as artists and multilingual designers. Supporting students' identities in this way has implications for how students

Teacher Professional Resource

To learn more about multilingual and multimodal literacies with young children, read the following:

- *Multimodal Literacies in Young Emergent Bilinguals: Beyond Print-centric Practices* (2022) edited by Sally Brown and Ling Hao

- *Story Workshop: New Possibilities for Young Writers* (2021) by Susan Harris MacKay

- *Rooted in Strength: Using Translanguaging to Grow Multilingual Readers and Writers* (2021) by Cecilia M. Espinosa and Laura Ascenzi-Moreno

- "Cultivating a Critical Translingual Landscape in the Elementary Language Arts Classroom" (2020) by Angie Zapata

see themselves as knowing members and valuable contributors to the well-being of their communities.

Enlivening a Critical Literature Response Framework: Starting Your Journey

In sum, imagine the possibilities for our children if they had access to these dynamic literature-based practices (see Figure 2.1) in the context of a Critical Literature Response Framework (see Figure 1.3). So exciting! Remember, it isn't the practices themselves that make for a critical literature response classroom, but rather the broader framework conditions and teacher commitments that guide these practices; these are what matter the most when supporting children's critical interrogations of literature. Enacting these practices in and of themselves cannot do the work of bringing awareness to social justice–related issues. What these practices can create under the right conditions are invaluable opportunities to dig deeply into those issues. Similarly, implementing book floods, picture readers, and multimodal and multilingual literature response and having wide and varied picturebook collections does not make us critically oriented educators. I want to emphasize again the importance of our own beliefs and understandings, our stances against racism, linguistic shaming, and, more broadly, xenophobia, as the foundation for a Critical Literature Response Framework. Without first unpacking our own beliefs and practices and without recognizing our teaching as political, these practices cannot lead us to transformative literature discussions.

The NCTE *Preparing Teachers with Knowledge of Children's and Young Adult Literature* position statement (2018) similarly encourages us to address our professional stances and to consider four basic principles as teachers of literature:

1. Know the literature.
2. Be readers.
3. Affirm diversity and exercise critical literacy.
4. Use appropriate pedagogy.

By embracing these principles and situating our work within a Critical Literature Response Framework, we enhance our capacity to teach and advocate for literature in the hands of our children through the literature practices discussed in this chapter. What the teachers in this book and I learned through our time together and after deep reflection is that this work must be nested in our collaborative teacher communities that include the voices of People of Color in sustained reading, professional discussion, and deep humility. The opportunities to debrief and engage in these principles, commitments, conditions, and practices truly are the critical areas of growth we need as educators.

As a teacher collective over several years, Lottie, Kara, Whitney, and I have gathered alongside other early childhood and elementary educators to learn more about children's literature and how to support the teaching and reading of books that represent cultures different from our own and how to support critical interrogation of texts with young children. We've familiarized ourselves with titles and authors and critiques, tried things out in our classrooms, failed, reassessed, and tried again. I think what sustained us was the opportunity to be together in conversation, to debrief what was happening in our classrooms with a focus on both how our students were responding and how we felt doing that work. No matter how long we've been doing the work, we recognize that we are each still en route, moving forward on our journeys as critical social educators. Constant self-reflection and the boldness to know that we all have limits to our knowledge were our touchstones. Here we provide access to our reflections and real transparency in those moments of reassessment of instruction.

Along the way, we familiarized ourselves with readings and thinkers who inspired, challenged, and pushed us. I share a sample of those readings and thinkers below as resources for you and other colleagues to explore and dig into. At the end of this book is an annotated bibliography of select resources as well. I am a firm believer that no one list can be held up as authoritative or complete. Keeping that in mind, I hope you receive this collection of resources as a place to start and grow alongside others interested in joining a critical literature response journey with you.

Professional Resources to Support a Critical Literature Response Framework in the Classroom

Social Media

As I mentioned in Chapter 1, the ongoing conversations around better representation in children's literature are now accessible to us all through social media. I am often asked who I follow and what I read; my answer changes frequently, as you can imagine, but I share some resources below that have impacted me at some point in my journey. As a reminder, this list is not comprehensive and is intended to serve as a launching pad for entering and participating in the critical literature discussions that are unfolding online. Check out these sites below as a place to start building your social media resources. Thank you to Sarah Reid and Mary Adu-Gyamfi, who helped me to gather and format the following resource list.

- Blogs
  - American Indians in Children's Literature—Debbie Reese & Jean Mendoza
    https://americanindiansinchildrensliterature.blogspot.com
  - Anansesem [Caribbean Children's and Young Adult Literature Publishing]
    www.anansesem.com
  - Booktoss—Laura Jimenez
    https://booktoss.org
  - The Brown Bookshelf
    https://thebrownbookshelf.com
  - De Colores: The Raza Experience in Books for Children
    decoloresreviews.blogspot.com
  - Disability in Kidlit
    disabilityinkidlit.com
  - Edith Campbell
    https://crazyquiltedi.blog
  - Hijabi Librarians: We've Got It Covered
    https://hijabilibrarians.com
  - Indigo's Bookshelf: Voices of Native Youth
    https://indigosbookshelf.blogspot.com
  - Latinxs in Kid Lit
    https://latinosinkidlit.com
  - Maya Gonzalez Blog
    www.mayagonzalez.com/blog/
  - The Open Book Blog—Lee & Low Books
    blog.leeandlow.com
  - Reading While White
    readingwhilewhite.blogspot.com
  - Sarah Park Dahlen
    sarahpark.com
  - We Need Diverse Books
    https://diversebooks.org/blog/
- Social Media Feeds (including X, formerly known as Twitter)
  - Children of the Glades (@OfGlades)

- Debbie Reese (@debreese)
- Ebony Elizabeth Thomas (@Ebonyteach)
- Hijabi Librarians (@hijabilibrarian)
- LatinoBooksMonthRI (@LatinoBooksRI)
- Latinxs in Kid Lit (@LationsInKidLit)
- Laura Jimenez (@booktoss)
- Lee & Low Books (@LEEandLOW)
- Reading While White (@ReadWhileWhite)
- Rich in Color (@Rich_in_Color)
- Sarah Park Dahlen (@readingspark)
- WeNeedDiverseBooks (@diversebooks)
- Some Authors and Illustrators to follow:
  - Isabel Quintero (@isabelinpieces)
  - Jacqueline Woodson (@JackieWoodson)
  - Juana Martinez-Neal (@Juanaartinez)
  - Lulu Delacre (@LuluDelacre)
  - Margarita Engle (@margaritapoet)
  - Minh Lê (@bottomshelfbks)
  - Monica Brown (@monicabrownbks)
  - Rafael López (@rafaellopezart)
  - Vashti Harrison (@VashtiHarrison)
  - Yuyi Morales (@yuyimorales)
  - Zetta Elliott (@zettaelliott)

- Hashtags
  - #BuildYourStack
  - #DisruptBooks
  - #OwnVoices
  - #ReadingTheK8Rainbow
  - #WeNeedDiverseBooks
- Websites
  - Diverse Futures—Stephanie Toliver https://readingblackfutures.com

- Raising Luminaries
  https://booksforlittles.com
- Social Justice Books: Booklists
  https://socialjusticebooks.org/booklists/
- Social Justice Books: Freedom Reads: Anti-Bias Book Talk Series
  https://socialjusticebooks.org/freedom-reads/
- Social Justice Books: Guide for Selecting Anti-Bias Children's Books
  https://socialjusticebooks.org/guide-for-selecting-anti-bias-childrens-books/
- Social Justice Books: See What We See: Children's and Young Adult Book Reviews
  https://socialjusticebooks.org/reviews-by-theme/
- Teaching for Change
  https://www.teachingforchange.org
- We Are Kid Lit Collective
  https://wtpsite.com
- We Need Diverse Books
  https://diversebooks.org

• Other
  - Debbie Reese: An Indigenous Critique of Whiteness in Children's Literature
    https://www.pbs.org/video/indigenous-critique-of-whiteness-in-childrens-books-iiquyq/
  - Ebony Elizabeth Thomas: The Dark Fantastic: Race and the Imagination in Youth Literature, Media, and Culture
    https://www.youtube.com/watch?v=b2NE773RNPw
  - Ebony Elizabeth Thomas: Race and the Imagination
    https://www.youtube.com/watch?v=YGJsdugoNoY

Publishing Houses

I've always found that Zetta Elliot has smart things to say about publishing houses, and she pushes us to seek out independent publishers. Check out this link to hear her compelling thoughts on the matter: https://booksforlittles.com/zetta-elliott/. Listed below are publishing houses for you to begin to get to know as you seek better representation in your collections. I'm still working to meet Zetta's call to better support independent publishers and bookshops investing in better representation in children's literature. I hope you'll join me!

- Agate Bolden
  https://www.agatepublishing.com/imprints/agate-bolden
- Amistad
  http://amistad.hc.com
- Baobab Publishing
  https://baobabpublishing.com
- Barefoot Books
  https://www.barefootbooks.com
- Beachhouse Publishing
  http://www.beachhousepublishing.com
- Caribbean Reads
  https://www.caribbeanreads.com
- Con Todo Press
  https://www.contodopress.com
- Flamingo Rampant
  https://www.flamingorampant.com
- House of Anansi and Groundwood Books
  https://groundwoodbooks.com
- Just Us Books
  https://justusbooks.com
- KitaabWorld
  https://kitaabworld.com
- Latana Publishing
  https://lantanapublishing.com
- Lee & Low Books
  https://www.leeandlow.com
- Mango & Marigold Press
  https://mangoandmarigoldpress.com
- Orca Book Publishers
  https://www.orcabook.com
- Plum Street Press
  https://www.facebook.com/search/top?q=plum%20street%20press

- Portage & Main Press and HighWater Press
  https://www.portageandmainpress.com/HighWater-PressReflection Press
  https://reflectionpress.com
- The RoadRunner Press
  https://www.theroadrunnerpress.com
- Salaam Reads
  http://salaamreads.com
- Yali Books
  https://yalibooks.com

Resources for Text Selection

As promised in Chapter 1, here is a list of the text selection guides from Lee & Low you might lean on to launch a deep assessment of the collections you already have in your classrooms. I particularly appreciate the invitations to include your young readers in this process along the way.

- https://blog.leeandlow.com/2016/03/01/classroom-library-5-things-to-consider/
- https://blog.leeandlow.com/2016/07/07/part-1-having-students-analyze-our-classroom-library-to-see-how-diverse-it-is/
- https://blog.leeandlow.com/2016/07/21/part-2-having-students-analyze-our-classroom-library-to-see-how-diverse-it-is/
- https://blog.leeandlow.com/2017/05/22/classroom-library-assessment-how-culturally-responsive-is-your-classroom-library/
- Henderson, J. W., Warren, K., Whitmore, K. F., Flint, A. S., Laman, T. T., & Jaggers, W. (2020). Take a close look: Inventorying your classroom library for diverse books. *The Reading Teacher*, *73*(6), 747–55.

Professional Reading

Building your collection of professional reading on children's literature in early childhood and elementary settings will be an ongoing process, as new work is always being published. The following texts are staples to stretch your learning, and I also encourage you to attend to the authors and researchers writing these texts so that you can be on the lookout for their future works as well.

Books

Ada, A. F. (2003). *A magical encounter: Latino children's literature in the classroom* (2nd ed.). Allyn & Bacon.

Ahiyya, V. (2022). *Rebellious read alouds: Inviting conversations about diversity with children's books.* Corwin.

Briceño, A., & Rodriguez-Mojica, C. (2022). Conscious classrooms: Using diverse texts for inclusion, equity, and justice. Benchmark Education.

Dunbar-Ortiz, R. (2019). *An indigenous peoples' history of the United States for young people* (Mendoza, J., & Reese, D., Adaps.). Beacon Press.

Ladson-Billings, G. (2009). *The dreamkeepers: Successful teachers of African American children.* Jossey-Bass.

Leland, C., Lewison, M., & Harste, J. (2013). *Teaching children's literature: It's critical!* Routledge.

Love, B. L. (2019). *We want to do more than survive: Abolitionist teaching and the pursuit of educational freedom.* Beacon Press.

Muhammad, G. (2020). *Cultivating genius: An equity framework for culturally and historically responsive literacy.* Scholastic.

Muhammad, G. (2023). *Unearthing joy: A guide to culturally and historically responsive teaching and learning.* Scholastic.

Nieto, S., & Bode, P. (2018). *Affirming diversity: The sociopolitical context of multicultural education* (7th ed.). Pearson.

Short, K. G., & Cueto, D. W. (2022). *Essentials of children's literature* (10th ed.). Pearson.

Souto-Manning, M. (2013). *Multicultural teaching in the early childhood classroom: Approaches, strategies, and tools, preschool–2nd grade.* Teachers College Press.

Thomas, E. E. (2019). *The dark fantastic: Race and the imagination from Harry Potter to the Hunger Games.* New York University Press.

Vasquez, V. (2010). *Getting beyond "I like the book": Creating space for critical literacy in K–6 classrooms* (2nd ed.). International Reading Association.

Research Articles

Bazemore-Bertrand, S. (2020). Classroom voices: Using children's literature to discuss social issues in the classroom. *Talking Points, 31*(2), 22–25.

Bishop, R. S. (1990). Mirrors, windows, and sliding glass doors. *Perspectives: Choosing and Using Books for the Classroom, 6*(3), ix–xi.

Braden, E. G., Gibson, V., & Taylor-Gillette, R. (2020). Everything Black is NOT bad! Families and teachers engaging in critical discussions around race. *Talking Points, 31*(2), 2–12.

Compton-Lilly, C. (2006). Identity, childhood culture, and literacy learning: A case study. *Journal of Early Childhood Literacy, 6*(1), 57–76.

Crisp, T., Gardner, R. P., & Almeida, M. (2018). The all-heterosexual world of children's nonfiction: A critical content analysis of LGBTQ identities in Orbis Pictus Award books, 1990–2017. *Children's Literature in Education, 49*(3), 246–63.

Cueto, D., & Corapi, S. (2019). Critical inquiries into politicized issues. *Journal of Children's Literature, 45*(1), 38–49.

Fontanella-Nothom, O. (2019). "Why do we have different skins anyway?" Exploring race in literature with preschool children. *Multicultural Perspectives, 21*(1), 11–18.

Gardner, R. P. (2017). Discussing racial trauma using visual thinking strategies. *Language Arts, 94*(5), 338–45.

Goodman, D. (2006). Language study in teacher education: Exploring the *language* in language arts. *Language Arts, 84*(2), 145–56.

Gultekin, M., & May, L. (2020). Children's literature as fun-house mirrors, blind spots, and curtains. *The Reading Teacher, 73*(5), 627–35.

Henderson, J. W., Warren, K., Whitmore, K. F., Flint, A. S., Laman, T. T., & Jaggers, W. (2020). Take a close look: Inventorying your classroom library for diverse books. *The Reading Teacher, 73*(6), 747–55.

Ishizuka, K., & Stephens, R. (2019). The cat is out of the bag: Orientalism, anti-Blackness, and white supremacy in Dr. Seuss's children's books. *Research on Diversity in Youth Literature, 1*(2).

Jones, S. (2006). Language with an attitude: White girls performing class. *Language Arts, 84*(2), 114–24.

Kesler, T., Mills, M., & Reilly, M. (2020). I hear you: Teaching social justice in interactive read-aloud. *Language Arts, 97*(4), 207–22.

Kibler, K., & Chapman, L. A. (2019). Six tips for using culturally relevant texts in diverse classrooms. *The Reading Teacher, 72*(6), 741–44.

Kleekamp, M. C., & Zapata, A. (2019). Interrogating depictions of disability in children's picturebooks. *The Reading Teacher, 72*(5), 589–97.

Lo, R. S. (2019). Resisting gentle bias: A critical content analysis of family diversity in picturebooks. *Journal of Children's Literature, 45*(2), 16–30.

McNair, J. C. (2016). #WeNeedMirrorsandWindows: Diverse classroom libraries for K–6 students. *The Reading Teacher, 70*(3), 375–81.

Mendoza, J., & Reese, D. (2001). Examining multicultural picture books for the early childhood classroom: Possibilities and pitfalls. *Early Childhood Research & Practice, 3*(2), 1–38. https://files.eric.ed.gov/fulltext/ED458040.pdf

Möller, K. J. (2020). Reading and responding to LGBTQ-inclusive children's literature in school settings: Considering the state of research on inclusion. *Language Arts, 97*(4), 235–51.

Newstreet, C., Sarker, A., & Shearer, R. (2019). Teaching empathy: Exploring multiple perspectives to address Islamophobia through children's literature. *The Reading Teacher, 72*(5), 559–68.

Quast, E. (2019). "And he could wear a dress?": A preschool transformative book conversation. *The Reading Teacher, 72*(4), 445–51.

Quast, E., & Bazemore-Bertrand, S. (2019). Exploring economic diversity and inequity through picture books. *The Reading Teacher, 73*(2), 219–22.

Rodríguez, N. N. (2017). "But they didn't do nothin' wrong!": Teaching about Japanese-American incarceration. *Social Studies and the Young Learner, 30*(2), 17–23.

Rodríguez, N. N., & Kim, E. J. (2018). In search of mirrors: An Asian critical race theory content analysis of Asian American picturebooks from 2007 to 2017. *Journal of Children's Literature, 44*(2), 17–30.

Rogers, R., & Mosley, M.. (2006). Racial literacy in a second-grade classroom: Critical race theory, whiteness studies, and literacy research. *Reading Research Quarterly, 41*(4), 462–95.

Ryan, C. L., & Hermann-Wilmarth, J. M. (2019). Putting read-alouds to work for LGBTQ-inclusive, critically literate classrooms. *Language Arts, 96*(5), 312–17.

Souto-Manning, M. (2009). Negotiating culturally responsive pedagogy through multicultural children's literature: Towards critical democratic literacy practices in a first-grade classroom. *Journal of Early Childhood Literacy, 9*(1), 50–74.

Toliver, S. R. (2018). "Imagining new hopescapes: Expanding Black girls' windows and mirrors." *Research on Diversity in Youth Literature, 1*(1).

Van Horn, S. E. (2015). "How do you have two moms?" Challenging heteronormativity while sharing LGBTQ-inclusive children's literature. *Talking Points, 27*(1), 2–12.

Ward, N. A., & Warren, A. N. (2020). "In search of peace": Refugee experiences in children's literature. *The Reading Teacher, 73*(4), 405–13.

Webber, K., & Agiro, C. P. (2019). Not from around these parts: Using young adult literature to promote empathy for the immigrant experience. *Talking Points, 30*(2), 2–9.

Wissman, K. K. (2019). Reading radiantly: Embracing the power of picturebooks to cultivate the social imagination. *Bookbird: A Journal of International Children's Literature, 57*(1), 14–25.

Zapata, A. (2020). Cultivating a critical translingual landscape in the elementary language arts classroom. *Language Arts, 97*(6), 384–90.

Zapata, A. (2022). (Re)animating children's aesthetic experiences with/through literature: Critically curating picturebooks as sociopolitical art. *The Reading Teacher, 76*(1), 84–91.

Zapata, A., Fugit, M., & Moss, D. (2017). Awakening socially just mindsets through visual thinking strategies and diverse picturebooks. *Journal of Children's Literature, 43*(2), 62–69.

Zapata, A., King, C., King, G., & Kleekamp, M. (2019). Thinking with race-conscious perspectives: Critically selecting children's picture books depicting slavery. *Multicultural Perspectives 21*(1), 25–32.

Zapata, A., & Laman, T. T. (2023). Reconditioning a new linguistic normal for children's classrooms through critical translingual literacies. *Language Arts,100*(3), 245–53.

Zapata, A., & Van Horn, S. (2017). "Because I'm smooth": Material intra-actions and text productions among young Latino picture book makers. *Research in the Teaching of English, 51*(3), 290–315.

National Book Awards

American Indian Youth Literature Award
Awarded in even years, this award honors authors, illustrators, and literature about and by American Indians.
https://ailanet.org/activities/american-indian-youth-literature-award/

Américas Award
This award honors children's and young adult books that depict Latin America, the Caribbean, or Latinx experiences in the United States.
http://www.claspprograms.org/americasaward

Asian/Pacific American Award for Literature
This award honors books about Asian/Pacific Americans and their culture.
http://www.apalaweb.org/awards/literature-awards/

Carter G. Woodson Book Awards
This award honors children's books that authentically portray ethnicity/ethnic minorities and topics related to race relations.
https://www.socialstudies.org/get-involved/carter-g-woodson-book-award-and-honor-winners

Coretta Scott King Book Award
These awards honor young adult and children's books written or illustrated by African American authors and illustrators that express the African American experience.
http://www.ala.org/awardsgrants/coretta-scott-king-book-awards

Dolly Gray Children's Literature Award
Awarded in even years, this award honors authors, illustrators, and publishers of books that appropriately depict individuals with developmental disabilities.
https://www.dollygrayaward.com

Jane Addams Children's Book Awards
 These awards honor books that engage children in topics of peace, social justice, and equity.
 http://www.janeaddamschildrensbookaward.org
Pura Belpré Award
 Awarded annually, this award honors Latino/Latina writers and illustrators of distinguished children's and youth literature that celebrates and depicts the Latino cultural experience.
 http://www.ala.org/alsc/awardsgrants/bookmedia/belpremedal
Schneider Family Book Award
 This award honors authors and/or illustrators of books that represent the disability experience.
 http://www.ala.org/awardsgrants/schneider-family-book-award
Sydney Taylor Book Award
 Awarded annually, this award honors authentic children's literature about the Jewish experience.
 https://jewishlibraries.org/Sydney_Taylor_Book_Award
Tomás Rivera Mexican American Children's Book Award
 This award honors authors and illustrators of books about the Mexican American experience.
 https://www.education.txstate.edu/ci/riverabookaward/book-award-winners.html

Children's Literature Cited

Bang, M. (2016). *Picture this: How pictures work* (Rev. & Exp. ed.). Chronicle Books
Buitrago, J., & Yockteng, R. (2015). *Two white rabbits*. Groundwood Books.
Colón, R. (2014). *Draw!* Simon & Schuster.
Laínez, R. C. (2019). *My shoes and I: Crossing three borders / Mis zapatos y yo: Cruzando tres fronteras* (F. V. Broeck, Illus.). Pinata Books/Arte Publico Press.
Morales, Y. (2018). *Dreamers*. Neal Porter Books/Holiday House
Smith, B. (1992). *A tree grows in Brooklyn*. HarperPerennial.
Tonatiuh, D. (2013). *Pancho Rabbit and the coyote: A migrant's tale*. Abrams.

Chapter Three
Becoming Critical Picture Readers

Lottie, a first-grade teacher, has a way of reminding her students that what they have to say is important and valuable. It is not uncommon to hear her articulate her admiration for their capacity to listen to one another. In doing so, she sets the stage for the important task of listening and thinking about the story to be shared and what fellow readers have to say in response to the book. "What is special about you all is that you can be thoughtful readers and listeners" is what she tells her twenty students as they settle on the carpet to participate in a read-aloud of a *Case for Loving: The Fight for Interracial Marriage* (2015) by Selina Alko and illustrated by Sean Qualls. Before reading, Lottie asks, "What is 'loving'?"

    Brayden thinks it means hugs and kisses.
    Aria says it's "like you like someone."
    Maliyah adds that it means "doing something nice for someone."
    Elena shares that it is "someone you want to live with . . . instead of just stay for the night."
    Lottie reads aloud the subtitle, "The fight for interracial marriage." She reads the author's and illustrator's names and mentions that the class will talk about them more later. Lottie then asks, "Why does the endpaper look like this . . . with hearts on it?" A student quickly interrupts to ask why it is called the endpaper, to which Lottie responds, "Because it is at the 'ends' of the book."

Elena thinks the endpapers have hearts on them because the "whole book is about loving someone . . . and about marriage too."

Luke adds, "Because Black and white people used to not be able to marry each other."

"How did you know?" Lottie asks.

Brayden explains how he inferred that meaning from the subtitle that she read aloud.

Lottie tells him, "Kiss your brain. It's a good one."

After reading aloud this line from the text, "where people every shade from the color of chamomile tea to summer midnight made their homes," Lottie wonders aloud, "What does that sentence mean?" As the children take a moment to reflect and talk to one another about the imagery in the written text and the skin shades they evoke, Lottie projects visuals of chamomile tea and summer night for students to interpret. Already a habit in their classroom, children immediately begin reading the visuals alongside the printed text as part of their work as readers. They note the variations in brown and white and tan and closely look at their own skins. In this case, reading both the written and illustrated texts positions students to notice and explore skin shade representations further. Lottie asks again, "So what does that tell you about the people that live there? Does it *look* like our classroom?" Students respond enthusiastically, "Yeah!"

Lottie does not always interrupt to ask questions during the first read-aloud of a text, but when she does, it is for a reason. In this case, she pauses to guide her young readers to visualize the imagery in the written text while also attending to the illustrations featuring those skin shades they see in their classroom every day. In Lottie's classroom, visuals are an entry point to critical interrogation of text.

In this chapter, I share a bit more about Lottie and provide deeper insight into the way she and her students live, learn, and make meaning together around picturebooks through a Critical Literature Response Framework. I then offer a brief overview of the focused literature exploration and literary arrows Lottie shared with the children and conclude with a series of critical literature encounters the children and Lottie entered to specifically highlight the role of visual thinking strategies. I hope that as you move through this chapter and reflect on how this work can look in your own classroom, you'll be reminded of the depth and capacity young children bring to critical literature discussions and that you'll find the art of navigating critical literature discussions with picturebooks as rewarding and hopeful as it is complex and humbling.

Featured Picturebook Summary

The Case for Loving: The Fight for Interracial Marriage (2015) was written by Selina Alko and co-illustrated with her husband, Sean Qualls, and offers history that was, until 2015, not accessible to young children in picturebook form. The Supreme Court decision in the *Loving v. Virginia* case is one part of our history that, unfortunately, most students do not encounter in elementary school. The picturebook offers a dynamically illustrated narrative of how Mildred Jeter and Richard Loving fell in love and were married in Washington, DC. Upon returning to their home in Virginia, they were arrested for not abiding by the state's laws against interracial marriage. Together, the Lovings fought to dismantle this law, taking their case all the way to the Supreme Court. They ultimately won, affirming their love and their family, and ensuring that others would not have to endure the same battle in court.

One important note: I recently learned that Mildred Jeter came forward in 2004 to say she did not identify as Black, although this picturebook indicates otherwise. According to Reese (2007), Jeter told [the interviewer], "I am not Black. I have no Black ancestry. I am Indian-Rappahannock" (para. 10). (To learn more about Dr. Reese's analysis of this book, scan the QR code to uncover more about the complexity of racial politics, the language of color blindness, and missing claims to Native identity that children will encounter when reading *The Case for Loving*.) In an effort to be transparent in my own learning and journey, I want readers to know that had I been aware of this critique at the time I would have shared it with Lottie and our team so that we could provide Mildred Jeter's complete Indigenous history and invite children into discussion on the matter. Even with our best efforts and intentions, we can make mistakes when selecting picturebooks for children. How we respond and work to repair is part of our work as well.

Entering Lottie's First-Grade Classroom

The first thing you should learn about Lottie as a teacher is that she is honest, open, and interested in the world. Together these qualities make it easy to see why young children are so comfortable around her. Her deep curiosity about nature and global phenomena is contagious, and her belief in young children as capable and competent is inspiring. As an avid birder, for example, Lottie knows so many varieties of birds and their songs. She shares her genuine interest in birds and every creature under the sun, a disposition of inquiry that the children are quick to take up. Among my most memorable times in her classroom was a moment when she talked to the children about caring for the corn snake that was visiting the class for an extended period. She modeled her own questions about the snake and the importance of providing a quiet and still environment for its safety, and she expressed great confidence in the children as observers, inquirers, and stewards of the earth. She extended the experience with informational texts on snakes, inviting the children to act as scientists: recording their observations and discussing those noticings with one another. These authentic engagements with literacy positioned the children to use reading and writing as tools for inquiry, learning, and life.

Lottie, a veteran teacher in her final year of teaching first grade before retirement, garnered much respect from all of us in the group for her rich experience as an educator, deep care for teaching young children, and humility. She in many ways was just starting her journey as a critical social educator. Lottie would be the first to say that she had something to learn, a sentiment very much in keeping with her desire for personal and professional development. For example, after sharing picturebooks with our group and discussing representations of skin shade in picturebook illustrations, Lottie shared, "I just think it's really charming that first graders don't really notice skin color, especially when it comes to choosing friends." A few months later, after engaging her students in interrogations of skin shade in illustrations and as children began illustrating their own families, reflecting variance in skin shade, Lottie brought her own reflection to our attention. "Remember when I said I thought first graders don't notice skin color? Well, I take that back," and she held up students' hand-drawn family portraits reflecting a diversity of skin shades. It was Lottie's trust in her young students, in their ability and power to enter these conversations, and her determination to truly listen to what these brilliant children were sharing that changed Lottie's mind.

As I provide more insights into Lottie's classroom and how critical literature discussions unfolded, I invite you to continue to reflect on your own practice. Where are you in your journey as a critical literacy educator? What are your passions and interests personally and professionally? Areas of strength and development? How might you enact the work similarly with your students? How might it look different? And why? What role does your journey as a critical literacy educator play in your classroom work, and in what ways are you leaving room for humility and reflection as guides for your journey? Keeping these questions in mind as you move through this chapter will help you begin to imagine what this work can look like in your classroom and to consider the way your journey as a person and critical literacy educator shapes what unfolds in your classroom.

Enlivening a Critical Literature Response in an Early Childhood Classroom

In addition to living out a culture of inquiry as well as professional and personal growth, Lottie made a Critical Literature Response Framework come to life in her classroom in two specific ways:

- Valuing young children as knowing and capable
- Supporting an expansive view of early reading

I briefly share more about these two classroom approaches below to provide even more context for how critical literature response unfolded in Lottie's classroom.

Classroom Approach 1: Valuing Young Children as Knowing and Capable

Too often we as adults perceive young children as too innocent for critical conversations about race, injustice, or diversity more broadly. Yet we know that children, especially our People of Color and LGBTQ+ children and youth and their families, navigate these topics daily in their lives. There is substantial research (Adu-Gyamfi et al., 2021; Fontanella-Notham, 2019) that supports having critical conversations with young children as viable and needed work that can directly impact the ways they navigate encounters with racial differences, for example, in the future.

Because questions of discomfort and appropriateness of diverse literature for young children persist, I have found that when I follow up by asking, "Who is uncomfortable? What do you mean by appropriate? For whom?," it is often we adults who fear making young white children and their families uncomfortable. Lottie sees every child as capable of entering these discussions and understands that silence only recenters racism and xenophobia as children are left to draw their own conclusions based on what they see and hear daily (see Figure 3.1).

Lottie knew her students were ready and able to talk about racial injustice and didn't hesitate to scaffold these discussions as children asked questions. When she revisits *A Case for Loving* later in the year, for example, she invites the children to make predictions about final rulings for interracial marriage based on what was presented to the court. She asks the children to reflect on what they think should happen and to share their personal responses to racial injustice.

Aria thinks they changed the law "because it's actually not fair."

Elena explains that "the color of people's skin doesn't matter.... On TV shows at home sometimes real people get married even though they don't have the same skin color.... Skin color doesn't matter for marriage." She adds that she thinks that the Lovings "are going to win their case."

Lottie asks if she has seen that in real life.

Elena replies, "Yes, in my family."

Teacher Professional Resource

Check out "Your Kids Aren't Too Young to Talk about Race: Resource Roundup" by Katrina Michie and the NASP statement on ending racism.

FIGURE 3.1. Children can talk about race.

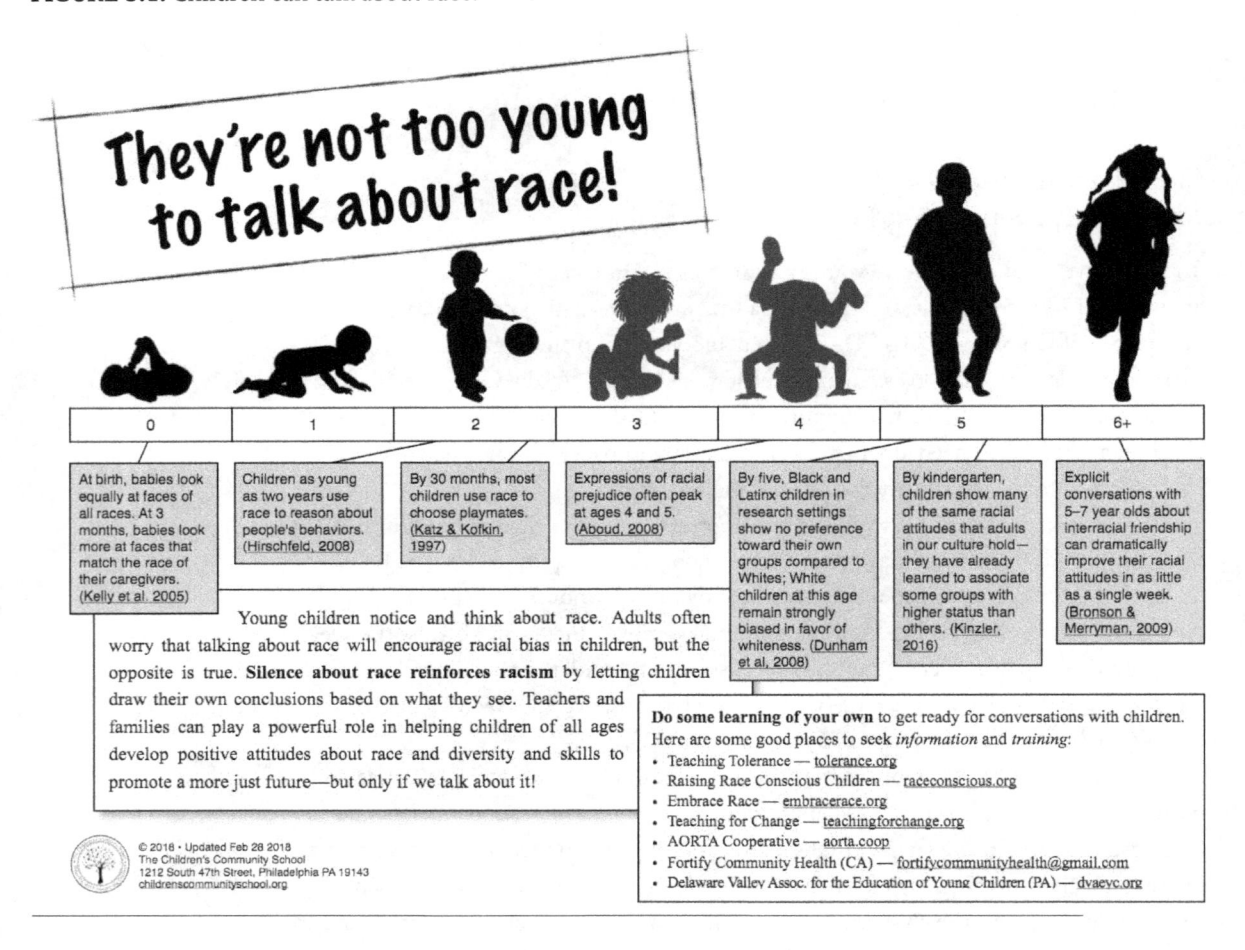

They're not too young to talk about race!

Age	Description
0	At birth, babies look equally at faces of all races. At 3 months, babies look more at faces that match the race of their caregivers. (Kelly et al. 2005)
1	Children as young as two years use race to reason about people's behaviors. (Hirschfeld, 2008)
2	By 30 months, most children use race to choose playmates. (Katz & Kofkin, 1997)
3	Expressions of racial prejudice often peak at ages 4 and 5. (Aboud, 2008)
4	By five, Black and Latinx children in research settings show no preference toward their own groups compared to Whites; White children at this age remain strongly biased in favor of whiteness. (Dunham et al, 2008)
5	By kindergarten, children show many of the same racial attitudes that adults in our culture hold—they have already learned to associate some groups with higher status than others. (Kinzler, 2016)
6+	Explicit conversations with 5–7 year olds about interracial friendship can dramatically improve their racial attitudes in as little as a single week. (Bronson & Merryman, 2009)

Young children notice and think about race. Adults often worry that talking about race will encourage racial bias in children, but the opposite is true. **Silence about race reinforces racism** by letting children draw their own conclusions based on what they see. Teachers and families can play a powerful role in helping children of all ages develop positive attitudes about race and diversity and skills to promote a more just future—but only if we talk about it!

Do some learning of your own to get ready for conversations with children. Here are some good places to seek *information* and *training*:
- Teaching Tolerance — tolerance.org
- Raising Race Conscious Children — raceconscious.org
- Embrace Race — embracerace.org
- Teaching for Change — teachingforchange.org
- AORTA Cooperative — aorta.coop
- Fortify Community Health (CA) — fortifycommunityhealth@gmail.com
- Delaware Valley Assoc. for the Education of Young Children (PA) — dvaeyc.org

© 2016 · Updated Feb 28 2018
The Children's Community School
1212 South 47th Street, Philadelphia PA 19143
childrenscommunityschool.org

Maliyah predicts that the "law will be changed because right now in our time, white people can marry Black people, but also Black people and white people."

What I hope you learn about young children who participate in a Critical Literature Response Framework discussion is that they can! Like the children in Lottie's classroom, your young readers have experiences and nascent understandings of how the world works around them, ideas waiting to be explored and expressed. Young children also have a developing sense of justice, a disposition toward what they understand as fair and not fair. By focusing on building awareness of issues and developing skills for interrogating texts, we are guiding children to develop their own perspectives and laying a foundation of critical literacy skills that can be built on toward antiracist and anti-oppressive pedagogies. This is possible when we value young children as capable.

Classroom Approach 2: Supporting an Expansive View of Early Reading

Literacy learning in Lottie's classroom was more than just work with alphabetic print and reading pictures. Alongside valuing her students as picture readers, Lottie valued early reading as inclusive of their bodies, voices, print, maker materials, and other multimedia to make meaning. Every day and across content area learning, Lottie modeled reading pictures, centered using her hands and body to express meaning, and expected her young readers to try different multimedia in the class when available.

One example focuses on their reading of *Drawn Together* (2018) by Minh Lê. Lottie projects the illustrated panels from this book onto the SMART Board. Reading the pictures, she notes how the grandson is grabbing his drawing. Elena reads the illustration too and similarly notes that the grandpa is wondering what the grandson is doing. Lottie agrees: "It looks like they both like to . . ." and students all reply, "Draw!"

Featured Picturebook

Drawn Together (2018) is written by Minh Lê and illustrated by Dan Santat. As the Thai grandfather and grandson featured in the book negotiate linguistic difference, they discover how their shared love of art can bring them together.

Lottie then asks if they can read more things in the illustration that show how the two characters are different or how they are the same.

Kaylesia describes how there is color on one character and no color on the other.

Hanh explains that there are more differences than similarities between the two, similarly citing color on one character, the grandson, and no color on the other, the grandfather.

Cora notices the difference in materials and tools they use to draw.

Mateo states that they both have hats on.

Kaylesia notices one has a wand and one has a paintbrush.

Cora says they both have a tool.

Reading the illustration, Aria adds that both the grandfather and the grandson look like they are ready to begin something. Lottie gasps, immediately asking all of the children to jump up and take the same pose as the grandfather and grandson in the illustration (see Figure 3.2).

As they do, Lottie asks, "How do you *feel* in this pose?" Sofia, who tends not to share in whole groups, smiles and says, "Creative." Lottie excitedly asks if they feel weak or powerful. Many respond with "powerful!" Donnie, who is similarly reticent in whole-group discussions, explains, "It feels like the grandson is saying, 'Bring it on!'," to which Lottie agrees enthusiastically. Lottie then tells the children to sit down, asking if the grandson and grandpa were feeling the same in that position—"Both powerful?" The students nod in agreement.

By expanding what counts as early reading in the classroom and varying the opportunities to respond and make meaning from literature, Lottie nurtures a

FIGURE 3.2. Embodied literacies at work to support literature response.

welcoming space for all of her readers—including those who are often unsure how to contribute to whole-groups discussions—to enter into literature discussion. This is possible when we value both print *and* more expansive views of literacy. And when we value children as capable of literature discussion and bring to our teaching more expansive views of early reading, we find a classroom space ripe for critical literature response.

Focused Literature Exploration: What Makes Family?

Informed by a desire to develop her own and her students' growing understanding of families, Lottie elected to build a literature collection focused on exploring the question "What is a family?" Through guided inspections of visual and written portrayals of families in picturebooks, Lottie aimed to nuance the assumptions and conceptions young children bring about family and how that focus might help students build awareness about different family structures and experiences. Doing so lays a powerful foundation for children to build on as they develop critical stances to both interrogate the narrow depictions of families they encounter in picturebooks and consider how intersections of race, ethnicity, class, and other sociocultural aspects of family might inform those interrogations.

As a focused literature exploration to start the year with her first graders, Lottie shared a wide and varied picturebook collection to help identify the vast array of family experiences in the world as well as in the classroom, building awareness of those differences and inviting the children to consider how their own family experiences are similar to or different from others, with careful attention to the everyday ways families are together. The literacy arrows for this literature exploration included the following:

- What makes a family?
- Who is your family?
- Do you see your family in these books?

- How is your family like those you see in the illustrations and narratives? How are your families different?

Through the four- to six-week literature exploration, Lottie and her students read picturebooks to personally connect with, experience, respond to, inspect, and interrogate depictions of diverse representations of families. From the stack, Lottie immersed the children in a book flood for the first few days and then selected touchstone texts to share as a whole group during whole-group read-aloud and critical literature discussions.

How might you too launch similar work in your classroom? In the sections that follow, I dig deeper into the book flood experience and then conclude with a closer look at three critical literature response experiences that emerged from this work in Lottie's classroom. A list of our top ten favorite picturebooks shared for this literature exploration can be found at the end of this chapter.

Teacher Professional Resource

In *Reading the Rainbow*, researcher Caitlin L. Ryan and educator Jill M. Hermann-Wilmarth ask us to "shift our understanding of LGBTQ people away from sex and toward who people are, including how they live, whom they love, and with whom they build family and community" (p. 2). In speaking to the many facets of sexual and gender identity, you can share a fuller perspective of what it means to be LGBTQ+ with children ways. To learn more about their book, check out the following QR code.

Launching Book Floods and Picture Reading with Picturebooks

The first days of a book flood have always set the tone for the literature discussions that follow. Lottie thoughtfully scheduled four consecutive days for the children to familiarize themselves with the families in the literature collection before them.

Day 1 Book Flood—Immersive Experience: What do you notice in the book? What do you like? How do the story and illustrations make you feel?

Day 2 Book Flood—Immersive Experience: What do we do with our family?

Day 3 Book Flood—Close Inspection: How is your family like those you see in the books?

Day 4 Book Flood—Close Inspection: How is your family different from those you see in the books?

I'm often asked, "How do you get a book flood going with young children?" In a context where reading books is part of the daily work you do to build a literacy life, book floods unfold quite nicely. But if creating space for little ones to read independently is new for you, I share a classroom experience here for you to see how Lottie carefully guides young children toward independence and critical inspection of picturebooks. These initial explorations can feel quite simple or perhaps too open-ended at first, but you'll see that over the course of the literature exploration, book floods can play a profound role in the way young children enter a Critical Literature Response Framework over the days that follow.

Sharing Literary Arrows

On the second day with their book flood focused on family, Lottie gathers the children on the floor in a circle around the books and invites them to join her in making a list of what we "do" with our family.

Aria: We eat together.

Jolene: We play games together.

Mark: We watch movies together.

The books are carefully displayed in the middle of the circle, and the children's eyes are big as they take in the sight of such a large collection. Lottie explains, "Today, let's really read the books, including pictures, to focus on what the families are doing that's really fun. I'm going to give you each two sticky notes so that you can mark the pages you notice that really capture this."

Lottie then moves over to a table to sit down and model for the students what this process could look like. She encourages them to find a comfortable spot. She specifically asks them to "watch my eyes" as she looks at the books, reading all of the pictures. She then models through think-aloud how to make connections from what she is seeing in the book to her own experiences. She then models laying the sticky spot on a note onto a page in a certain way, much like a bookmark, so that she can find the sticky note quickly. Lottie reassures them that it's perfectly fine to change your mind and put the sticky note on another picture. As she finishes, she reminds the children that they will be sharing their findings and encourages them to use this time to really look for what families are doing together in the books. Lottie takes time to provide this guidance as a scaffold toward building these note-taking habits among her students and valuing the work of being a picture reader as well as a reader of print. This is the work of guiding children to independently select and read from the literature stacks before them.

To help students transition into independent reading time, Lottie asks them to put their eyes on a book that looks interesting to them, and then she dismisses them one by one to grab the book. As students select books, she reminds them that they may find they are not the only one who wants to read a particular book, encouraging them to wait patiently until their friend is through reading and to look for another book in the meantime. Within minutes each child has a book they have self-selected, reading with sticky notes in hand and looking for the just-right illustrated spread to share later. Some of the children partner-read with each other, a practice Lottie welcomes and encourages.

Conferring with Readers during Book Flood

Witnessing young children self-select books and exercise their agency to read pictures, read print, and read pictures and print together is always a sight to behold. A good rule of thumb is to wait a good ten minutes before beginning to confer with young readers, giving them time to settle in and step into storyworlds. During the book flood on this day, both Lottie and I move around the room to confer with readers, to listen, provide feedback and guidance, and collect their noticings to build on during whole-group debrief.

Hanh and Cora were partner-reading *Under My Hijab* (2019). To learn about their self-selection process, I ask, "Can you tell me why you all picked this book?" The girls reply in unison, "Because," and then giggle. They take turns sharing with me that after skimming the pages, they selected it because they like how the little girls make cookies with their grandmothers. They open the book and point to this illustration as they speak. Like many young children, these readers are guided by their personal connections to the book, one of many guiding principles Lottie encourages her students to keep in mind as they self-select books.

I then ask, "How do you know this is a family?," wanting to know more about their initial conceptualizations of family. They hesitate, but Cora ultimately shares, "They both kinda have the same skin." Hanh clarifies by saying that it's not the "exact same," but that it is similar. She notes that the daughter is a little lighter and the grandmother is a little darker. I ask them to tell me more and suggest flipping through the book to find a page that will spark ideas. Hanh adds that she thinks the fact that they live in a house and that the book contains images of planting flowers could show that they are a family. The girls return to the illustration of grandma making cookies with the granddaughter, and Hanh shares that, as in the picture, she cracks the eggs for the cookies in her own family when they cook. Clearly, as a picture reader, Hanh is accustomed to reading the little details in an illustration as well as the visual narrative as a whole. Hanh further notes how in her family they put some things on one side of the table and some on the other as they make cookies. I ask her to elaborate on how her family is different from the families in the book. She explains that the family in the book has a table next to the kitchen, but her family doesn't have a table next to the kitchen because they live in an apartment. She adds that they also don't have the

> **Featured Picturebook**
>
> *Under My Hijab* (2019) is written by Hena Kahn and illustrated by Aaliya Jaleel. Crafted in rhythmic verse and vividly illustrated, *Under My Hijab* celebrates the diversity of contemporary Muslim women and girls, their deep family connections, and their shared joy in their culture and faith.

design of the tiles in their kitchen, nor windows. Quietly thinking, Cora adds that the grandmother's skin is Black but that Cora's grandmother's skin is not like that.

With access to illustrated portrayals of different racial and ethnic families, look at what young children respond to! Guided by one literary arrow focused on family and access to picturebooks to self-select and respond to, these two young readers, in addition to many noticings about families in the kitchen, explored notions of family as related to skin shade. Cora noted how family members share the same skin shade, and Hanh clarified that some family members have different skin shades. Hanh and Cora were clearly comfortable initiating discussion of skin shade in this smaller, familiar conference setting with me. The book flood provides needed, valuable openings in discussions for children to share their understandings of race and ethnicity in the classroom; now Lottie's job was to nurture the spaces for those conversations to grow.

Whole-Group Share

After twenty-five minutes of independent and partner reading from the book flood collection, Lottie invites the children back into the classroom circle on the floor. She asks them to continue to think about "what the families are doing" in the illustration as a place to start sharing (see Figure 3.3).

FIGURE 3.3. First graders engaged in whole-group sharing of picturebooks.

Kaylesia shares from *So Much!* (2008) by Trish Cooke and illustrated by Helen Oxenbury. She picks an illustration of a family "because it's more like my dad and my mom."

Mateo picks an illustration from *Yo, Jo!* (2007), written and illustrated by Rachel Isadora, because it "reminds me of my family." He points out the hat and sunglasses on the featured characters as something his family has in common; he picked this picture of a crowd of people in a street because they look like him and remind him of his family. The characters look like his family and share the same Brown skin.

Hanh talks about picking the illustration of the grandmother and granddaughter baking cookies in *Under My Hijab*. She also notes that the kitchen is arranged differently than her own.

The students' comments remind us that children will look for their own families in the books they are reading, and when they see their families represented in those texts, they will readily engage with them and won't hesitate to share their thoughts. When children don't see their families represented in the books they are reading, we are failing to engage them fully in our literacy classrooms. We are also denying them the opportunity to center their experiences as part of literacy learning in ways that stretch the imaginations of everyone participating in the classroom community. Literature scholar Ebony Elizabeth Thomas (2019) describes this as "the imagination gap," the failure to imagine what is possible for diverse communities: "When youth grow up without seeing diverse images in the mirrors, windows, and doors of children's and young adult literature, they are confined to single stories about the world around them and, ultimately, the development of their imaginations is affected" (p. 6). Picturebooks with diverse representation offer children more possibilities for the world they live in.

When children see themselves in texts, under the right conditions such as the encouraging atmosphere of a book flood, they may offer critical noticings that emerge organically from their responses to picturebooks. These critical noticings become the perfect platforms for launching critical literature discussions. For example, after Mateo explained that the characters look like his family and that they share the same Brown skin shade, he continued to inspect skin shade representation and notice variance across other books.

Teacher Professional Resource

To learn more about Ebony Elizabeth Thomas's work on the imagination gap, follow this QR code:

On this day, unlike Mateo, Hanh and Cora elected not to share their noticings of skin shade in their book. Lottie always follows her students' leads on personal connections to race, ethnicity, and other sociocultural differences. Students must have the agency to welcome us into their worlds on their own terms. The invitation to note what the families in the picturebooks "do" together during the debrief was a perfect opening for students to publicly make connections to their own families—or not. It was open-ended enough for those who wanted to share more about their families to do so on their own terms.

Creating a space in the book flood for children to share their aesthetic responses is invaluable and gives momentum to picturebook explorations. In a short period, a book flood debrief can introduce children to new titles, new authors, and new illustrators while also exposing them to new realities, new possibilities, and grander imaginings. Book floods also allow readers to make personal and critical noticings to build on and to put their knowledge as readers to work. The children's noticings of skin shade in illustrations are impactful points of discussion for the whole group, for both students of color and those who are not, as it creates an authentic pathway to normalize talk of race, ethnicity, and skin shade. I wasn't surprised that the discussion in the following days continued to focus on those concepts, and Lottie followed the children's lead.

In the section that follows, you'll explore three critical encounters that unfolded in the days following the book flood. You'll also see an example of our[3] personal "reflection toward change" when we looked back at what unfolded. To illustrate that the work is always negotiable, I share insights into the personal challenges and negotiations we encountered and how we navigated them in the classroom.

Critical Encounters with Picturebooks

As a reminder, I characterize critical encounters with literature as those moments when a text elicits a response that urges deeper discussion into a justice-oriented issue or an interrogation of power, or that potentially becomes a transformative moment that changes a reader's previously held beliefs. These are the moments, microbursts of collective meaning making, that are ultimately the heart of critical literature response because these moments produce fissures in book talk that can ultimately make for a better world.

Critical Encounter 1: Interrogating Skin Shade through Visual Thinking Strategies

The first graders in Lottie's classroom were well into the second semester of their year together. Many of her students were decoding and making meaning of print narratives, and all were well versed as picture readers and discussants of texts. By this time of the year, students had already participated in literature explorations and discussions about civil rights, racism, and important figures in civil rights movements, all very much in keeping with standards and scope and sequence for first grade in the state. To provide further context for the topics of prejudice and civil rights, particularly as they approached the MLK Day holiday, when texts of this nature would abound, Lottie wanted to share a text that would invite her readers to explore these themes in a more contemporary setting. She selected *Sulwe* (Nyong'o, 2019) to contextualize judgments around skin shade in today's world, an issue that isn't unique to the civil rights era. Lottie had found that her young readers believed that civil rights advocacy happened only "a long time ago" and wanted to give her students access to narratives that reflected the realities of People of Color today.

Entering the Critical Encounter

On this day, their second read of *Sulwe*, students are focused on the illustration of two sisters, Day and Night. Leading up to discussion, Lottie holds up the illustration

---

Featured Picturebook

Sulwe (2019), written by Lupita Nyong'o and illustrated by Vashti Harrison, offers a heartfelt experience for children to reflect on their own unique beauty. Harrison's exquisite and luminous illustrations animate Sulwe's story with magic and love, particularly as Sulwe negotiates her feelings about her skin shade. This is a powerful picturebook about colorism, self-esteem, and uncovering true beauty from within, recipient of a Coretta Scott King Illustrator Honor Award and an NAACP Image Award for Outstanding Literary Work for children.

of Sulwe lying in her bed. Many of the children comment on the big feelings Sulwe is negotiating at this stage of the book, particularly her sadness about the darkness of her skin in comparison to that of those around her, especially her sister Day.

Building on students' noticings of the narrative, Lottie asks, "What was she sad about?"

Cora: Sulwe was sad about wanting to have lighter colored skin.

Elena: Sulwe wanted to have friends like her sister who had lighter skin.

Kaylesia: I have mixed skin because my dad has white skin and my mom has Brown skin.

Brayden: Some babies are born with lighter skin that gets darker over time.

Lottie expresses her desire to talk more about that with them and invites the children to consider the terms they have heard used to describe skin shade. The students quickly talk about having variations of Black and white skin and draw on their growing expertise in visual thinking strategies to infer meaning from the illustrations.

Lottie then projects a double-page spread from *Sulwe* so the children can read both the written and the illustrated narratives (see Figure 3.4). The image offers an enlarged view of Day on the left, surrounded by positive words, juxtaposed with Night on the right, surrounded with negative words. She asks them to turn their eyes to the screen and to share what they notice.

Hanh reads a word on the left side of the page, "nice." Mateo reads "ugly" on the right side. Other students continue reading the words aloud: "bad," "scary," "lovely."

FIGURE 3.4. Lottie sharing *Sulwe* with first graders.

Lottie: What do you think about those words they chose?

Cora: The bad words in the illustration seem rude and the light side seem nicer.

Maliyah: Not nicer, because the words they say on the dark side are not nice AT ALL.

Elena stands up and approaches the screen. She uses her hands as she explains that she sees a bad side and a good side in the illustration. She adds that there is a contrast between the color of the words on the dark side being a lighter color and the words being dark on the lighter side. Elena interprets a color binary presented in the illustrated spread quite literally and in doing so elicits more noticings and challenges to the interpretations of some of her peers.

Maliyah also notes that Night's body is shown in whole but that only the Sun's face is shown. She asks everyone to turn their eyes to the screen projecting the illustration and study it for a minute. Taking up her invitation, Trey looks at Day and says, "She is light so we can see it and she is dark so we cannot see it." Trey adds that Night is "dark and pretty" and that she can't be seen because she is dark. Maliyah agrees that Night is beautiful.

Once again centering their initial noticings of the illustration, Lottie asks, "Why do you think people use words like *scary, bad,* and *ugly* for Night?" The children talk among themselves and conclude that the negative words don't make sense to them for Night (see Figure 3.5).

Lottie then says, "I love what Maliyah said about the illustrator—did the illustrator draw Night like she was 'scary, bad, and ugly'?" Students respond, "No." In an effort to highlight how arbitrary the words are as descriptors of Night, Brayden adds, "They could have switched the words to read 'lovely, nice, and pretty' on the other side and 'scary, bad, and ugly' on the other." Maliyah clarifies further, adding, "But still, that [Sun] one is nice, but the Black one, she's not bad and ugly and scary, I bet she's still lovely and not bad."

Nodding in agreement, Connor evokes a theme from the book and stands up to explain, "If there was no light, there would be no dark, and if there were no dark, there would be no light." He adds, "If one thing is gone from your life, it makes it so it

FIGURE 3.5. First graders interpreting metaphor using visual thinking strategies with projected images of picturebook illustrations.

changes. You would not have those memories anymore if that thing or person was gone." As he walks back to his seat, he emphasizes, "There wouldn't be any of these," pointing to books on the easel. The books displayed include biographies of Rosa Parks, Ruby Bridges, and Martin Luther King Jr.

As the students and Lottie respond to the image, they are deftly deconstructing a black/white binary presented in the visual and written narratives. Doing so elicits critiques of social constructs that position darkness/Blackness as "scary, bad, and ugly" and lightness/whiteness as lovely and somehow "nicer." Through this critical encounter, students and Lottie also reinforce an important foundation that normalizes listening to insights and responses from Students of Color. Without Elena's initial noticings and Maliyah's follow-ups, the discussion could not have unfolded the way it did. Learning from Elena and Maliyah nudges Connor to note that light and dark would not really exist without each other, and then take it a step further to explain that the stories on our easel are not complete without stories of Black history. In Lottie's classroom, discussions of equity are centered on more than themes of kindness for all (Turner, 2019) but also involve active critiques of constructs and systems that too often limit the stories we share in the classroom.

As they transition out of discussion, Lottie encourages students to write down their responses to *Sulwe* (see Figure 3.6). After responding to the text in their reader-response notebooks, Kaylesia reads her writing aloud: "The story of Sulwe is how I feel. I was born Nov 13. I love my skin. I am the color of dusk. I never try to mess up my skin ever in my life because I like my skin very very much."

It is powerful to hear Kaylesia take up the metaphors from *Sulwe* to describe her skin as the "color of dusk." She shares pride in her mixed skin color and a desire to "never try to mess" it up. Reading, writing, feeling, talking, and questioning the written and illustrated text in *Sulwe* was a generative literacy experience for these young children. This critical encounter offered the students a space to explore skin shade variation and how our identities are tied to our skin shade. It also fostered an appreciation of the beauty of varied phenotypes and having a positive sense of self.

Teacher Professional Resource

Interested in learning more about when teaching kindness isn't enough?

FIGURE 3.6. First graders adding to their reader-response notebooks as they interpret skin shade representation in *Sulwe*.

Critical Encounter 2: Inferring Critical Meaning from Illustration

In this critical encounter, the first graders in Lottie's classroom are well into their third read of *The Case for Loving* (Alko, 2015). Rereading a shared text that children feel invested in allows the class to dig deeper into the themes that emerged from their discussion and layer in more interpretation of the illustrated narrative. Earlier in this chapter, I shared some of what happened in the first and second read. On this day, Lottie focuses on launching visual thinking strategy work to invite discussion around the court case portrayed in the book and to engage students in the work of inferring meaning from illustration. She selected this moment given the richness of the illustrated scene and poignancy of the moment.

Entering the Critical Encounter

As Lottie gathers her students on the carpet, she asks them to recall their read-aloud of *The Case for Loving* from yesterday and what the book was about (see Figure 3.7).

Hanh: Two people wanted to marry each other but they were different skin colors.

Kaylesia: One was "creamy caramel colored" and one was "a type of tea" but one was Black and one was White and they couldn't get married because they were different colors.

Cora: They had to move somewhere else, but the police came to arrest them.

Lottie: Why did they get arrested? Do you remember?

Brayden: Black and white people were not allowed to marry each other.

Lottie: Where did they want to live?

Alicia: They wanted to live with their family in Virginia.

Julie: They hired lawyers to change the law.

After engaging students in this retelling to reestablish a shared narrative, Lottie projects another double-page spread on the screen. She focuses on the illustration showing the skin shade rainbow between Mildred, whose nickname was String Bean, and Richard. Lottie asks the children to "please study the picture."

After a few moments, Lottie asks, "What do you see going on in this picture?"

Julie: They talked about loving each other.

Maliyah: He is at one side of the rainbow and String Bean is at the other.

Lottie: Why call it a rainbow?

FIGURE 3.7. First graders' critical encounter with *The Case for Loving*.

> Maliyah: Rainbows don't have to be red, orange, yellow, green, and blue, and violet too (in singsong fashion) . . . but it is in the shape of a rainbow.

Lottie asks for any thoughts about that. Connor says, after coming up to the screen, that Richard has the bottom two shades of the rainbow and Mildred's skin shade is the top two shades of the rainbow. Using his hands to highlight his point, he adds that the rainbow is showing "the colors of skin you can have . . . like light skin (pointing to his own skin) and dark skin like Maliyah (while walking over to and pointing at Maliyah). Maliyah adds, "Or even darker like Elena and Mateo." Maliyah then takes it further, inferring the illustrator's intentions. She explains that the illustrator used these colors on purpose. If it wasn't on purpose, "it would probably be like a regular rainbow. But instead, they used two skin colors that would go together and two Brown ones—like Black and Brown, they are alike—Brown is a little lighter."

It is clear on this day: children have grown accustomed to talking about and noticing skin shade differences. It is important to note that this conversation did not happen on the first day of the literature exploration or on the first day of school. Rather, this kind of talk has been normalized after repeated and extended opportunities to explore skin shade representations in picturebooks and to reflect on the skin shades they see in their classroom. The relationship of mutual respect and trust in the classroom provided a safe context for students to talk to one another about their skin shades; in Lottie's classroom, students had the agency and choice to respond to conversations about skin shade, as well as the choice not to participate in the discussion.

Lottie builds on Connor's and Maliyah's offerings to emphasize the unique variance and dimensions of skin shade. She explains, "And we've talked about that before—even if we name a color, it's all different, isn't it, and we're all somewhere, as Maliyah notes, in 'different parts of the rainbow.'" Lottie extends the conversation by inviting other noticings, and students find themselves standing up and using their bodies to point to parts of the illustration on the screen or in the book to help emphasize their noticings about skin shade variance. Rather than asking the children to remain seated, Lottie welcomes this movement because she understands that students are learning how to use their hands and expressions for emphasis and how to use the illustrated texts as "proof" of their claims.

To move the children into inferring, Lottie extends Maliyah's comment about the illustrator's intentions. In doing so, she is encouraging them to think about artist/illustrator's craft. "Why did the artist use that shape with those colors in it?"

Elena: That's kinda crazy; she's a little bit of each of the top and he's a little bit of each on bottom. I agree with Connor.

Cora: If you flip the rainbow over, it would be a smile.

Maliyah: Yeah! Maybe because it's a happy moment.

Julie: Rainbows are kinda happy colors too, I mean happy things.

Lottie: So are you thinking that the artist wanted to show they are happy? If this is your job, making picture books, do you think it's an accident when you paint things?

Many students: "NO!"

Lottie: So you all agree that this is not a regular rainbow but one that shows skin shades.

Becoming Critical Picture Readers 77

Kaylesia: It's a skin color rainbow!

Lottie: Looking at that picture, why do you think the rainbow is like it is? Think about it for a minute. Why do you think the artist put characters on opposite sides of the rainbow instead of together underneath the rainbow?

After time to turn and talk, the children come back ready to share their inferences.

Sadie: We think Mildred and Richard are on opposite sides because they can't get married.

Elena: It looks like they just met each other.

Connor: The skin colors are pushing them apart. If you don't have the right skin color, they push them apart. So the rainbow is what separated them.

As he explains this, Connor uses his hands to trace the opposite arcs of the rainbow to emphasize his point (see Figure 3.8).

FIGURE 3.8. First graders interpreting critical themes on the projected screen through visual thinking strategies.

Through visual thinking strategies, Sadie infers that the illustrator separated Mildred and Richard to show the legal barriers to interracial marriage. This first grader is noting symbolism within the illustration by inferring meaning visually. Connor similarly interprets the skin shade rainbow as a symbolic barrier, explaining that at this time, "if you don't have the right skin color," couples like Mildred and Richard are pushed apart. With the invitation to read illustration, Connor articulates the societal racial constructs that limit what is possible for interracial families. Through this critical encounter, young children are noting and naming the injustices experienced by one interracial couple and learning about history in relation to their own responses to the picturebook.

Critical Encounter 3: A Teacher's Reflections toward Change[4]

In this critical encounter, students had finished reading from *Rosa* (Giovanni, 2005), *The Case for Loving* (Alko, 2015), and other relevant picturebooks focused on civil rights. Here, Lottie creates an opening for students to consider the role of fear in relation to the racism experienced by the protagonists in these narratives.

Entering the Critical Encounter

Lottie: Hmmm, I wonder who was scared in these books.

Elena: People were scared in *all* of these books!

Lottie: What were they scared of? . . . You think people were scared in all of the books? . . . You think they're scared there? Hey, did being scared help? Didn't help many people, being scared, did it? What could we do instead of being scared? What could we do instead of being scared? . . . What could we do, if we're scared of something, what instead of, saying it's bad and making it illegal, what could we do instead?

Cora: Be brave.

Lottie: How would you be brave? How could you be brave when you're scared of something?

Cora: Stand up and say, like, . . . "I don't wanna move to a new seat."

Maliyah: Or get off the bus.

Lottie: So, okay, so, feeling strong, convicted, say, "It's okay for me to sit here, I'm gonna sit here" instead of being scared, okay.

Maliyah: 'Cause saying, "No," like yes, that's a good idea, but just saying, "No," like you should say more than, like, "Please can I stay here?"

>   (sighs) 'Cause, this is the neutral section so Black *and* white can sit here.

Talking about fear in these texts is an important step toward recognizing injustice and disrupting whiteness. In response to the invitation to consider fear, students centered a Black perspective, calling on stances of bravery and conviction that were needed to enact change and decenter whiteness. Specifically, Lottie asks, "Did being scared help?" and "What could we do instead of being scared?," which moves the discussion toward agency and hope. Maliyah takes up the work of centering Black hope (Duncan-Andrade, 2009) and bravery and states, "You should say more. . . . Black and white can sit here." In this way, she is also emphasizing the need for strategy and planning a fuller response to racist encounters. When our collective later *reflected toward change*, we noted the need for caution when centering Black perspectives and experiences. We don't want students to reenact fear or experiences that awaken trauma or perpetuate Black suffering. In these instances, it is essential to center Black experiences in ways that recenter hope and bravery and intellect, as Lottie and her students did.

Lottie: Let me ask this question: Is it Black people . . . or is it white people who are scared in this book?

Maliyah: White. *White*. Black?

Lottie: Who's scared? White. So, Sadie, what are they scared of?

Sofia: Um, the Black people.

Lottie: Yeah. Hmmm.

Aria: That's why they have to go to the back. 'Cause [the white people are] scared.

Lottie: Hmm, so I wonder what white people could've done, instead of being scared.

Cora: Be brave?

Maliyah: Well, they could be brave but—

Lottie: What do you think white people could do instead of being scared?

Elena: They can be, like, stop (holds her hand out in the "stop" gesture), that is e—nough, I am going to try to be brave now, instead of scared.

Maliyah: But in those times, like, white people were kind of like the wrong people, like, Black people they just want freedom! Just *freedom*! That's not too much to ask, is it?

>   **Elena:** Why do people treat Black people the wrong way, but white people are scared of Black people, but they treat Black people the *wrong way*? But that doesn't make sense 'cause they treat Black people the wrong way, and they're *scared* of Black people. That doesn't make sense at all.
>
>   **Lottie:** How many of these books happened because people were scared. What do you think?

Here, we initially focused the conversation on the fear white people have of Black people and what white people should do instead of being scared. Despite our intention of inviting students to identify white people's racism and fear as the root of injustice and considering alternate behaviors, students' responses to the question "Who is scared?" produced a narrative of "fear of Black persons" and ultimately recentered whiteness. Through reflection toward change, we noted that a focus on what white people *could* have done reinforced white gaze rather than disrupt it. Asking what white people could have done rather than should have done may have suggested that white people's fear was justified. Ultimately, it was Elena and Maliyah who shifted the conversation toward Black freedom and justice, noting how white people's racist behavior "doesn't make sense at all." From our *reflection toward change*, we also reminded ourselves that to disrupt whiteness, we must remain open to the offerings our young students, especially our Children of Color, make in response to injustice.

What Critical Encounters Can Teach Us

Collectively, these critical encounters with picturebooks affirm how capable young children in early childhood settings are of engaging in a Critical Literature Response Framework and how powerful picturebook illustrations are as text to read and interpret. Lottie builds on the noticings children share and offers literary arrows to help guide their investigations. I invite you to reflect on a few relevant tips for enacting a Critical Literature Response Framework with young children. Ask yourself: How did the classroom commitments and conditions Lottie values enhance students' learning? How might the classroom practices, specifically book floods and picture reading, enhance your student learning in a Critical Literature Response Framework? And—most important—how might you make this work your own?

Tips to Support Critical Encounters in Literature with Young Children

As you refine your practice based on your reflection, consider eliciting children's authentic responses to picturebooks as Lottie did by trying the following:

- Offer literary arrows that nudge reflection:
    - What makes you say that?
    - Can you show me what/where in the text/illustration made you think that?
    - Tell me more.
- Model considering new perspectives in response to picturebooks.
- Welcome students' personal experiences and insights as they respond to picturebooks, particularly those experiences and insights that are different from your own. Devaluing children's stories is devaluing children and their family experiences.
- Avoid exoticizing children's experiences by creating space for children to choose if/when/how/where to share their personal histories in response to picturebooks. Students have the agency to share (or not) their lives in the classroom.
- Honor space and time for children to talk to one another, to move, and use their bodies in response to picturebooks (turn and talk, debrief circle without interrupting others, writing, acting out, standing up and pointing, interacting with materials and screens).
- Engage in reflection toward change—how can the language we use and the consciousness we bring to the work of a Critical Literature Response Framework inform positive changes in the questions we ask and themes we determine to be important?

Top Ten Favorite Picturebooks Shared for Family Study

1. Alarcón, F. X. (2017). *Family poems for every day of the week / Poemas familiares para cada dia de la semana* (M. C. Gonzalez, Illus.). Children's Book Press.
2. Beer, S. (2018). *Love makes a family*. Penguin.
3. Cabrera, C. A. (2020). *Me and mama.* Denene Millner Books/Simon & Schuster Books for Young Readers.
4. Khan, H. (2019). *Under my hijab* (A. Jaleel, Illus.). Lee & Low Books.
5. Look, L. (2006). *Uncle Peter's amazing Chinese wedding.* (Y. Heo, Illus.). Atheneum Books for Young Readers.
6. Morales, Y. (2015). *Niño wrestles the world.* Square Fish.
7. O'Leary, S. (2016). *A family is a family is a family* (Q. Leng, Illus.). Groundwood Books.
8. Quintero, I. (2019). *My papi has a motorcycle* (Z. Peña, Illus.). Kokila.

9. Saeed, A. (2019). *Bilal cooks daal.* Simon & Schuster Books for Young Readers.
10. Tahe, R., & Flood, N. B. (2018). *First laugh—Welcome, baby!* (J. Nelson, Illus.). Charlesbridge.

Children's Literature Cited

Alko, S. (2015). *The Case for Loving: The fight for interracial marriage.* (S. Qualls & S. Alko, Illus.). Arthur A. Levine Books.
Khan, H. (2019). *Under my hijab* (A. Jaleel, Illus.). Lee & Low Books.
Lê, M. (2018). *Drawn together* (Santat, D., Illus.). Little, Brown Books for Young Readers.
Nyong'o, L. (2019). *Sulwe* (V. Harrison, Illus.). Simon & Schuster Books for Young Readers.

Chapter Four

Talking to, with, and across Wide and Varied Picturebook Collections

On this day, as they launch into their literature exploration focused on depictions of border-crossing experiences in picturebooks, Kara and her fourth graders are already noting connections across *Dreamers* (2018) by Yuyi Morales and *The Journey* (2016) by Francesca Sanna. Nine-year-old Jennifer notes how border crossing from one "home" to another can happen voluntarily, as it did for Yuyi in *Dreamers*. Zack responds that border crossing can also happen involuntarily, as it did for the characters in *The Journey* due to "famine, war, or something bad happening, and they don't usually go back." It was important to Kara that students develop insight into the nuances and complexities of border-crossing experiences, some of which Zack and Jennifer noted in their examples. The wide and varied collection of picturebooks in their classroom book flood certainly reflects Kara's commitment, as do her invitations to identify relevant border-crossing themes on this day.

To scaffold the work of identifying relevant connections across texts, Kara lifts themes from the picturebooks that students are already reading from the collection. She reminds her students that borders can be both visible and invisible, and highlights the large wall featured on the cover of Zack's self-selected picturebook, *The Wall* (Sís, 2007), as an example of a visible wall. She concludes by inviting them to look at the list of books they have each read so far: "Here's what I want you to think about: What are some other messages or themes or ideas that you have noticed in these books? I'm going to give you two minutes to go around your table to share one theme that you noticed."

As they shift into discussion at their tables, students begin to share their initial efforts at theme generation (see Figure 4.1).

> **Jane:** I read *Dear Primo* (Tonatiuh, 2015), and it's about overcoming and crossing invisible borders from language to language.
>
> **Luke:** I think *From Far Away* (Munsch & Askar, 1995) is about borders. There was a border when the character was at her old home and the civil war was holding her back from learning. She *had* to cross that border; she didn't have friends and she learned how to speak a new language in her new school.

Kara is helping students to focus on the idea that border crossing can be a physical experience or a metaphorical one in order to identify more robust themes, and she draws on familiar texts in the collection to do so. She knows that students will deconstruct these initial themes as they read more texts from the collection but welcomes these nascent understandings. What results is a chart in grid form that holds a list of border-crossing themes.

FIGURE 4.1. Initial border crossing themes generated by Kara's students.

Initial Border-Crossing Themes Generated by Students

- If you're far away from home, you still have a home.
- Overcoming invisible borders is possible.
- If you don't understand at first, just try.
- Being in someone else's shoes helps you understand.
- Overcoming a mental border
- Hard work pays off.
- Family is important.
- Learning from history
- Going somewhere else for a better life

Upon seeing the completed chart, Mahoma quickly says, "I know what we're going to do! You read some books and then if you think it's one of those themes you add the title!" Kara nods and adds, "Or you can add your own theme if it's not there. Now tiptoe back to your tables and let's get started."

As students work on reading and thinking across texts with shared themes, they talk to one another and share their responses to the narratives.

> **Alyssa:** I think this book (holding up *From North to South* [2013] by René [Colato] Laínez is about borders.... There are sometimes when you can't understand what borders are, but in time you might understand them.
>
> **Genna:** What you said, it made me think about the book we just read (*From Far Away*); the author was kinda trying to . . . make you feel in her shoes . . . if you were her.

In Kara's classroom, reading from a robust and focused collection of picturebooks and identifying points of intersection between them is an entry point for responding to text. She scaffolds her fourth graders to make text-to-text connections by focusing on shared themes that they generate together. She welcomes students' nascent interpretations, including "Hard work pays off," knowing that she has examples in the collection that will offer an alternate perspective to consider. In the weeks that follow, Kara will draw on students' responses to the wide and varied collection to critically interrogate the representations in the literature.

In this chapter, you'll learn more about Kara and her fourth graders, and I'll share more about how they experienced picturebooks through a Critical Literature Response Framework. In addition to a brief overview of the border-crossing literature exploration Kara shared with her students, I highlight three critical literature encounters they worked through together. As always, when reading about Kara and her students, consider how this work can look in your own classroom. Where might a literature exploration focused on border-crossing experiences and immigration unfold in your classroom? What can it look like? The primary aim of this chapter—beyond learning more about how Kara introduces students to the theme of border crossings—is to convey the power of having a wide and varied picturebook collection when launching a Critical Literature Response Framework by highlighting the intertextual connections children can make after being immersed in such a collection. I also hope that you'll be moved by the profound insights children offer when discussing border-crossing themes in children's picturebooks—we have much to learn from the questions they ask, the conclusions they draw, and the critiques they offer.

Entering Kara's Fourth-Grade Classroom

Kara's teaching through literature is truly focused on reading, thinking, and talking across texts. She thoughtfully plans and offers literary arrows that nudge children to make meaning across the books they encounter in the classroom. Watching how Kara lives with children, books, opera, art, writing, and talk (and more) in the classroom makes it easy to understand why her fourth graders are so invested in literature. Students truly "enter" storyworlds that come alive as Kara reads aloud the carefully crafted narratives she selects. "Being in and moving through" a storyworld and our responses, as Judith Langer (1990, p. 238) has taught us, is a powerful literary orientation that positions us as readers to explore both our own and characters' emotions, relationships, motives, and reactions, ultimately urging us as readers to draw on what we know about being human. As Langer (1994) explains:

> Even when we finish reading, we rethink our interpretations—perhaps at one time taking a psychological and at other times a political and at still other times a mythic stance toward the characters' feelings and actions. Thus, throughout the reading (*and even after we have closed the book*) our ideas constantly shift and swell. Possibilities arise and multiple interpretations come to mind, expanding the complexity of our understandings. (p. 204, emphasis added)

The models, the experiences, and the time Kara provides for her students to "be in and move through storyworlds" has nurtured students' capacity to understand, reflect on, and critique characters and any injustice they perceive in the story landscape. Even after Kara finishes reading aloud *Front Desk* (2018) by Kelly Yang, for example, her students cannot help but continue to rally behind the Tang family as they help immigrant families and question Mr. Yao's unethical behavior as he exploits immigrant employees like the Yangs. Kara's students were so invested in the Yang family and Mia's commitment to a better world that they consistently made connections back to *Front Desk* as they read from other book flood texts focused on border-crossing experiences. What results is a truly immersive experience in storyworlds for the readers in Kara's classroom, one in which they approach literature with incredible depth and great empathy and develop their own perspectives on

---

Featured Read-Aloud

Front Desk (2018) is a chapter book written by Kelly Yang. This young adult novel unfolds at a motel in Anaheim, California, during the 1990s where Mia Yang, a ten-year-old Chinese immigrant, works at the front desk. Mia narrates her family's struggle to manage a motel while adjusting to life in their adopted country. Readers will find themselves rooting for the Yangs as they explore themes of immigration exploitation, exclusion caused by racial intolerance and financial hardship, and the way persistence can overcome resistance in realizing one's dreams.

complex issues again and again through discussion, *even after they have closed the book.*

Genuine passion is how I can best characterize Kara's approach to sharing wide and varied literature collections and why the students in her classroom are equally invested in the characters they encounter in texts. Her authentic enthusiasm goes a long way toward motivating the readers in her classroom, and students' responses to her excitement are undeniable. The room sits still in anticipation when she reads aloud, and the students gasp in response to a character's plight or an unexpected turn in the plot. Kara's eyes widen and her smile grows bigger as students talk reader to reader with her about characters and share their challenges with the plot. What animates such energetic discussion in her class is Kara's love of character-driven literature and the authenticity with which she receives children's responses to texts. Research (Baker, 2006) has consistently pointed to the teacher, not the curriculum, as the most significant variable in a student's experience of and learning in school, and Kara makes real what we have learned from this research. Paired with her commitment to better representation in the literature she shares and a deep desire to center the experiences of People of Color in her instruction, Kara's literature instruction is as effective as it is passionate.

> **Inviting Teacher Reflection**
>
> After this initial introduction to Kara's classroom, here are some reflective questions to consider:
>
> - What role does reading aloud for pleasure play in your language arts classroom?
> - Do you read aloud for strategy instruction? With what frequency does it happen and under what conditions?
> - Do you find you are able to both read for pleasure and teach reading at the same time?
> - What qualities in literature do you seek to help children invest in characters' lives and experiences?
> - How often do you model your personal connections, questions, and critiques of injustice in literature?
> - How do you raise questions in response to characters or injustice portrayed in the narrative while also leaving room for students to draw their own conclusions?

Kara is a veteran teacher of twenty-plus years, an avid reader who remains current with new titles and emerging authors who are publishing stories with diverse representations. Kara has usually read the newest titles before I have. As a white, female educator, Kara understands the power she has to decenter status quo narratives in children's lives through literature, and that by doing so, she is helping children develop more robust and nuanced understandings of the world they live in, as well as providing needed examples of racially, ethnically, linguistically, and culturally diverse protagonists.

As you learn more about Kara and her classroom and how a Critical Literature Response Framework can look, I invite you to continue to reflect on your own practice. What are your literature passions and interests personally and professionally? What are your preferred literary genres and formats? Whose experiences do you center in your collection? Which do you find you avoid? How might you impart your own journey as an avid or growing reader of diverse picturebooks with your students? What role does your journey as a reader play in your classroom work and in what ways are you leaving room to continue to develop your literary diet? Reflecting on these questions as you read this chapter will help you reconnect with your own reading life and consider the way a commitment to better representation in children's literature and a Critical Literature Response Framework can come to life in your classroom.

Enlivening a Critical Literature Response Framework in an Elementary Classroom

A Critical Literature Response Framework is not only enhanced by Kara's enthusiasm for a robust literature collection, but it is also enlivened by Kara's commitments to the following:

- Eliciting more in-depth talk from readers
- Growing students' vocabulary to talk about complex issues

In the sections that follow, I share more about these two classroom practices through examples to help you better understand the way Kara's desire to hear from her students as readers and her attention to vocabulary impacts the classroom conditions for critical literature response work.

Classroom Approach 1: Eliciting More In-Depth Talk from Readers

Digging deeply into complex issues of immigration, refugees, and border-crossing experiences through picturebooks occurs as Kara expresses genuine interest in knowing what her fourth graders have to say as both readers and community citizens. She takes time for their responses and invites further comments, consistently asking students to "Tell me more. . . . Tell us more." What a simple but profound way to invite children to elaborate on their thinking. When Kara shares literary arrows, she sincerely wants to be in discussion with children, not just initiate a call-and-response. Thus, the invitation to "tell us more" works because her readers know they are talking with someone who is just as excited about the book as they are. "Tell me more" also nudges students to slow down, return to the text, or pause to process their responses with more depth as they elaborate and talk across storyworlds.

When reading *Dreamers* (2018) by Yuyi Morales, for example, Kara engages her students in visual thinking strategies as she projects a scan of scenes from *Dreamers* for the children to read. On one of these pages, the mother and son characters are looking at a map, and in the other they are in a fountain with a police officer, a speech bubble emerging from the mother's mouth exclaiming, "¡Ay!" Kara starts by asking her students this simple question: "What is happening in this picture?"

Brittany explains Yuyi's use of "¡Ay!" in the illustration, describing it as the equivalent of saying, "Oh!" As she struggles to explain, Kara asks her to "tell me more." Kara's invitation gives Brittany pause, and she turns back to the illustration to gather data, returning to her explanation to note how frustrated the mother must be to be found in the fountain by a police officer. She decides that the man must be a police officer because of the badge, belt, and uniform he has on. The invitation to "tell me more" nudges Brittany to return to the text to gather context clues as she makes inferences about a different language.

> **Featured Picturebook**
>
> *Dreamers* (2018) is written and illustrated by Yuyi Morales, who drew on her own immigration story to craft this picturebook narrative about becoming an immigrant in the United States. Through her discovery of the library and beloved picturebooks, she reclaimed her voice to become the storyteller and artist she is today. *Dreamers* weaves together the stories you carry with themes of resilience, your dreams, your hopes, and history.

In the same exchange, Kara asks, "What more can we find?"

Ethan states, "I'm pretty sure they're in San Francisco." Kara asks, "What do you see that makes you say that?" Ethan points to the map in the illustration showing a bridge and says he thinks this is a famous bridge in San Francisco and that the mother must be trying to call someone. Kara again requests, "Tell me more." Ethan goes on to explain that maybe "Ay!" could mean "What?" and that perhaps she is confused and trying to call someone.

Zack then suggests that he's "pretty sure that's not San Francisco because it's not connected to Mexico." Kara gets out a map to show which states border Mexico. She asks Zack to "tell me more." Zack thinks perhaps Yuyi and her son were in the fountain because she thought the running water looked like a shower for them to bathe in.

Areif mentions that "she's probably trying to get back to Mexico. When you are looking at a map, you're trying to get somewhere. . . . Since she is an immigrant, she couldn't go back." Kara asks, "What do we know about her story that shows us that Areif is right and that [Yuyi] could not go back?" Students note that the written narrative says she could not return home at that time, but that clearly Yuyi can go back and forth now as a published author and illustrator. Though, Kenan notes, that it is quite expensive.

Kara continues to repeat, "What else do you see? Tell me more!" And as she does, the children continue to find even more to visually interpret.

Asking children to "tell me more!" and leaving space for them to do so encourages them to take up that space to develop and share their hypotheses. The readers in Kara's classroom know they can keep mining the meaning available in both the written and the illustrated narratives for clues to support claims and inferences they are making, and the repeated invitation produces multiple peer-to-peer modeling of this process. Students also know there is someone in their classroom very interested in learning about what they find. "Tell me more!" elicits hypotheses that can be confirmed or challenged as readers are compelled back into the storyworld again and again. It is not surprising that many different books are evoked in one conversation given how often and deeply the children go back to revisit texts. When we ask children to share more of what they are thinking and provide space and time for them to revisit and rethink, they will surprise us with the ease, intellect, and savvy with which they do so.

Classroom Approach 2: Growing Vocabulary to Discuss Complex Issues

Kara centers attention on vocabulary with her students not only as a scaffold for making meaning from text in general, but also to help her readers navigate topic complexity. For Kara, building vocabulary offers an entry point into a new topic of inquiry. Her instinct to pursue vocabulary as a pathway for students' comprehension is very much in line with what reading research has revealed. As Jim Baumann (Baumann, 2014; Baumann et al., 2007) has suggested, teaching vocabulary in meaningful collections and supporting children's curiosity about new words and their meanings is a powerful steppingstone toward vocabulary growth and reading comprehension. When children uncover new words and develop different strategies to unpack their meanings, they have an effective impetus for digging deeply into text. Moreover, relevant terms and the way they work together to make meaning provide a helpful scaffold to framing discussion of new and complex inquiries.

For example, to prepare students to navigate discussion of border-crossing experiences in children's picturebooks, Kara introduces four terms: *migration*, *immigration*, *borders*, and *refugee*. She previews these four related terms by inquiring first into what students already know about them. She lists each word at the top of separate pieces of chart paper and invites students to add what they already know about the words' meanings and to add the titles of any books they think might be related to the terms. Kara specifically explains, "Here's what you're going to write: If you think you know what that word means, I want you to write it down. . . . If that word reminds you of something, if that word reminds you of another word, anything that pops into your head, I want you to write it down. It's okay to write nothing if you have zero ideas about that word. This is just to see what you already know." Kara then asks a student to explain the directions in her own words.

Before the students begin writing, Kara briefly models what she might think about each term and adds her thinking to the charts. At this point, the students are dismissed from the carpet one by one with a marker in hand, and they circulate for several minutes to share their thinking about each vocabulary word, placing check marks by things already written on the posters with which they agree (see Figure 4.2).

After students have added their initial understandings of the terms to the charts, Kara gathers students together on the carpet to focus on the term *migration*, elaborating on what the children have added what they know about animal migration to the chart.

She reminds them of what they know about "butterflies migrating to ... [waits for students to answer] Mexico."

Kara notes that the concept of "migration" presented in the literature is "talking about people," not animals. She reads student answers from the chart and thinks aloud as she interprets their contributions, synthesizing their ideas to explain that the people in the books "move from place to place," and she writes this down. Kara adds that maybe, as the students have noted, migration is within a country, or from country to country. She agrees with students' discussion of migration as something that usually happens in order to find work, but not always. She pauses to ask if "you think that is migrants' choice to migrate." A student says, "No," and Kara says, "Tell me more."

FIGURE 4.2. Fourth graders collaborating to learn new and relevant vocabulary about immigration.

Kezia: Most people would not want to leave their home where they have grown up.

Jennifer: Some might choose to migrate to the beach, better conditions.

Zack says that his family migrated here because his dad's job caused their move from Oregon to Missouri. This prompts Kara to add to the chart that people "sometimes migrate ... typically by choice but not always." She notes that they will continue adding to this chart as they develop their understandings.

Kara builds on what her students already know about relevant vocabulary by gathering their emerging understandings of the word, asking them to draw on their experiences and their inferences from the literature collection (see Figure 4.3). To scaffold their learning, she connects the word *migration* to their previous study of the migration of butterflies. Kara understands that learning is fluid and continuous as she helps students refine their initial definitions of these new

FIGURE 4.3. Kara guiding her fourth graders through vocabulary learning.

vocabulary words over time as they encounter them in the collection. Kara presents new terms and reviews the definitions day to day to frame class discussion, helping students discern the meanings of new words by "chunking" their parts and attending to morphemes. I saw how this scaffolding led students to learn complicated terms such as *transnationalism* and *digital transnationalism* as they quickly made both personal and picturebook connections to these terms. Kara offered students a place of inquiry and experience to scaffold generative classroom activities that allowed them to identify new words and enter critical conversations with confidence.

By eliciting further talk about literature and developing students' understanding and use of relevant terms as they discuss complex issues, Kara is priming her classroom for a Critical Literature Response Framework. Asking students to "tell me more" and supporting vocabulary development are not practices unique to a Critical Literature Response Framework, but they are truly beneficial practices that can only enhance students' interactions in discussions that occur both within and outside of the literature classroom. Through these practices, students in Kara's classroom feel empowered to engage in conversations as informed citizens and readers, ready to work for a better world.

Focused Literature Exploration: Border-Crossing Experiences in the United States

Kara was required by her district curriculum to engage her fourth-grade students in the study of immigration in the United States. Understanding the great responsibility of the task, keeping in mind the district objectives, and desiring to nuance the learning beyond the traditional immigration narratives students would encounter, Kara gathered a collection of titles that reflected these aims. Through a wide and varied literature collection and well-planned literary arrows, Kara's students entered this book flood in ways that ultimately put different border-crossing experiences in conversation with one another and produced opportunities for the children to explore the impact that socioeconomics, policies, privilege, and hope can have on so many.

Within this focused literature exploration that occurred in the spring of the academic year, the picturebooks available provided written and illustrated portrayals of immigration, migration, and refugee experiences from across the globe. Kara helped her students to build awareness of the differences among these experiences and invited the children to consider how their own family experiences are similar or different from others'. She also encouraged keeping a close eye on empathy and injustice that arose in those narratives. The literacy arrows for this literature exploration included the following:

- What do you know about immigration? Migration? Refugee experiences?
- How are you making sense of the term *border crossing*?
- What communities are most represented in these border-crossing narratives? Which are missing?
- In what ways are the experiences portrayed in _____ like or different from the experience in_____?
- After reading this book, what do you now understand about immigration? Migration? Refugee experiences?

Through this four- to six-week literature exploration, Kara and her fourth graders read deeply into and across this robust collection of border-crossing experiences. Kara immersed her readers quickly in their inquiry and selected touchstone texts to complement their reading engagements with the wide and varied collection.

How might you too launch similar work in your classroom? In the sections that follow, I dig deeper into the power of having a wide and varied focused picturebook collection through many examples of Kara's students at work pairing texts; I do so as a way to support you as you build your own stacks. I conclude with a closer look at three critical encounters that emerged from their reading of this collection. A top-ten list of favorite picturebooks from this collection can be found at the end of this chapter.

Preparing and Launching Wide and Varied Picturebook Collections

Building a wide and varied picturebook collection takes time, but the best place to start the process is by closely examining the book stacks you already have. Much like a chef's pantry of staples and recipes that are refined over time, the process of developing a wide and varied picturebook collection requires patience and experimentation. We learn over time, practice, and reflection which texts can enhance student learning and which do not necessarily complement the work in productive ways. The texts you select to share with children are the rich ingredients for a robust literature discussion, and it's okay— actually, it's more than okay, it is absolutely necessary— to be discriminating about which titles you include and which you leave behind. Refining and continuous curation can help keep the collection fresh, responsive, and meaningful for your students. Kara developed her collection focused on border-crossing experiences by drawing on texts she already had access to as well as new titles she uncovered through discerning social media recommendations and book awards, as well as through conversations with other teachers who offered their experiences with specific texts. Even today, if you were to ask Kara about her collection, she could share the newest titles she has added and name those she omitted. Just today she shared, "Angie, I just finished *The Last Cuentista* (Higuera, 2021). It is a perfect book to layer into this focused literature exploration!"

As I shared extensively in Chapter 1, the text selection process is an essential part of launching a Critical Literature Response Framework classroom. There is so much to consider around authenticity of racial, ethnic, linguistic, and broader cultural representation in children's picturebooks for the classroom bookshelves. It can often be a welcome challenge to narrow and develop just one focused collection to support inquiry. The focus allows you time to commit to and develop expertise on a topic to guide your text selection. I highly recommend working on a focused collection as a place to start if you are just beginning to build your overall collection. A focused picturebook stack ideally coheres around a topic of inquiry that considers multiple relevant lines of inquiry. For example, Kara nuanced her collection on immigration to include portrayals of migration and refugee experiences. She worked to ensure that the collection reflected border-crossing experiences across different countries and under different conditions. Narratives reflected documented and undocumented experiences, physically arduous and underprivileged conditions of border crossing, as well as narratives that offered insights into both transnational and more migrant communities that settled into a new country of residence. What resulted is a book flood ready for children to read across, interrogate, and learn from.

One week after having had multiple guided engagements to read from the collection (which I explain further in the section that follows), for example, students quickly begin to share their initial noticings about different border-crossing experiences. Kara reads aloud *Friends from the Other Side* (Anzaldúa, 1993) and shares her emerging hypothesis about Joaquin's movement across the border: "I wonder if he crosses back and forth between Mexico and the United States every day, hmmmm." A few pages later, Kara reviews the written description detailing how Joaquin and his family had moved to the United States, and in doing so, disconfirms her previous wondering. She pauses the read-aloud to ask her students to think about how Joaquin's border-crossing experience in *Friends from the Other Side* compares to Yuyi's and her son's experiences in *Dreamers*. Some students use hand motions from the "Itsy Bitsy Spider" to show they are weaving connections as they think.

Featured Picturebook

In *Friends from the Other Side / Amigos del Otro Lado* (Anzaldúa, 1993), Prietita befriends Joaquín, who has just arrived in the United States from the other side of the Río Grande. This picturebook captures both the beauty and the hardships of life on the border and the solidarity, bravery, and care that many who live on the border share to survive.

Kezia:	They're different.
Areif:	Neither of the stories show them having that much money.
Ethan:	*Friends* is more about migration and *Dreamers* is immigration. In *Friends*, the family "could go back [home]" and in *Dreamers*, it said that she and her son "Couldn't go back."
Daniel:	Joaquin has to worry about the border patrol, but Yuyi didn't.

Kara builds on Daniel's noticing to ask, "Do you think Joaquin and his mother feel safe in their home?" Many students answer no, leading Kara to think aloud and introduce the concepts of documented (Yuyi) and undocumented (Joaquin) persons and how undocumented persons might have worries (e.g., border patrol) that documented persons do not. She finishes reading the book, and the children continue to share their noticings about the similarities and differences of the border-crossing experiences they have read about.

A wide and varied picturebook collection allows Kara and her students to think across multiple storyworlds as shared context to uncover the nuances of border-crossing experiences and provides authentic and humanizing narratives for students to interrogate. Having rich picturebook examples like *Dreamers* and *Friends from the Other Side* provides important written and illustrated narratives to notice how immigration experiences are similar and how they are different.

Importantly, Kara considered a variety of text formats and literary genres as part of her text selection process. In the border-crossing picturebook collection Kara curated, children encountered fiction, biographies, fictionalized histories, and poetry. She broadened the collection to include text formats such as graphic novels, chapter books, and staged musical scores. Kara has developed a process for building a focused inquiry literature collection that is inclusive of diverse representation, informed by work in the field, and considerate of varied texts structures and literary genres.

As a final consideration about building a wide and varied picturebook collection for a focused literature exploration, I want to emphasize how a process of text selection requires great humility. It is highly likely that despite your best intentions and thoughtful, careful research, you will include a text that must be reconsidered. As I shared in the previous chapter, I want to be transparent about the many ways I have been humbled by the text selection process, especially around the book *Loving*. As another example of this, we included *One Green Apple* (2006) by Eve Bunting in the border-crossing picturebook collection. It was only later in the process that we encountered the numerous critiques of this book by literary critics, scholars, and cultural insiders who challenge its assimilation metaphor. When something like this happens, you can choose to pull the book from the collection when the portrayals are deeply troublesome in ways that cause deep trauma and harm. This is where having colleagues and teachers who identify as members of the community portrayed in a text to debrief with can be most effective since they can help you make an informed decision, especially if *you* are not of that community. In other cases, we can, as Yoon and colleagues (2010) suggest, thoughtfully share some select critiques of the text to guide students through well-planned critical discussions of ideology and social actions. Whatever path you pursue, the capacity to recognize the limits of our knowledge, or our humility, is what makes repair possible.

Clearly, wide and varied text selection is a complex process that demands our time and commitment to do no harm to children. An *informed and inclusive* text selection process affords classroom conditions for a Critical Literature Response Framework that facilitates both whole-class and individual areas of exploration. For Kara's classroom, the process helped children surpass the curricular objectives focused on immigration by taking up a more global perspective of border-crossing experiences. The wide and varied collection of texts offers nuanced and humanizing representation of lived experiences in text, as well as opportunities for students to consider similarities and differences among them and to interrogate depictions of power and identity they encounter in the written and illustrated narratives. Through more authentic portrayals of different border-crossing experiences, the children encountered a diversity of border-crossing narratives that disrupted stereotypes and encouraged text-to-text connections. In the section that follows, I highlight three different approaches Kara used to amplify students' reading across the narratives found in her wide and varied collection.

One affordance of a wide and varied picturebook collection is that it entices readers to disrupt singular narrative representations and to think across storyworlds. Here I highlight just some of the most significant (and unexpected!) ways Kara and her students engaged with this focused picturebook collection about border-crossing experiences.

Interpreting and Interrogating Motifs and Symbols in Illustrations

One thing that each of the teachers featured in this book does well is engage children as picture readers. In this example, Kara invites children to read illustrations more deeply through visual thinking strategies to interpret visual symbols and the impact they have on their growing understanding of immigration. After a week of reading from the collection, Kara returns to *Dreamers* as she notices how frequently the children keep referencing Yuyi's journey. She projects one of the illustrated spreads onto the screen for students to interact with and read. With Kara's invitation, "What more do you see?," the children share.

Zack: Towards the bottom left corner there is a book podium thing.

Serena: There are books in the stroller. . . . Books are everywhere. She's reading everywhere.

> Kezia: There's a brown thing in the middle.... It's a moon.
>
> Mahoma: I notice in the other pictures she doesn't have a backpack ... but here she does.
>
> Areif: There are leaves everywhere. Yuyi uses the leaf to represent freedom because leaves can go anywhere.

Building on Areif's attention to symbolism, Kara labels a piece of chart paper with "Yuyi's Symbols." She asks, "What's a symbol?" John explains that it's "something that represents something else." Kara mentions that Yuyi uses lots of symbols and shares an example. "Look at this page. Is the leaf representing a tree? Just a leaf? What else could the leaf be besides freedom?"

> Ellie: The leaf could represent traveling.
>
> Jane: I think the butterfly also represents travel and freedom because they migrate.

Certainly, if you are familiar with Yuyi Morales's *Dreamers*, you can confirm that her depictions of bats, monarch butterflies, and other wildlife are intentional metaphors for migration and immigration. When you have a strong picturebook collection that is rich in authentic visual portrayals, so much meaning can be mined for deeper conversation. On this day, Areif's hypothesis of Yuyi's use of leaves in the illustration launched a great discussion about symbolism. Kara built on his offering to engage students with the author-illustrator's intentions with certain visual motifs. Reading symbols in illustration (see Figure 4.4) for their "hidden" meanings became a popular and productive way that students engaged with the picturebook collection moving forward.

FIGURE 4.4. Students' interpretations of illustrated metaphors.

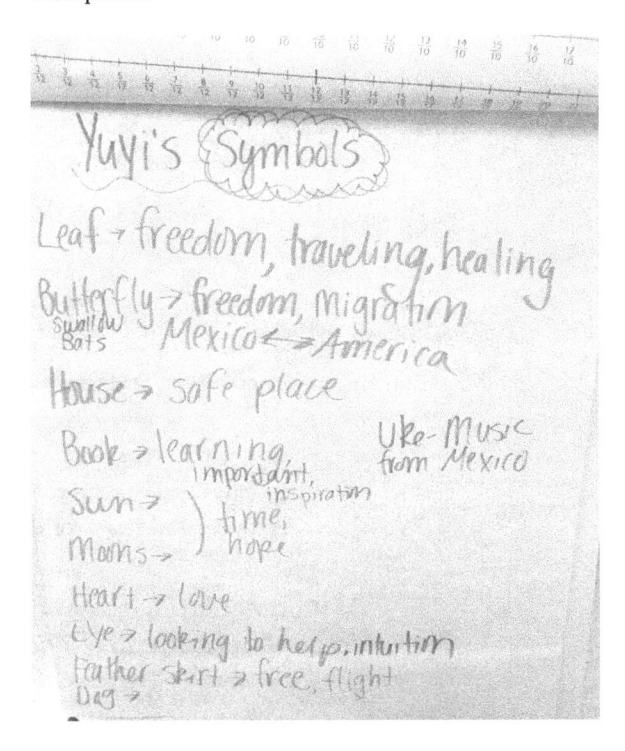

Musical Pairings

One surprising and generative engagement with the border-crossing picturebook collection was Kara's integration of music and theater as parallel texts to think across. She introduced carefully selected scenes from the musical *Hadestown* to her students. *Hadestown* weaves together the mythic tale of Orpheus and Eurydice and that of King

Hades and his wife, Persephone, and takes audience members on a visual and musical journey across and in between the borders of the underworld and the natural world. Kara explains that the musical describes the mythological setting of Hades as "the underworld, the dark place" and how this musical paints Hades as a good place, even though we often think of it as dark and scary.

The song "We We Build the Wall" is performed much like a call-and-response between a leader figure and children building a wall. After listening to the song, which elicited snapping and swaying from the students, they repeatedly referenced the following call-and-response lines from the lyrics for closer inspection; these are the lines that stood out to them the most:

> We build the wall to keep us free.
> The wall keeps out the enemy.
> The enemy is poverty.
> Because they want what we have got, we build the wall
> What do we have that they should want?

Kara asks, "What is happening during these lines and what do you hear—for instance, voices, words, volume—that makes you say that?"

Luke suggests that the singers are singing about why they need to build the wall, and that because the singers do not answer that question, it provides the "space" for the listeners to think about that.

Zack reminds everyone about the line focused on how the wall was trying to keep out the enemy and that he thought it mentioned poverty. He explains that the leader probably wanted to keep his job and didn't want an "overflow" of people. He concludes that the leader is probably worried that a "bunch of rich people get pushed out and then THEY don't have jobs."

Ashley notes that she was confused when the singers said they "build the wall to keep us free" because she knows that walls are usually built for separation.

For this discussion, students are using auditory clues, or reading sound, to help them understand the text and to provide evidence for their developing interpretations of text based on the lines they lifted. By broadening the collection to include this multimodal text, Kara has given students the opportunity to consider the tension and negotiation of different perspectives within the song and how borders keep some from entering Hades and some trapped within the walls. This experience also offered another shared narrative and storyworld to connect to across their discussions.

Amplifying Students' Everyday Connections across Literature and Their Lives

Kara knows that if she wants to encourage students to read across and beyond the picturebook collection, she must be sure to provide models of readers doing just that.

As students make connections to other shared reads (such as to *Front Desk*, the whole-class chapter book read-aloud), independent reading, vocabulary, and current events, Kara takes time to restate and amplify what they are doing, at times even using their examples as models to teach explicitly. In the following classroom discussion, Kara does just this as students dig deeper into the concepts of immigration, refugees, and borders in the following ways: through connections to students' independent and shared reading, to concepts students already know, and to current events and their own lives.

Connecting to Students' Independent and Shared Reading

As Kara reads from *Dreamers*, she notes that Yuyi's permanent immigration was unexpected because she hadn't realized she would not be able to go back and forth given the way US policies were at the time. Kara reads about Yuyi's feelings of not being understood or understanding everything around her. Areif shares that Yuyi's feelings remind him of *Pie in the Sky* (2019) by Remi Lai in which the character Jingwen struggles to understand what surrounds him. Kara smiles and restates Areif's text-to-text connection for all to hear, names it as a valuable meaning-making strategy, and encourages students to similarly make connections to their independent reading and other chapter books.

In the discussion that follows about Yuyi's feelings, Ashley explains that some families want to immigrate from their country to America, but the borders won't let them. Kara responds, "Oooh, hold onto that!" as she once again holds up their shared read-aloud, *Front Desk*. She asks, "Did they immigrate?" referring to the families in the book. Students nod and say yes. Ashley then begins to elaborate on the limitations of national border policies by connecting across characters' experiences from their shared read-aloud as an example of how border policies shape immigrant experiences. Kara facilitates further discussion by amplifying students' connections to books they have been reading in class.

Connecting to Concepts Students Already Know

As students continue to offer their understandings of *immigration*, Kara draws on their comments as she uses an oversized chart to record a basic definition of immigration. She writes that immigration is "people moving to another place, typically another country, to find a better life or because they want to." Genna claims that sometimes when people immigrate they are forced to, because of war or something. Kara notes, "That's coming, hold on to that!" to suggest that perhaps Genna's statement relates better to another term they have been exploring.

Luke adds that immigration reminds him of the word *immigrant*. Kara agrees and clarifies that the action is *immigration*, and the immigrant is a person or a noun.

Kara models referencing their previous work by flipping to the chart they had created focused on refugees and asks Genna to repeat what she said earlier about a person being forced to go to another country because of war. Genna elaborates on her noticing, and Kara then reads the comments on the refugee chart and states, "Genna was on the right track. This [leaving a place due to devastating conditions] is a similar experience for many migrants and many immigrants."

By drawing on students' authentic connections to concepts they bring to the discussion, Kara helps them learn new vocabulary in relation to familiar concepts from books they have read and discussions they have held.

Connecting to Current Events and Students' Lives

Kara adds the children's language to the chart, sharing that immigration might also happen when someone must leave their country because of war, famine (which she describes as not having enough food to feed the people that are there), or natural disaster. She connects "natural disaster" to news of Puerto Rico facing a hurricane, a current event that students were eager to discuss earlier that morning.

She then asks, "Do you think, based on this definition, might anyone go back after fleeing their country?" Joshua says no and Kara acknowledges that typically refugees are unable to return to the unsafe conditions they left. Genna says they might return after the famine or natural disaster is over or gone. Ashley then talks about what she saw at the state historical society museum about a person who had to leave their state. Kara notes that we often think of refugees as coming from another country.

Kara then invites the children to begin to think more deeply about the concept of borders. She reads aloud the responses students had left on the chart: "Forcefield, splitting things, wall between countries." She pauses and asks, "Can we always see borders?" Luke says sometimes and Kara asks him to "tell me more." He explains, "There are two types of borders in my head, one that you can see, like the Great Wall of China was at one time, and another kind of border, like the one in the room I share with my brother. We can't see it, but we know it's there." Kenan explains the idea of invisible borders using the game capture the flag, in which "you have to protect your base." Ashley talks about the border between Kansas and Missouri. Kara adds "Invisible borders" to the chart. She ends by inviting her fourth graders to continue making connections to current events and their lived experiences. "Here's your takeaway—if your parents have the news on, ... think about those words.... If you see newspapers in the checkout line, look for those words—*immigration, refugee, border*. Tell us what you learn."

In just this one discussion in which Kara and the children are digging deeper to understand the terms *immigration*, *refugee*, and *border*, the students showed us so much. When we pause to make room for children to show us how they think across the texts they read and live both in the classroom and outside of school, we learn so much about how they make meaning of complex topics in relation to their lived experience and current events.

It makes sense that as readers uncover new meanings and explore complex concepts, they connect to what they have read, link to familiar terms, and share the relationships they see between the literature, their lives, and the world around them. As a bilingual teacher in Texas, sharing border-crossing picturebooks elicited so many personal connections for my first graders who were growing up in immigrant families, just as I did. Depictions of various physical border-crossing journeys were familiar, as were the negotiations of living in the in-between or liminal spaces of language, culture, and identity. Here in the Midwest, sharing border-crossing picturebooks did not elicit the same experiences from the children of immigrant families, which made sense as I reflected on our distance from the United States and Mexico border. Making a journey by plane or by car does not happen with the same frequency here in the Midwest as it does in Texas given the additional costs, commitment of time, and distance. I find that many in the Midwest are surprised when the Latinx immigrant children, for example, are not as transnational as they assumed they were. They are surprised that the children of Mexican heritage don't always identify with border-crossing picturebooks or have stories to share from their heritage country, and they don't understand why the experiences the children do share are fuzzy for them. In Kara's classroom, during one of their discussions about border crossing, Ethan enthusiastically talked about his family's trip to Mexico from Texas and visiting people who came back and forth. He shared about his family members and how his uncle got pulled over when he crossed the border even though he was not speeding. When Ethan finished sharing his connections to the collection, Kara asked if his family goes back across the border often. He was unsure. Kara didn't press him further or shame him for not knowing. Instead, she valued his personal connection as a valuable experience for him personally and as an appreciator of the books they were reading. Kara understood that when you read border-crossing stories, it can evoke students' own border-crossing stories, and with that comes the great responsibility to receive children's experiences in humanizing ways. As children encounter border-crossing experiences in texts, they will begin to interrogate the borders they navigate in their lives and encounter in the world more generally, which demands that we be ready to receive their journeys, whatever they might be, without assumptions or prejudice.

In the section that follows, you'll find three critical encounters that unfolded in the days following the book flood. You'll also see an example of our personal reflection toward change when reviewing what unfolded. To

Inviting Teacher Reflection

- How might you listen to, lift, and locate the way students engage a wide and varied collection of picturebooks with diverse representation?

- In what ways are students' organic responses to a wide and varied picturebook collection creating pathways for deeper interrogation of text?

- What seems to matter most for students' engagements with a wide and varied picturebook collection?

- Whose immigration/refugee/border-crossing narratives are most represented? Which are missing?

- If you do not observe students make these moves in their discussion, how can you plan to model them yourself?

illustrate that the work is always negotiable, I share insights into the personal challenges and negotiations we encountered and how we navigated them in the classroom.

Critical Encounters with Picturebooks

As a reminder, I characterize critical encounters with literature as those moments when a text elicits a response that urges deeper discussion into a justice-oriented issue or interrogation of power, or that potentially becomes a transformative moment that changes someone's previously held beliefs. These are the moments, microbursts of collective meaning making, that are ultimately the heart of critical literature response because these moments produce fissures in book talk that can make for a better world.

Critical Encounter 1: Questioning Themes of Meritocracy through Picturebooks

In this critical encounter, Kara is revisiting the initial list of themes the students generated from the border-crossing picturebook collection. By this stage of the focused picturebook exploration, students have been reading from the book flood and are ready with many titles, characters, authors, and illustrators from their collection to layer into the discussion. In an effort to trouble the themes of individualism and meritocracy (a system in which advancement is based on individual ability or achievement) that emerged in response to their reading, Kara revisits *Friends from the Other Side / Amigos del otro lado* (1993) by queer feminist writer Gloria Anzaldúa and illustrated by Consuelo Méndez. Kara found that the work of developing themes from the book flood had generated discussion with her fourth graders, but that the deeper, underlying complexities were still waiting to be uncovered. To dig further into their reading, she sought a touchstone text to help students continue to nuance their understanding of "hard work pays off" that emerged in their discussion.

Entering the Critical Encounter

On this day, Kara points to the student-generated list of themes that emerged in response to the book flood and says, "This is the one I want us to think about today: *Hard work pays off*." She asks the students to take a moment to reflect on an occasion when hard work paid off, encouraging them to consider an experience at school, at home, or with their family, and asks them to keep this moment in their head for just a moment. After they have a few moments to reflect, students respond.

She asks, "So what is something that you've done in your life when you think hard work paid off?" Jane shares a hypothetical example in which she really wants a pair of shoes but has half of the amount of money; then she would need to go to work to make enough money to buy the shoes. Areif shares his example of learning English. When he was six years old, his mom told him to learn English and he did so by watching TV in English and working hard to learn new words. Mahoma then talks about his hard work with his soccer teammates. He uses details to explain that they lost their first game 1–7, but after "running a bunch," they have now "scored a bunch."

After hearing a few examples. Kara poses an additional layer to the question by asking, "Does hard work *always* pay off?" Kara doesn't let them answer this question right away but instead uses the question to pique the students' interest, giving them time to think and come up with an answer on their own. Kara understands that her students must first situate this issue in their own lives to interrogate it further.

Kara invites the children to return to their desks to write in response to the question, "What happens if you work hard, and it doesn't pay off?" She tells them to take a few minutes to think about this and then to think of an example in a book or in their personal lives when hard work didn't pay off. She adds that "you may have read a book . . . I'm thinking about *Front Desk* right now, where hard work does pay off." She talks about how the character in the book works hard to learn English, but she asks again, "But does hard work always pay off?" Kara continues asking questions to help students come up with an idea or to redirect their attention and help them narrow down ideas to write about.

After they finish writing, she again asks, "Does hard work always pay off?" to frame their discussion.

    Genna: Not *all* the time because sometimes you do stuff and the plan changes.

    Kara: Give me an example.

    Genna: Okay, my older sister worked hard to go to a local magnet school, but a spot opened up at another magnet school, so we moved and plans changed.

    Kara: So hard work doesn't always pay off because conditions and plans change.

    Zack: You can work hard, but you stop, so nothing happens. If you stop, then nothing good will happen.

    Jane: Could other people affect your hard work?

    Ethan: You can work hard, then someone by accident trips you in a marathon, you might get hurt.

    Alyssa: No, because sometimes no matter how hard you try, it still might not happen. I studied really hard for the spelling bee, but I never get in.

> **Kara:** I hear you all are saying no, hard work doesn't always pay off, so I want you to keep brainstorming the reasons and more examples as to why you are saying no. As I read *Friends from the Other Side*, I want you to listen for this theme, something doesn't pay off. And I want you to be thinking about why.

Throughout the read-aloud, students share their connections to Kara's questions.

> **Zack:** Yes, hard work pays off because they made it to America, but they came from Mexico to America hoping they could find work and they couldn't, and the border patrol looked for them. They were living in a shack and not so good environment. Their hard work paid off in some ways, but not in all of the ways the characters hoped they would.
>
> **Jane:** Joaquin, he worked hard, but the hard work didn't pay off, it just didn't happen.
>
> **Luke:** Joaquin was carrying firewood, and [I] don't think he sold a lot, so I agree, just because you work hard, it just doesn't happen.

Kara then reflects on how these responses relate to *Front Desk* and says, "Mia worked really hard for something, but it did not pay off." Kenan agrees and shares, "She got scammed." At this point, Kezia shows the "connection symbol" with her hands, linking her fingers one by one to signal the text-to-text connections that are unfolding. Taking this cue, other students begin to reflect on the question of hard work and meritocracy through other texts they have read. Luke offers an example of one of the state award books he's reading in which the main character reads a lot of books but gets sent to the principal's office because he was reading when he shouldn't be. Luke notes that reading does not pay off for this character. Zack discusses *Undocumented: A Worker's Fight* (2018) by Duncan Tonatiuh and highlights points from each page, including the illustrated spread depicting an apartment cramped with five people. He adds that he thinks the border patrol "picked up all their relatives." Zack notes that the families in *Undocumented* were working hard but not getting to live in a nice place because they weren't getting paid enough. As Zack holds up the accordion-style picturebook and points to the image of the undocumented workers protesting, the other students and Kara connect the experience to the discussion of protesting they had earlier in the year during social studies.

As this critical encounter reveals, children can lean into discussions to challenge messages of meritocracy when we offer rich examples to think with and interrogate. When Kara asks, "We'd like to think hard work pays off, but what if it doesn't?," she invites children to trouble the theme of meritocracy that emerged in their discussion. She makes room for children to first situate this question in their young lives as a way to make the conversation more accessible. She scaffolds their meaning making through constant modeling and posing questions to prevent possible confusion. Students not only reflected on this topic in the context of their own lives, but also adeptly troubled the notion of meritocracy in other picturebooks they had read to challenge normative views of meritocracy on their own terms.

Critical Encounter 2: Reading Power in Illustration

In this second critical encounter, children interrogate meanings in the illustrations of *Dreamers* to reflect on positions of power presented in the book. Kara has noted how much the children depend on picture reading when thinking across texts and interpreting color, line, perspective, and other semiotic meanings in illustrations. Just earlier in the week, after being invited to share their noticings about immigration across both *Dreamers* and *Friends from the Other Side* (which they soon began to call "Friends"), the students expressed so much based on the illustrations alone.

Daniel: *Dreamers* shows more passion in the illustrations and shows more illustrations, and *Friends* is more realistic.

Luke: The characters and stories are both from Mexico and the illustrations' color reminds me of Mexico.

Building on their noticings, Kara then asks if their understanding of the narratives would be different if the illustrations were done differently. The students agree.

Entering the Critical Encounter

Kara revisits the image from *Dreamers* featuring Yuyi and her son playing in the fountain, with a speech bubble coming from her mouth that says, "¡Ay!" From the reader's perspective, the expression on Yuyi's face is one of uncertainty and possible embarrassment, and only the back of the policeman is seen, with his hands firmly placed on his hips as if in disapproval.

Zack: Yuyi's face makes me think that she did not know not to get in the fountain.

Daniel: The policeman must be mad, because he has his hands on his hips.

Kara asks her students to stand up off of the floor and embody the policeman's position. As the children stand with their hands on their hips, Kara asks what they think a policeman in this position would be saying (see Figure 4.5).

Some students: "Stop!"

Ashley: "Ma'am, that is public property."

Kara then asks, "Who do you think has power in this picture?" Some students agree that both Yuyi and the policeman are powerful in the illustration.

Areif: At first I thought it was the policeman, but now I think it's Yuyi.

Jane: I agree. Yuyi is taller and bigger in this first illustration and must be more powerful.

Kara uses this idea of size as equal to power to connect to *The Journey* (Sanna, 2016), in which size also represents power among the characters. Kara points to the left-hand side of the projected picture that shows Yuyi as taller and larger. She then compares that to the right-hand picture in which the officer is taller and Yuyi is smaller. She asks if the students think Yuyi the illustrator did that on purpose? Many of the students comment that Yuyi must feel less powerful in the fountain, which is why she illustrated herself smaller in size there (see Figure 4.5).

Mahoma: No, I don't think power is about size. See, Yuyi is background here, way back, like she's less important.

Daniel: I think Yuyi and the policeman both have power. She has the courage to walk across the border, but the policeman can arrest you in this case?

FIGURE 4.5. Kara and her fourth graders interpret representations of power in illustrations.

In this critical encounter, the children interrogate visual representations of power across *Dreamers* and other texts they had read together. Focused on the size and placement of the characters in the illustrations, the children read into the semiotic meanings to trouble notions of power as static and residing solely in a particular position (e.g., the policeman). Noteworthy is Daniel's suggestion that power is not only physical (in a stance or position) but also metaphorical, reminding us that there is great power in the courage that immigrant communities often display.

Critical Encounter 3: Challenging Misconceptions of Blackness

In this short but powerful critical literature encounter, Kara brings the students back together to reflect on the books they have read and the other books they have discussed. In doing so, she elicits a snapshot of students' thinking as a way to check for understanding. Students' responses to the literature serve as data for her teaching; Kara knows that the thinking her students share will inform what happens next in her instruction. During this critical literature encounter, students are ten days into their reading from the collection focused on border-crossing experiences and they already have strong familiarity with multiple titles, authors and illustrators, characters, and storyworlds.

Entering the Critical Encounter

To launch the discussion and invite the children to think across the border-crossing storyworlds they have read, Kara asks, "What are the cultures, countries, and maybe people here in the stories?" She points to the physical collection of picturebooks flooding the room. Zack immediately responds that he notices that all the characters featured in the books are Black. Kara asks him to "tell me more," and he repeats that all the characters are Black. Kara realizes that her invitation doesn't elicit further reflection given how familiar he is with the storyworlds that inundate the classroom. In response to his claim that all the characters featured in the collection are Black, Kara asks, "But are they?" Zack appears to conflate all People of Color featured in picturebooks as Black. Kara challenges that with "But are they?" to suggest that maybe he needs to rethink what he is saying. She wants him to consider that not all the characters featured in the picturebooks are Black but are instead portrayed with more nuance to reflect Indigenous, Afro-Latino, mixed race, or mixed ethnicity peoples. In my role as classroom book lady, I join the discussion to share that often people who have Black or Brown skin, like me, call ourselves People of Color. I talk about being a Person of Color and having South American heritage and how I prefer being called a Woman of Color or Latina. Kara records the terms discussed throughout the conversation for the children to see in written form; these introductory terms include *Black/African American*, *Mexican*, *People of Color*, and *Indigenous*. Students continue to discuss, and Luke then shares that he sees People of Color in the books flooding the room.

> **Teacher Professional Resource**
>
> To learn more about BIPOC and POC, check out the following QR code.

In this critical encounter, Kara challenges Zack's misconception about diverse racial and ethnic representation in the picturebooks the class has read. In doing so, she treats Zack and his peers as intellectually capable of rethinking the language they use to talk about people and capable of negotiating the nuances of the issue. As children are introduced to these considerations, individual students like Luke make the decision to take up new learning and use the term *People of Color* in their talk. By introducing relevant terms to discuss specific groups and sharing the complexity of this work, Kara is helping children enter further discussion on the topic with a more informed and inclusive perspective.

This critical encounter sets up a future discussion in which we further complicate the term *People of Color* (which has been contested as suggesting erasure of ethnicity and race). Discussions could also explore the critiques around the term *BIPOC* (Black Indigenous People of Color), which similarly raises questions for those who see the term as establishing conflict among racial and ethnic groups given the way distinct communities are grouped together as one, further causing harm and erasure of certain communities. Ultimately, the discussion around the language we use to discuss People and Communities of Color and other marginalized groups (so complex and important!) requires that we be transparent about what we mean and why we use the terms we do. I have found that many students, particularly those who claim membership in the very groups we are discussing, are quite comfortable with these negotiations of multiple perspectives and can draw their own conclusions about the language they use and why. For those who find themselves as outsiders to the discussion, the opportunity to witness the ways People of Color are racialized, gendered, and discussed through labels (and how others are not) brings needed awareness to the additional labor and everyday complexities that so many People of Color experience around our identities.

What Critical Encounters Can Teach Us

Together, these critical encounters with picturebooks amplify the significance of offering a wide and varied collection when enacting a Critical Literature Response Framework in an elementary classroom. Kara sees her students as capable readers able to navigate multiple perspectives and storyworlds and doesn't hesitate to encourage them to interrogate themes of power that emerge or to reconsider unfounded claims. I invite you to reflect on a few relevant tips for enacting a Critical Literature Response Framework with elementary children. Ask yourself: How did the classroom commitments and conditions Kara values enhance students' learning? How might the classroom practices, specifically selecting wide and varied literature collections, enhance your students' learning in a Critical Literature Response Framework? And—most important—how might you make this work your own?

Tips to Support Critical Encounters in Literature with Young Children

I invite you to consider how the following practices unfolded in the three critical encounters shared in this chapter, how they enhanced the experience when present, and how they *could have* enhanced the experience when they were not present.

Reminders

- Contextualize the picturebooks shared. Be sure to humanize the author and illustrator by sharing their stories and recognitions. In doing so, you bring awareness to the realities of the storyworlds shared and how they are often grounded in personal experiences.

- Make time to get informed and learn about the current events that children are relating to. What are the global and local issues that children seem to care about and connect their reading to? What are the different perspectives on the matter? How can you bring awareness to bigger issues in the world that students can connect to?

- Assume that immigration stories exist in the families or extended families of the children in your classroom. This will help you more readily receive the stories they choose to share.

- Believe in the capacity, intellect, and awareness your students bring as citizens of the world. Children can lean into the complexities of current events and their lives.

- If you see children as capable, challenge their misconceptions that repeatedly arise.

Top Ten Favorite Picturebooks Shared to Explore Immigration

1. Anzaldúa, G. (1993). *Friends from the other side / Amigos del otro lado* (C. Mendez, Illus.). Children's Book Press.

2. Binford, W. (Comp.). (2021). *Hear my voice: The testimonies of children detained at the southern border of the United States.* Workman.

3. Buitrago, J. (2015). *Two white rabbits* (R. Yockteng, Illus.). Groundwood Books.

4. Laínez, R. C. (2013). *From north to south* (J. Cepeda, Illus.). Children's Book Press.
5. Laínez, R. C. (2019). *My shoes and I: Crossing three borders / Mis zapatos y yo: Cruzando tres fronteras* (F. Vanden Broeck, Illus.). Arte Público Press.
6. Mateo, J. M. (2014). *Migrant* (J. M. Pedro, Illus.). Abrams Books for Young Readers.
7. Morales, Y. (2018). *Dreamers*. Neal Porter Books/Holiday House.
8. Sanna, F. (2016). *The journey*. Flying Eye Books.
9. Yang, K. (2018). *Front desk*. Arthur A. Levine Books/Scholastic.
10. Young, R. (2016). *Teacup* (M. Ottley, Illus.). Dial Books for Young Readers.

Children's Literature Cited

Anzaldúa, G. (1993). *Friends from the other side / Amigos del otro lado* (C. Méndez, Illus.). Children's Book Press.
Bunting, E. (2006). *One green apple* (T. Lewin, Illus.). Houghton Mifflin.
Higuera, D. B. (2021). *The last cuentista*. Levine Querido.
Lai, R. (2019). *Pie in the sky*. Henry Holt.
Laínez, R. C. (2010). *From north to south / Del norte al sur* (J. Cepeda, Illus.). Children's Book Press.
Morales, Y. (2018). *Dreamers*. Neal Porter Books/Holiday House
Munsch, R. N., & Askar, S. (1995). *From far away* (M. Martchenko, Illus.). Annick Press.
Sanna, F. (2016). *The journey*. Flying Eye Books.
Sís, P. (2007). *The wall: Growing up behind the Iron Curtain*. Farrar, Straus and Giroux.
Tonatiuh, D. (2015). *Dear primo: A letter to my cousin*. Abrams.
Tonatiuh, D. (2018). *Undocumented: A worker's fight*. Abrams ComicArts.
Yang, K. (2018). *Front desk*. Arthur A. Levine Books/Scholastic.

Inviting Multilingual and Multimodal Literature Response

Chapter Five

As Whitney prepares to read aloud a poem from the illustrated collection *Hey You! C'mere! A Poetry Slam* (2002) by Elizabeth Swados and Joe Cepeda, she explains to her fifth-grade students that she will invite them first to simply listen to the poem; she will not be sharing the illustrations just yet. She asks her students to visualize who and what they hear in their minds as they listen to the poem, a familiar comprehension practice in their classroom (see Figure 5.1). She states, "As I read, you will make the picture in your mind. And if you can't visualize it completely [touches the right side of her head with her right hand] then you can at least start to plan [makes a listing motion with her right hand] like, 'Okay. I would draw somebody with this type of hair, and this age, and this skin color, and all of that. Maybe this gender; this is where this person would live or work....' I want you to draw the picture in your mind. Are you ready?"

The selected poem, "Tough Kids," features two voices: one of a bully and another of a kid receiving and responding to the bully's words. After reading the poem, with great emphasis on varying voices and volume for the two protagonists, Whitney asks students to consider what the characters in the text "sounded" like. Students respond,

"He *sounds* like a bully."

"It's a *he* because the author used that word."

"He uses the word *c'mere*."

"I thought he had lighter skin."

"I thought he had darker skin."

Whitney records these initial visualizations on a public document using the SMART Board as the children speak, making sure to capture their words as well as which parts of the written narrative elicited their visualizations.

To extend the conversation, Whitney then reveals the illustrated double-page spread and asks her students to compare what is presented on the page with their initial visualizations (see Figure 5.1). She nudges them to confirm whether the visual portrayals of the protagonists align with their thinking. Students start to make comments as Whitney slowly moves the book so that all of the students can examine the illustration more carefully.

"The bully has a square-ish head."

"He's got darker skin. That's different than what I thought."

"Yeah, his head is kind of like something hard like a brick or a cinder block; those are tough too."

Whitney reflects on their comments and shares, "So, a bigger [bulks up her body like a bodybuilder] head, a bigger body maybe because they're tough? To show that dominance, maybe? And then [points to the bully in the illustration], do we see a bigger

FIGURE 5.1. Whitney invites her fifth graders to visualize the speakers in *Hey You! C'mere!* (Swados, 2002).

body? And some of you noticed that the illustrator chose a different skin color for the character than what you had visualized."

While reading the illustrations, students read characters' shape and size and body language to infer aspects of their identities, and some students challenged their initial assumptions about the characters' skin shade. Whitney elected not to immediately invite deeper discussion about skin shade or linguistic diversity during this first discussion of the poem, instead only welcoming students' initial responses. She does this to nurture a space for students to continue sharing their responses. Whitney understands that to guide students toward interrogation of assumptions in a text as well as in their own lives, students must feel free to share those assumptions without fear of immediate rejection. She returns to their noticings about skin shade and identity in the days that follow, many of which we explore later in this chapter.

As she reads aloud, Whitney focuses on language diversity and visual representations of language differences through literary arrows to frame their upcoming picturebook encounter. Her purpose for these initial literature response discussions is to position students to reflect on how the author and the illustrator work together to "show" a character's identity through language and illustration. This practice helps students understand how individuals and communities are depicted in picturebooks through different multimodal and linguistic features (what I'm calling multimodal and multilingual features of picturebooks).

Ultimately, through the course of this literature exploration in Whitney's classroom, many students concluded that, indeed, the visual, the embodied, the auditory and other sensorial features in a picturebook can complement or disrupt the printed narrative. Through these foundational conversations, the fifth graders in Whitney's classroom also tackled the notions that (1) we can make assumptions about people based on the way they are portrayed in illustration; (2) we can make assumptions about people based on the way they "sound" or how they speak in the narrative; and (3) we must be flexible and acknowledge that we *have* assumptions and understand that our assumptions are not always right.

In this chapter, you'll get to know Whitney and how language study through picturebooks and opportunities to explore the relationship between language and identity through multilingual and multimodal invitations unfolded in her classroom. You will also find a brief description of their focused literature exploration. And, to foreground the importance of multimodal and multilingual literacies in supporting critical encounters with picturebooks, I conclude the chapter with descriptions of three critical literature encounters Whitney and her students experienced. As always, whether teaching our youngest children or teaching fifth graders, I hope you consider how this work can be tailored to create literature discussion entry points for your own readers. I also hope you experience the depth of student learning that amplifies the powerful relationship among language, identity, and power.

Entering Whitney's Fifth-Grade Classroom

When sharing picturebooks, Whitney doesn't just read aloud to her fifth-grade students; her students truly engage in collaborative learning that entails more than taking Standardized English Print[5] approaches to literacy learning. Part of what keeps bringing me back to Whitney's classroom is the abundant literacy life and learning that thrives among her students. Every time I walk in, her students are busy reading, writing, making, thinking, looming, moving, crafting, singing, dancing, painting, questioning, discussing, reflecting … the list can go on. The room feels full of life as bodies and minds are busy and focused on making meaning together.

It's easy to think this passionate engagement just happens, especially in a designated expressive arts school, but as experienced teachers know, so much care and feedback goes into nurturing a vibrant learning space like this. Whitney dedicates the first weeks of school to building community with a focus on "being together" around text, providing ongoing feedback and spaces for students to reflect on their community building as well. At the heart of their learning and work together is not just listening but responding to literature and to one another, as well as crafting texts. Whitney's students know how to talk about books they've read after spending just a few weeks with one another, and they value that time. As they transition into responder, conversant, interrogator, and creator of texts through picturebooks, students are guided by the literary arrows and other reader-response invitations Whitney offers as she reads aloud.

> **Inviting Teacher Reflection**
>
> - What kind of movement do your students experience in the classroom? How comfortable are you with students moving around the classroom? Under what circumstances?
>
> - How do you build community during the first few weeks of school? Do you integrate experiences around literature as part of that work?
>
> - In addition to talk and writing, what other kinds of text making do you invite, mentor, and encourage in your classroom?
>
> - How might you begin to stretch the movement and text-making opportunities your students encounter in the classroom?

Getting the "Long Conversation" Started as Readers and Writers

It was not uncommon to see Whitney confer with her readers about books while sitting on the floor or at their tables. During independent reading time, she positions herself as both a fellow reader and a teacher, ready to receive their thoughts about the book while also providing guidance and instruction. What enhances her instruction as a language arts teacher is that she consistently positions students to respond to picturebooks not only as readers but also as composers-writers and artists. For example, after inviting students to visualize characters just by listening to the narrative, she asks them to consider how characters portrayed in the double-page spread might "sound" (see Figure 5.2). As Whitney shares the poem "Aunt Evelyn" from the same collection, the children read the illustration (rather than the text), which features a Woman of Color who appears to be a grandmother figure.

Whitney: So, if you were the author, what would Aunt Evelyn's voice be? Brainstorm just a couple of things: What would she be saying? Maybe in this illustrated context or just how she would talk in general.

Ivy: Because I just thought . . . I know her voice, but I didn't think I should write it. I can, like, say it out loud, but I couldn't, like, write it.

Whitney: What will you have to think about if you're the writer, though? If you're going to write Aunt Evelyn's talking [stands up and touches the SMART Board], her English, what will you have to be careful of and think about?

Jaylen: First you wanna know what Aunt Evelyn is going to look like. And who she is.

Whitney: Okay. So it helps to understand who she is, what she looks like, all of the attributes and experiences of that person. Okay. [starts to write on the SMART Board] So, to write a character, you want to understand who they are. What else do we need to think about if you're going to write from her English? Do you have to have that same language, or have the same race or gender or age as the character? [turns away from SMART Board and looks at students] Or her words?

Katie: Well, if you're writing it and it's like a shaky grandma voice, but you could like make it shaky.

Whitney: Okay. So, you will want to think about how [steps back from the SMART Board, looks at their language definition chart, and gestures to the chart with the book] their register or their pitch would be?

Katie: Yeah.

Ivy: We should know about her accent or her body language she uses.

Jameila: Her accent and grammar might be different.

FIGURE 5.2. Children can talk about race.

Some students begin to speak with a scratchy high-pitched voice, simulating what they believe a grandmother might sound like. Riley listens and then interrupts the conversation to share.

> Riley: Well, for starters I know that my grandma doesn't really ever talk in a grandma voice. She sounds just like you, maybe. But that's because she's not really, like, old. But my abuelita doesn't sound like that. She lives on a farm. She's got a very strong voice. And then, my grandma she sings a lot, so she never has a very scratchy voice. It's always very nice.

To facilitate this initial conversation, Whitney builds on students' responses to define important terms relevant to the learning, such as *pitch* and *register*. The freedom students like Riley feel to disrupt the stereotypes shaping the discussion speaks to the community of mutual respect and trust fostered among this group of readers. Ultimately, this is what we look for among a collaborative meaning-making community, a space for students to notice, interrogate, share, and raise questions when talk is guided by singular or stereotypical narratives of characters or communities.

I want to highlight how Whitney positions her students as writers and illustrators and encourages them to think about their responsibilities as picturebook makers and writers who are capturing lives and languages on paper. Because troubling appropriations of language dominate book publication, this literature discussion remains essential in language study. Who gets to write which languages? Why? Under what conditions, if any? What responsibilities does an author or picturebook maker have when crafting portrayals of diverse languages? How can you ensure that the representation is not replicating tropes and stereotypes of Communities of Color? It is a complex conversation, and Whitney is asking students to pause to consider these issues as writers and picturebook makers. Although students do not take up her invitation to reflect on these questions as they relate to race and gender, they do reflect on age. The conversation here is the first of many. This is Whitney's way of getting the "long conversation" going as she understands that these considerations require repeated discussion and examples, not just one mini-lesson.

Whitney is considered a teacher leader in her school, mentoring early career educators and gathering teachers interested in developing literature-based experiences in their classrooms. She has also been a significant learning and research partner for me as we think together about ways to share picturebooks with portrayals of diverse communities and languages. As a critical social educator, she asks questions I don't always know the answers to and pushes me to consider perspectives I had not considered. We have learned a lot over our time together, made plenty of mistakes in practice, and learned lessons that now, of course, feel so obvious. Above all, Whitney wants to do better by her students and is willing to give of her time and heart to do so. This desire fuels her commitment to sharing diverse literature in her classroom and developing her practice.

Perhaps you are like Whitney—you have teaching experiences under your belt and are yearning to do more in your classroom to effect change and to resist societal prejudice and racism. You've got more questions than answers, but you have made the commitment to do better by your students and to develop your practice. Below I share a bit more about Whitney's classroom and overview her focused literature exploration on linguistic diversity. As you read more about Whitney's classroom, consider the ways a multimodal and multilingual approach to literature response can support *your* students' critical reading of picturebooks.

Enlivening Critical Literature Response in an Upper-Elementary Classroom

In addition to positioning her students to respond to picturebooks as readers and composers, Whitney enlivens critical literature discussion in other ways. Although this chapter highlights multilingual and multimodal invitations, Whitney's Critical Literature Response Framework instruction is also enhanced by the following:

- Supporting an expansive view of language
- Exploring relationships between language and identity

In the sections that follow, I share more about these two approaches through examples to help you better understand the way Whitney's beliefs about language, literacy, and identity impact the classroom conditions for critical literature response.

Classroom Approach 1: Supporting an Expansive View of Language

Exploring portrayals of language in children's picturebooks in the classroom is only possible when a teacher values language diversity as an integral aspect of children's reading and writing lives both in and out of the classroom. Given the increasing pressure so many of us face to bring students to a Standardized English form of literacy, the place for exploring our different Englishes, language varieties, and home languages is easy to delegate as enrichment or as an after-school experience, or to just ignore completely. Yet when more expansive views of what counts as language are not a part of language arts learning, we miss the opportunity to guide young children to understanding language(s) as a system(s), we withhold occasions for students to leverage their rich linguistic repertoires as readers and writers, we refuse them the opportunity to connect to the broader aspects of their identities, and we deny them exposure to languaging practices other than their own. Whitney did not hesitate to guide students through language study, support shared linguistic terms to help the class collectively enter these discussions, and lean on linguistically diverse picturebooks to do so.

In one classroom example, Whitney reads aloud *Yo, Jo!* (Isadora, 2007), choosing to frame this reading as an opportunity to explore different language varieties. Before reading, Whitney gives her students two questions to consider: As you hear the different Englishes in this book, (1) who do you think speaks like this? and (2) who do you think writes like this? As Whitney reads *Yo, Jo!* to the class, at certain points she stops reading to ask students to turn and talk about the two questions. After reading, she has students focus specifically on two spreads near the end of the book: (1) where Jo encounters Grandpa and (2) where Jo says "Yo, chillin'!" to Grandpa.

After taking time to reflect on Whitney's questions, Jada astutely shares, "They [Jo and Grandpa] both don't have the same language; because they do have the same

Featured Picturebook Summary

Yo, Jo! (2007) is written and illustrated by Rachel Isadora. A young Black boy named Jo walks through his neighborhood greeting each group of friends in a different way, exchanging greetings such as "Yo! Hey? Wassup?" Upon encountering his grandfather, Jo quickly pivots to Standardized English when his grandfather raises an eyebrow at Jo's language. But in response, Grandpa winks and replies, "Yo, chillin'!"

language, it's just that they speak it differently." Whitney smiles and builds on Jada's noticing to share, "That's so interesting. That you can speak the same language, but you can speak it differently? [addressing the class] Would you agree with that? *They're both communicating in English, but are they using different Englishes?*" Students unanimously agree and describe Jo's English:

"Jo's English is mixed and . . . I don't know how to say it."

"Jo's English is creative."

"Jo's English is hip-hop language."

"He's shortening the words, like *chillin'*."

Whitney masterfully builds on the brilliance of her students' noticings of linguistic difference among the characters in *Yo, Jo!* to center a more expansive view of language. The discussion of these two spreads was fertile ground to introduce the concept of multiple Englishes (Canagarajah, 2012; Young & Martinez, 2011), which becomes a critical concept as the class moves forward in this focused literature exploration. By doing so, Whitney sets a strong foundation for students as they turn their conversations toward understanding the relationship between language and identity.

Classroom Approach 2: Exploring Relationships between Language and Identity

We cannot study linguistic difference without acknowledging how our ways with words are completely entangled with who we are and where we come from. The relationship between language and identity has been well researched, with scholars emphasizing how families socialize us into language and how schooling subtracts from the rich linguistic repertoires and multilingual identities children possess before they even begin school (e.g., Anzaldúa, 1987; Heath, 1983; Zentella, 1998). More recent research also tells us that we can no longer ignore how language is deeply tied to racialized identities and how our identities are shaped by raciolinguistic and deficit assumptions that are imposed in certain contexts (e.g., Flores & Rosa, 2015; de los Ríos et al., 2021).

Classroom studies of language in literature with children can unfortunately quickly become an exercise in contrasting language differences as "academic language versus other," a model that can perpetuate a false binary between home and school language. Rather than juxtapose one language variety next to another, Whitney helps her fifth graders focus on the speaker, the context, the rhetorical purpose, and the impact the language achieves. She also helps them understand how race, power, ageism, and other features influence the way we receive that language as readers.

For example, as students initially entered these conversations about language and identity in picturebooks, Whitney quickly noticed that students struggled to name aspects of the characters' identities. She chose to be explicit in her guidance on the issue. She explained, "You might need to use words that involve somebody's gender; you might need to talk about somebody's race. Or what their skin tone looks like. Okay? You might talk about culture, and it might feel a little uncomfortable because you might not have those same attributes about you. So, when we're talking about something that we don't have, it's okay to still name it in a respectful way."

Whitney also does not hesitate to model talking about the way her identity affects her work as a reader. For example, when listening to the poem "Tough Kids" being read aloud by Whitney, Riley thinks that she hears Whitney read the character's voice in a particular way, possibly signaling a Person of Color. As Riley explains, "When you read *Hey You! C'mere!*," by the way you said it, it kind of seemed like he had dark skin to me." Whitney responds, "Do you think my voice and me reading it impacts what you visualize?"

Many students nod in agreement. Whitney thinks aloud, "Because my voice is coming from . . . [points to herself] a white, woman, thirty, teacher. And I'm reading somebody else's voice. Right? So, when you hear it, even if I try to change my voice, to maybe sound like a character, it's still like a white teacher pretending to be someone else. Right?"

As Riley notes conflict in the way the bully's voice was read aloud, Whitney highlights how her identity as a white, thirty-year-old woman impacts their reading experience. Here, Whitney raises an interesting theoretical question. Does the identity of the reader influence how listeners visualize characters? It's a question she often invites her students to consider. In this case, her reading of slam poetry evokes a hip-hop community, which Riley associates with Communities of Color. The dissonance Riley experienced in hearing her white teacher read slam poetry aloud was a powerful opening Whitney used to raise questions about language and identity for students to consider. The discussion on this issue that followed is presented as a critical encounter later in this chapter.

On a different occasion, Whitney asked her fifth-grade students to discuss whether she (a white woman) should be reading aloud *Yo, Jo!* Although students initially shared that it sounded "strange" or "awkward" when she read the book aloud, they quickly began to talk about how her age ("You're not a kid!"), her whiteness ("You're white, Mrs. Hoffman"), her position of power ("You're a teacher"), and so much more factor into their assessment. In sum, these classroom discussions of different language varieties, race, age, power, and more begin to decenter Standardized English as the only possibility for their literacy lives in school and set the stage for deeper interrogation of the ways our identities shape our reading and writing both in and out of school.

Whitney similarly brings aspects of her identity to her teaching of writing. She features her language and identity in the illustrated poem she worked on as a model for her students drafting their own poetry in response to the shared literature. Whitney generates examples of metaphors and similes for each of the parts she has listed in her writer's notebook. She writes:

> My eyes are "suppers" for lunch in Kansas.
> My hair is like the straight county roads leading to my aunt's house.
> I am NeNe to my nephews and my niece.
> I am Whit to my "Hey, girl!" friends. My "likes" skip like a broken record when I get nervous.

Acknowledging the ways in which her identity and her language shape her writing encourages her students to do the same.

As Whitney illustrates, when we teachers consider the racial, linguistic, cultural, gendered, and other sociocultural aspects of our identities and are willing to share how our resources shape our language and literacy lives, many children will feel the freedom to explore how their identities shape their language and literacy lives as well. Whitney does not demand or expect that children do this in the classroom; she does not force them to put their sociocultural resources and racial, linguistic, or ethnic identities on display. Instead, she fosters a space where children can express their identities and languages if they choose, rather than deny them the opportunity to do so.

Focused Literature Exploration: Linguistically Diverse Picturebooks as Mentor Texts

For the focused literature exploration, Whitney purposefully shared a collection expressing different languages (e.g., English, Spanish, Arabic, French), language varieties (different Englishes, regionalisms), and language formats (emojis, different fonts and styles of print and scripts) in picturebook form reflecting different literary genres. Such a collection makes for an exciting book flood that children can experience, respond to, inspect, and learn from as readers, writers, and illustrators. Aiming to cultivate a literature experience for students that centered the beauty and power of their different ways with words, Whitney intentionally ensured that these picturebooks articulated linguistic diversity not only in the print narratives but also in illustrations that reflected the vibrancy of the language lives represented in the books. Doing so helps our children to see that language is not used in isolation but instead is lived out in three-dimensional, embodied, dynamic, and vibrant ways across a variety of cultural, racial, and ethnic communities and in a wide array of settings for different purposes.

Whitney's fifth graders received this literature exploration enthusiastically. Their encounters with their own and others' languages launched personal explorations of their personal lives, languages, and literacies. Guiding questions, or literary arrows, from Whitney included the following:

> What do you notice about the way the author or illustrator crafted with language(s)?
>
> How are these language patterns similar to and/or different from your own?
>
> Why do you think the author or illustrator added that language(s)?
>
> How does hearing different languages make you feel?
>
> How are the author and illustrator working together to "show" a character's identity?

Launching Multilingual and Multimodal Literature Response

As a response to these extensive interactions with picturebooks, students were invited to craft illustrated self-portraits and poems (a multimodal and multilingual literature response invitation) that reflected their ways with words and identities. Through metaphor, color, and different languages and Englishes, students put their languages in conversation with a visual identity display.

In Whitney's classroom, multilingual and multimodal literacy (MML) invitations were entangled with children's explorations of linguistic diversity in picturebooks. In the sections that follow, I highlight how MML invitations such as reading voices, creating language maps, crafting self-portraits, and composing podcasts enhanced the literature exploration and nurtured important spaces for critical literature encounters.

Reading Voices, Reading Identities, Resisting Assumptions about Language and Identity

Because the students were engaged in their first encounters with the literature collection, Whitney asked a district parent, who happened to be a linguist, to come to the class to share his extensive collection of audio recordings of different voices reflecting a vast array of experiences, ethnicities, races, and ages. As the children listen to each voice, he prompts them to come up with three descriptions for each of the speakers and to match the voices to the portrait photographs he projects on the screen. Whitney adds, "Even if you think it is obvious who you think that voice belongs to, write it down."

Toward the end of the listening selection and after listening to children respond, he adds, "I've seen a couple of people write about the speaker's race. Can you tell someone's race from the way they talk?" It's a question that initially causes the students to pause, but soon enough they have much to say on the matter.

> **Aiden:** I try to think if I'm listening to the radio and I'm hearing a singer I've never heard, sometimes I like to *imagine* them. And sometimes I get them totally wrong, like a different race, and sometimes, like a different age and stuff. Yeah, I just do that a lot. It's something that I do.
>
> **Riley:** I mixed speakers; I thought that her accent matched with another picture. The girl with blond hair was going like this [poses like the person in the portrait]. And the background kind of looks like she was on a beach. So the audio where she talks about how she went home and washed her hair, I thought it matched the beach because it seemed like something you would do after you go to the beach. And she seemed like, "Oh, I'm reading something." She also had kind of light skin, a little bit of Black [skin]. She was kind of like an Indian color too. And I thought that's like what the accent matched up with.

The visiting parent agrees and says, "So, I think that's a *great* idea, that when we hear voices [makes a circular gesture with his right hand near his ear] we're always kind of doing this naturally, right? When you hear a voice, you're making a picture in your head of what you think that person might look like. But I think it's an important point: We might be right *a lot,* but we're not always right [shakes his head no]. Sometimes we're wrong. It's fine to notice and talk about what we hear in people's voices, but we want to do it in ways that lift people up. Not in ways that put people down. So that's something to think about."

The opportunity to read, listen to, interpret, discern, and debrief audio-recorded voices and to articulate the images we have of the speaker puts our assumptions on the table to interrogate and challenge. As students like Aiden and Riley reflect on the visualizations they created, they talk about how they ascribe to the speaker a particular race, skin shade, possible ethnicity, and/or age. Aiden also explains that sometimes his assumptions based on a person's voice are "totally wrong." He shares that he makes these assumptions frequently—"Yeah, I just do that a lot." Riley similarly shares how she ascribes a particular skin shade and activities to the speaker and associates someone's accent with a particular identity. For young children, reading voices and sharing assumptions about speakers' identities brings an initial awareness to the relationships between language, race, age, and experiences that can then be interrogated further over time through "long conversations" (Nichols, 2006). Reading voices and sharing assumptions also offers an opportunity to raise caution about assumptions that shape our assessment of speakers. Riley's description of the speaker's skin color as "Indian" or as a "little bit of Black," for example, provides a critical opening to talk about the relationships and differences between skin shade, race, and ethnicity. As the visiting parent shares, *"We notice [language] differences, but what we do about them is important."*

Indeed, we are asking children to explore language as listening subjects, putting the work of interpreting language differences on the listener rather than on the speaker (Flores & Rosa, 2015). In schools, linguistically minoritized children, often Children of Color, are categorized as having deficiencies in their language development despite the fact that their ways with words serve them well at home. As teachers of young children, what might it mean to acknowledge what Flores and Rosa identify as the "white listening subject" and the assessments (Ascenzi-Moreno, 2018) shaping how our children experience schools? How can inviting teachers and students to read voices challenge the mindsets and teaching practices that repeatedly identify our linguistically diverse children as having deficits?

Language Maps and Lists: Documenting Our Linguistic Toolkits

Soon after the class reads voices, I introduce the idea of a language map. Using markers and large chart paper, I craft a map that shows my languaging resources such as English, Spanish, Southern English, academic talk, and family talk. I do my best to feature not only the national languages I speak but also the regional and cultural language practices I engage in. As I document these resources on my language map, I describe my linguistic resources as language tools, emphasizing how everyone uses multiple language tools to communicate, even in situations where it may seem someone might draw on only one language variety (for instance, I speak Spanish in English dominant spaces). I share how I speak English and Spanish and French but have different kinds of Englishes, including Southern Texas English, what some call "Academic English," and Spanglish (speaking across both English and Spanish), which I speak with my family and friends. I also share that my mother has recently learned how to use emojis and GIFs (she's always sending me a random pizza emoji), adding to our language toolkit. After modeling, I invite students to create their own language maps or to list their language resources in their writer's notebooks. The fifth graders then use the end of class to work on their language maps (see Figure 5.3).

A closer look across even just three sample language maps reveals the rich linguistic landscape the students in Whitney's seemingly English-dominant classroom navigate daily. The varieties of Englishes (e.g., home English, school English) and registers (e.g., baby talk, parent talk) alone highlight how capable elementary students are of indexing their linguistic toolkits and provides a visual for students to begin to understand the complexity of language at work in their daily lives. For bi- and multilingual students like Bailey and Jameila, the opportunity to name their heritage

Inviting Multilingual and Multimodal Literature Response 125

FIGURE 5.3. Sample student language maps.

language as a viable resource in their life resists the tacit boundaries that too often silence their Spanish in schools. The visual representation of linguistic resources, like Jayda's, for example, also allows students to map the boundaries between home and school languages. In uncovering these linguistic borders, students are more likely to interrogate and resist them.

Language and Identity Self-Portraits

The next day, to center the deep connection between language and identity, I craft a self-portrait, keeping in mind the ways my languaging practices inform how I see myself with the children. As I draw, students who know me well give suggestions, such as adding "I ♥ TX" to the illustrated shirt, and as a longtime Texan I agree wholeheartedly. I also add a Peruvian flag in the background, like the one in my grandmother's home, as a symbol of my family and my heritage. Everything from the way I dress, how I hold myself, what I do during the day, the shape of my face and eyes, the texture of my hair, the color of my skin—I personally see these things in relationship to my language, my heritage, my family, and my daily practices. Crafting visual representations of ourselves through the lens of our linguistic toolkit brings awareness to the richness of the language repertoires and the diversity of tools we have at our disposal for reading and writing and how they are entangled in our everyday. As I create this self-portrait, I also connect the process to the work of picturebook authors and illustrators, who must similarly make decisions about the characters and communities they are depicting in their narratives. This helps the students understand how real-life language use does not happen in isolation but is part of a living constellation of resources that connects language with race and ethnicity, place, movement, the embodied, the visual, and so much more.

Whitney also creates a self-portrait, highlighting the process of linking language to the portrait to help scaffold the students toward engaging in a similar process (see Figure 5.4). I share a few of her guiding questions and modeling statements that really launched students into deep exploration of their language and identity through self-portraiture.

- What languages am I using in this self-portrait? Or what Englishes am I using to think about my self-portrait?

- Now, on that language map, I want you to circle or maybe put a star next to the Englishes or languages or your ways with words that you're using in your self-portrait. What are you thinking about with your language and your identity when you are drawing your self-portrait?

- What context do you need to be thinking about as you draw yourself? Where are you? What are you doing? What do you see?

- How are my hair and facial features a part of my identity? How do they connect me to a community and my family?

- Why don't you use the iPad, like Jameila does, to turn on the camera's selfie feature so that you can study your face? Examining your facial features as you illustrate might help you see new things.

- From the book flood, which mentor illustrators might you use to help you complete your self-portrait?

Inviting Multilingual and Multimodal Literature Response   127

FIGURE 5.4. Student self-portraits.

Jada
By Jada

My hair is cold like the Michigan icy roads
My curly hair like warm hot fries
My eyes are gleaming tord the shining sun
My yes is like success filling the air
My bye are like the moon rise up in the sky
My hand like the Michigan mitten
My skin color is smooth chocolate caramel melt

Chicago
By: **Riley**

My scarf blows in the wind when I step into the morning sun
My worn out shoes that hold a memory with every mud splatter

My pants hold every doggy hair in cuddle time

My eyes shimmer like the Chicago lake

My smile gives off a wave of happiness

My rosy cheeks like a new spring blossom

My hair bounces as I ride my bike along the bumps of the city

I am Bug to my family

I gaze at each word the crosses me

I stretch the words that feel long

I am **Riley** _____ when I'm in trouble

When I wake up
By: **Gabrielle**

When i wake up i talk rather groggy
Hair like a bush and cats practically talking
I whisper good morning and slip on my coat
Turn off my iPad so it doesn't make smoke
I reach for my glasses
Pick up a cat
Walk out my door
Having a grin
Reaching the living room and...
"Good morning!" i shout

MR. **Henry**
By: **Henry**

My eyes are as green as my jacket that sticks to me like glue
My stitches tied together like shoe laces,
My hair as rugged as old times.
My teaching is loud and clear like a drum.
I'm as focused as a hawk and as quiet as a library.

Together, the work of reading voices, language mapping, and self-portraiture constitutes an intersection of linguistic, aural, visual, and embodied literacies that set the stage for language study through picturebooks in Whitney's classroom. Whitney and her students attended to and used these multimodal and multilingual literacies in conjunction with the different modes of meaning and languages expressed in diverse picturebooks, to broaden their understanding of and thinking about language and identity. What resulted from this focused study of linguistically diverse picturebooks was a deep exploration of the self, family, place, language, and so much more. The details of the students' reading and composition work reflect a deeper understanding of the ties that bind them to their sociocultural and intellectual capital. But it is the synergy of their illustrated self-portraits that truly animates these students' self-inquiries. From their skin shades to the texture of their hair, the shape of their eyes and faces to the details of their setting and their clothes, these culminating compositions reflect a deeper understanding of the relationship between identity and language as mentored by linguistically diverse picturebooks.

Critical Encounters with Picturebooks

As in previous chapters, I detail here three critical encounters from a classroom engaged in a focused literature exploration. And again, I provide an example of our collective's personal reflection toward change, in which we share even more insights into how we navigated critical encounters in the classroom.

As a reminder, I characterize critical encounters with literature as those moments when a text elicits a response that urges deeper discussion into a justice-oriented issue or an interrogation of power, or that potentially becomes a transformative moment that changes someone's previously held beliefs. These are the moments, microbursts of collective meaning making, that are ultimately the heart of critical literature response because these moments produce fissures in book talk that can ultimately move anti-oppressive stances forward.

Critical Encounter 1: Rethinking Our Reading of Language Differences

In this critical encounter, we return to a literature discussion explored earlier in the chapter to follow up on a one-to-one conference that took place between Whitney and Maya in response to their discussion of the poetry slam collection *Hey You! C'mere!* (Swados, 2002). Mock languaging (Hill, 2009), or appropriating another person's language in stereotypical ways, was one concept Whitney and her students were mindful of throughout the language study. As they began to examine more closely their own and the characters' languages and identities, they realized they needed to attend to the way they approached someone else's language and identity so as not to replicate stereotypes or usurp a resource that was not their own.

Maya, a young Latina, wrestled with this idea from an oral miscue in Whitney's reading of the poem "Tough Kids" in *Hey You! C'mere!* In her reading, Whitney read aloud "beat 'cha" as "beat ya." Whitney acknowledged that her identity as a white woman made it a challenge to read aloud something that was outside of her linguistic experience. Afterward, Maya sought out Whitney to talk more about this.

> **Featured Picturebook**
>
> *Hey You! C'mere! A Poetry Slam* (2002) is written by Elizabeth Swados and vividly illustrated by Joe Cepeda. From the perspective of seven different children walking and playing in their neighborhood streets, Swados offers a collection of summer verses reflecting the unique voices and experiences of these children on one hot summer afternoon.

Maya was worried that someone with the same language and identity as the young boy of color in the poem might perceive Whitney's miscue as mock languaging. But Maya also recognized that it is understandable that someone who doesn't share the same language and identity as the character, such as Whitney, might "mess up" when reading the poem aloud.

Whitney asked Maya, "What does that mean if I make a mistake when I'm reading that voice?" Maya shared how it could be considered offensive or mocking to others if Whitney reads a voice incorrectly. They continued talking intently (see Figure 5.5).

Whitney: I also didn't want to try too hard. Why do you think I didn't want to try too hard?

Maya: Because that's not the language you speak in.

Whitney: Okay. And if I tried too hard, what would maybe . . .

Maya: You might like mess up on your, like your vocabulary if you don't pronounce it right, or like you might not say it the way that it's supposed to be said.

Whitney: Okay. And if I made that mistake, what does that mean if I make a mistake when I'm reading like that?

Maya: [thinking] [quietly] It means that you're not used to those words and you don't usually mash your words together.

Whitney: Mmm hmm. Do you think if somebody *did* speak like that and they heard me *trying* so hard . . .

Maya: It might be offensive to them. You'd like try really hard and it's like, it's a problem. [Whitney nods head] And they don't think it's a problem 'cause it's just a *word* and you're like stuck on their words. And you can't get, like, the right sound out.

Whitney: And then if I'm, you know, trying to be like somebody else and I'm not like them, then maybe it might seem like I'm also ...

Maya: [nodding head] Trying to mock them.

Whitney: ... mocking [nods head]. Yeah.

Maya: Mmm hmm.

Whitney: So it's hard, isn't it?

Maya: Mmm hmm.

Whitney: And you wanna read books that aren't like you, so that you can learn about new people and appreciate new languages.

Maya: Yeah.

Whitney: But then if you try too *hard* to do that and use a voice that's not your own ...

Maya: Mmm hmm [nods head].

Whitney: ... then it might be taken as like making fun and mocking.

Maya: Yeah. [nods head] It will.

Whitney: How do we deal with that? What do we do?

Maya: Well, just kind of do what you do, like don't get too like caught up in the word. Just kind of say it how you would say it and always be respectful.

Whitney: Okay. [nods head] That's good advice. I'm gonna keep trying to do that then.

FIGURE 5.5. Whitney and Maya confer to discuss mock languaging.

Maya's point is clear—reading aloud someone else's language from a picturebook is complicated. This is a tension when teachers and students closely examine language and identity in picturebooks. They will encounter books that reflect their own ways with words *and* books that are not written in their voices. However, when sharing these texts with young children, if we do not take the time to be thoughtful in our oral or written representations of someone's language and identity, we may find ourselves exoticizing languages and cultures that are not our own. From young children (Zapata, 2020), we have learned that exposure to different languages and language varieties feeds curiosity that can at times lead to mock languaging by white speakers (Hill, 2009) that reproduces racist caricatures. This does not mean that white teachers and young children should not read and appreciate picturebooks that reflect a wide array of languages and language varieties, but we must, as Maya teaches us, ask questions of ourselves and others, and be mindful to establish cultures of appreciation for the authors and their language.

Critical Encounter 2: Helping Students Deconstruct Assumptions

In response to an invitation from Whitney, Jada, who identifies as a Black girl, chose a picturebook to explore an identity unlike her own.[6] Jada commented that the Muslim female character "looks more white," using a questioning tone. Whitney followed up by rephrasing, "So you think the author or the illustrator didn't get her skin tone right?," to which Jada responded yes. Whitney recognized that Jada's perspective on the narrator was an opportunity for Jada to shift her understanding about a cultural identity unlike her own. Whitney took this opportunity to open a space for Jada to reflect on her assumption by modeling reflective questions.

Whitney: Let's see. Do you think the author or the illustrator might have that same language?

Jada: Yeah.

Whitney: Why?

Jada: It looks like they both have similar names as the people in the book.

Whitney: Okay. So, *maybe* the voices and the people that they're representing in here are actually people that they might know or are from their same culture or religion or family?

Jada: Mmm hmm. Yeah.

Whitney: So, looking back at we know, you think they look kind of pale, and like a little too light, but could people that speak this way and wear hijab like that be lighter? Yeah. It might be different than what we think. So this book really stretched what you maybe think about people that would wear henna or wear hijab or celebrate Eid, right? Because when you read this, you thought, "Oh! People that have henna, their skin wouldn't be this light." But throughout the book, maybe this kind of changes what you think a little bit.

Jada: [quietly] Mmm hmm. [nods head]

Through reflective questions, Jada quietly contemplated a new understanding—that perhaps there are people of the Islamic faith with lighter skin shades who identify with the language and identity being depicted in the picturebook.

At the conclusion of their conference, Whitney asked Jada to write down some of the thoughts they had discussed about *Golden Domes* in her writer's notebook. Writing as a tool for thinking afforded Jada a private space to process this learning. As she wrote, Jada grappled with her own thinking, as well as the perspectives that Whitney shared during their conference:

> It looks like they're light [the people in the book]. But in my perspective is that she [the girl in the book] is too light. But she might be real and light.

Through the reading of picture and word, talk, reflection, and writing, Jada was able to rethink her misconception and to articulate how her thinking evolved to include a new understanding about a cultural identity that was different from her own.

Featured Picturebook

In *Golden Domes and Silver Lanterns: A Muslim Book of Colors* (2012), written by Hena Khan and illustrated by Mehrdokht Amini, a young Muslim girl guides readers through the world of Islam as she visits special places in her neighborhood. Along the way, readers are introduced to colors that are a part of her Islamic culture, such as a blue hijab and a white kufi.

Critical Encounter 3: Making Claims into Your Language and Identity

Here I feature Whitney and Ivy's writing conference about the poem Ivy wrote after being mentored by linguistically diverse literature. The transformative act of mentoring a writer to craft with their own ways with words may seem everyday to some, but it is a radical act of love—made possible by Whitney's selection of diverse picturebooks that support her students' identities. It's not every day that linguistically minoritized children see their language(s) in print in books in the classroom and can hold up their language(s), race, ethnicity, phenotype, religion, gender, and so much more as resources for their literacy lives in the classroom. Putting your language to work as writing craft is a lifelong lesson that forever cements your language and identity as both beautiful and powerful.

On this day, Whitney confers with students about their writing as mentored by the linguistically diverse picturebook collection they have explored. She documents their language on a public chart beneath some of her own, much like a record of the rich diversity of languages in the classroom. Doing so sets the stage for writers to move beyond Standardized English in their writing. Just before this moment, Whitney had modeled her own process for developing a metaphor about her life and language and recorded those on the chart (see Figure 5.6).

When students break to write independently, Ivy approaches Whitney and asks to share her writing. They sit together at Ivy's desk as she reads aloud a draft of her poem from her writer's notebook.

FIGURE 5.6. Whitney explores and shares her language practices through poetry.

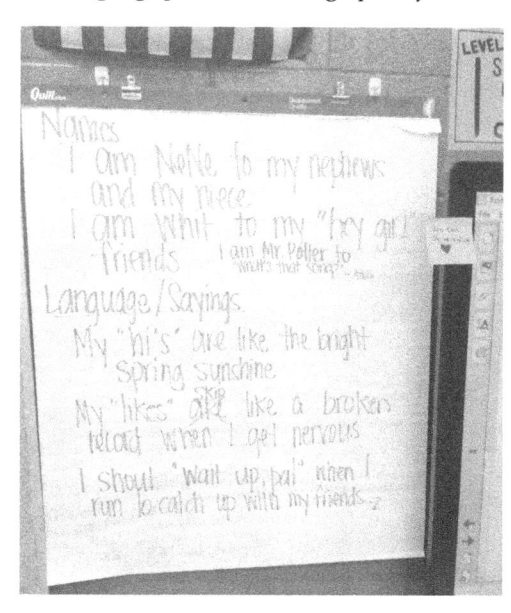

Ivy: "My hair is like my dad's side of the family. / My act is like my dad and his sister. / My outfits bust out in the sun. / When I go outside my dance moves move with the wind and beat. / When I talk to my cousin my wholesome language change."

Whitney: Mmm. I love that! Tell me exactly how they change.

Ivy: Well, I talk really louder, and I talk like, "What do you want?"

Whitney: Okay. I love it. When I talk to my cousins, I talk louder too.

Ivy: Yeah.

Whitney: Okay. Let's get that description in there. Take this one, okay? And we want to know *exactly* how your voice and language changes. Okay.

Ivy: All right. And when they get on my nerves, I be like . . .

Whitney: Use an example.

Ivy: . . . or my sisters like [louder voice; more emphatic] "Stop! Get out of my room! Leave me alone!"

Whitney: Love it! That's the next line! I love that because you said, "I be like" and that's your way with words, so let's include that. Okay? Don't worry about "Oh, it's at school it needs to sound like this." Don't worry about it sounding like your academic talk here, because the purpose here is to show your identity.

Access to linguistically diverse literature that modeled craft and prose beyond that of Standardized English cultivated a writing space where Whitney could value and encourage Ivy to put her ways with words to work. She nudges Ivy to consider writing what she would really say and not to switch to "academic talk" just because she's at school. Whitney is communicating that Ivy's Englishes are not reserved for a separate audience, and that all of her Englishes are welcome in her classroom language arts writing.

Upon reflection toward change, our collective wondered how this might also be a conversation that Whitney and Ivy could share (with Ivy's permission) with the class, inviting students to consider what Ivy's English achieves for her poem. What does crafting a poem with "I be like . . ." achieve that "I said . . ." does not? We note that Ivy's use of her voice communicated a closeness and intimacy with her family, authenticity of the moment, and playfulness. This is the affordance of language study rather than an exclusive focus on audience; attention to how language works and what it achieves attunes readers to craft and purpose. Rather than read and replicate a Standardized English form again and again, students are engaged in the more complex work of studying how languages work and what language can do for their writing.

What Critical Encounters Can Teach Us

The critical encounters I've shared showcase the complexity of linguistic and modal diversity and the capacity children have to build awareness around these dynamic literacies. A multilingual and multimodal approach to picturebook instruction helps children uncover the multiple languages, literacies, and lives at work in their classroom and in the shared literature. Whitney supports a Critical Literature Response Framework through multilingual and multimodal literature invitations, which in turn allow students to explore the relationships between language, identity, and power and to resist the Standardized English Print forms as the only viable communicative norm. I invite you to reflect on a few relevant tips for enacting a Critical Literature Response Framework with upper-elementary children. Ask yourself: How did the classroom commitments and conditions Whitney values enhance students' learning? How might the classroom practices, specifically multilingual and multimodal literacies, enhance *your* students' learning in a Critical Literature Response Framework? And—most important—how might you make this work your own?

Tips to Support Critical Encounters in Literature with Young Children

As you reflect on the following tips, consider how these critical encounters with picturebooks were (or could have been) enhanced by these suggested practices and perspectives.

- Build on children's authentic questions regarding linguistic difference, bias, racism, and stereotypes.
- Aim for the "long conversation" rather than one mini-lesson.
- Offer literary arrows that nudge reflection about language and identity.

- What do you know about communities or people who share the language(s) featured in this book? (This establishes a safe space to expose assumptions and misconceptions.)
  - How does the illustrator and/or author show us this character's identity?
- Model an appreciation for encountering new languages and language varieties and share authentic moments when you are negotiating your own language and identify in your writing.
- Cultivate spaces where students reveal initial assumptions as they respond to the languages and identities featured in the picturebooks, particularly those experiences and insights that are different from your own. Guide them toward interrogating those assumptions.
- Avoid shaming children's misconceptions by creating space for children to choose when/how/where to share any deficit thinking about language differences. Cultivate a space where children can interrogate rather than replicate their biases.
- Engage in reflection toward change. How can the language we use and the consciousness we bring to the work of critical literature response inform positive changes in the questions we ask and the themes we determine to be important?

Top Ten Favorite Picturebooks Shared for Language Study

1. Bennett, K. (2012). *One day I went rambling* (T. Murphy, Illus.). Bright Sky Press.
2. Bertrand, D. G. (2008). *Sip, slurp, soup, soup / Caldo, caldo, caldo* (A. P. Delange, Illus.). Piñata Books.
3. Brown, M. (2011). *Pablo Neruda: Poet of the people* (J. Paschkis, Illus.). Henry Holt.
4. Faruqi R. (2021). *Amira's picture day* (F. Azim, Illus.). Holiday House.
5. Feelings, M. (1992). *Moja means one: Swahili counting book* (T. Feelings, Illus.). Puffin Books.
6. Gilmore, D. K. L. (2014). *Cora cooks pancit* (K. Valiant, Illus.). Lee & Low Books.
7. Gonzalez, M. (2017). *Yo soy Muslim: A father's letter to his daughter* (M. Amini, Illus.). Salaam Reads/Simon & Schuster Books for Young Readers.
8. Isadora, R. (2007). *Yo, Jo!* Harcourt.

9. Khan, H. (2021). *Crescent moons and pointed minarets: A Muslim book of shapes* (M. Amini, Illus.). Chronicle Books.
10. Lindstrom, C. (2020). *We are water protectors* (M. Goade, Illus.). Roaring Brook Press.

Children's Literature Cited

Isadora, R. (2007). *Yo, Jo!* Harcourt.
Khan, H. (2012). *Golden domes and silver lanterns: A Muslim book of colors* (M. Amini, Illus.). Chronicle Books.
Swados, E. (2002) *Hey you! C'mere. A poetry slam* (J. Cepeda, Illus.). Arthur A. Levine Books/Scholastic.

Launching a Critical Literature Response Framework in Your Classroom

Chapter Six

One afternoon, as the students are gathered on the carpet in Kara's classroom, Zack asks aloud, "What does *diverse* mean?"

[Unidentified student]: It's a synonym for *different*.

Kara: I think a lot about what *diverse* means for the books for our classroom and how the books can look like *all* of us and center stories that we don't see enough in the library.

Zack: None of the state-awarded books this year would be considered diverse.

Another student: Our school is diverse because we have a lot of people from different countries.

Mohammed: Our school is focused on the arts so that also makes us diverse.

Genna: Skin color can show diversity too.

To extend the discussion, Kara builds on what the students discuss to name ethnic, racial, and linguistic identities as part of their discussion of the term *diverse*.

What the children's questions and responses remind us is that children are ready to explore diverse representation in picturebooks and they won't always wait for us. With a teacher's guidance, students can explore what *diversity* means and describe it in the ways they understand—by connecting to texts and their lived experiences. Participating in these conversations as educators, librarians, mentors, and parents can provide support and create a space for children's exploration of broader racial and cultural diversity, as Kara does here in ways that are authentic, accessible, and honest and that don't shame any particular person or group.

In this era of #BlackLivesMatter, #FamiliesBelongTogether, #Ican'tbreathe, #LoveIsLove, and countless other calls for resistance to xenophobia, injustice, and racism in our society, sharing picturebooks with diverse representation *and* engaging young children in thoughtful discussion of the critical issues at hand remain a moral and ethical imperative. Wanting better for our children means *doing* better for our children in the classroom. This effort insists on students' access to the voices, histories, and stories of culturally, racially, ethnically, and linguistically diverse communities and so many others notably absent on our bookshelves. For students who claim membership in the communities represented, the picturebooks are affirming. That fact alone makes sharing these texts in the classroom absolutely necessary. For students who do not claim membership in the communities represented, the picturebooks are often their first introduction to a world that is different from their own, which presents a powerful opportunity to build appreciation, empathy, and community with and for new voices. Together, these rationales urge us to share high-quality picturebooks with diverse representation to prepare our youngest readers to participate in our global, networked, multicultural, multilingual, multiethnic, multiracial, multimodal (and . . . and . . . and . . .) world (Leander & Boldt, 2013).

To help all children equip themselves with the tools needed to resist the status quo representation in children's picturebooks, diverse picturebooks must be paired with instruction that enthusiastically receives young children's evolving responses to the worlds they encounter in pictures and words. A Critical Literature Response Framework is designed to cultivate the very classroom conditions, teacher commitments, and classroom practices needed to do just that. The framework supports students' aesthetic responses to diverse portrayals of joyful living, loving, and being in the world. Reading critically is as much about appreciating and connecting to beautiful counternarratives as it is to interrogating structures of power in literature. As Gholdy Muhammed (2020, 2023) highlights through her work, cultivating genius *and* joy are integral aspects of any equity approach in learning and teaching efforts. Nurturing the joyful stories alongside our histories can only nuance and disrupt the negative tropes of diverse communities that are so pervasive within so many children's literature collections.

Because we early childhood and elementary school educators are continuously inundated with mandates to teach reading out of context, to teach letters and sounds in isolation, to reduce writing and social studies learning in the curriculum, and to address only Standardized English Print texts, these chapters are designed to illustrate how a Critical Literature Response Framework is both meaningful *and* intellectually demanding; it does not have to unfold in opposition to teaching children to learn to read. Supporting literature instruction guided by aesthetic and academic learning drives these efforts and can challenge the binary thinking that identifies teaching children to read as somehow separate from teaching children to respond to literature. We must pause once again to acknowledge the current and fluid sociopolitical landscape that continues to shape and narrow both what elementary teachers can teach and how they teach that content. As I shared in Chapter 2, Lottie, Kara, and Whitney (like you) live within the tensions between *both* adopted curricula, materials, and mandated schedules that privilege teaching Standardized English phonics out of context *and* their commitment to better representation in the materials they share with students. Should questions arise as they enact a Critical Literature Response Framework in their classrooms, these teachers can point to how learning vocabulary in meaningful collections can enhance children's discussions of border-crossing experiences. They can discuss how learning how to infer from visuals can enhance children's discussions of power in illustration. They can explain how learning to read from multilingual and multimodal texts like dual language picturebooks can enhance children's understanding of voice in writing. The courage to teach and speak back to the limits of a standardizing curriculum that fails to advocate for *all* voices in our classrooms, particularly those too often absent in our literature collections, is necessary in our current climate. Changing the stories in our classrooms demands that we change our instruction in ways that enhance academic learning, engage critical reading of texts, and cultivate a love of reading picture and word. Our children deserve to have their stories and histories as integral visual and print narratives in the classroom.

And *we* deserve the time, space, and resources to grow our craft, to uncover and address our hidden biases, and to refine our teaching beliefs to enliven a Critical Literature Response Framework thoughtfully and effectively for our students. It is essential to do so in the company of colleagues we trust, colleagues who will support and push us out of our comfort zone and invest in our codevelopment over time. We can certainly close our doors and do our work away from the gaze of others, but if we want to truly effect change, going public with a Critical Literature Response Framework is necessary. We can also challenge ourselves to find colleagues who bring voices and experiences to learn from, including those of People of Color. Feeling the support of a team of fellow educators and invested administrators through collaboration and outreach can give your work momentum and provide a network of affirmation when questions and challenges arise.

After providing a final review of the classroom conditions, teachers commitments, and classroom practices that compose a Critical Literature Response Framework, I suggest one additional component: collaboration and outreach. I conclude the chapter with a brief collection of questions that have emerged as I partnered with teachers to do this work, which may offer some guidance on how to respond should you encounter these same questions.

The book thus far has addressed the following components of a Critical Literature Response Framework:

🌱 *Conditions* for Enacting a Critical Literature Response Framework
- Embody teachers' critical stance.
- Embrace literature-based instruction.
- Enter critical encounters with text.

🤝 *Commitments* for Enacting a Critical Literature Response Framework
- Evoke aesthetic response.
- Invite critical interrogation.
- Impel public action/praxis.

📚 *Classroom Practices* for Enacting a Critical Literature Response Framework
- Share book floods.
- Prepare wide and varied collections.
- Scaffold picture reading.
- Explore multimodal and multilingual literature response.

I have presented these commitments, conditions, and classroom practices as a dynamic constellation that *as a whole* produces an ideal landscape to live out a Critical Literature Response Framework. I hope you have experienced the Critical Literature Response Framework and the classroom vignettes in this way, rather than as a prescribed set of teaching beliefs and practices, and that you walk away with new energy for your diverse literature instruction. Within each classroom chapter, we observed how Lottie, Kara, and Whitney, respectively, enacted their classroom practices with diverse picturebooks through a unique approach. For example, Lottie's valuing of young children as knowledgeable, Kara's efforts to elicit more in-depth talk from readers, and Whitney's support of a more expansive view of language each reflected their commitments to the work and enhanced the classroom conditions for a Critical Literature Response Framework. Collectively, their work showcases how a Critical Literature Response Framework can be refined for different contexts, students, and teachers. We are all unique, so it was important to showcase how a Critical Literature Response Framework is not a curriculum to implement but rather a set of classroom practices that thrives under certain conditions and teacher commitments and is then individualized by a teacher's unique classroom approaches. With these understandings in mind, I conclude by drawing attention to a fourth and final component of a Critical Literature Response Framework: collaboration and outreach.

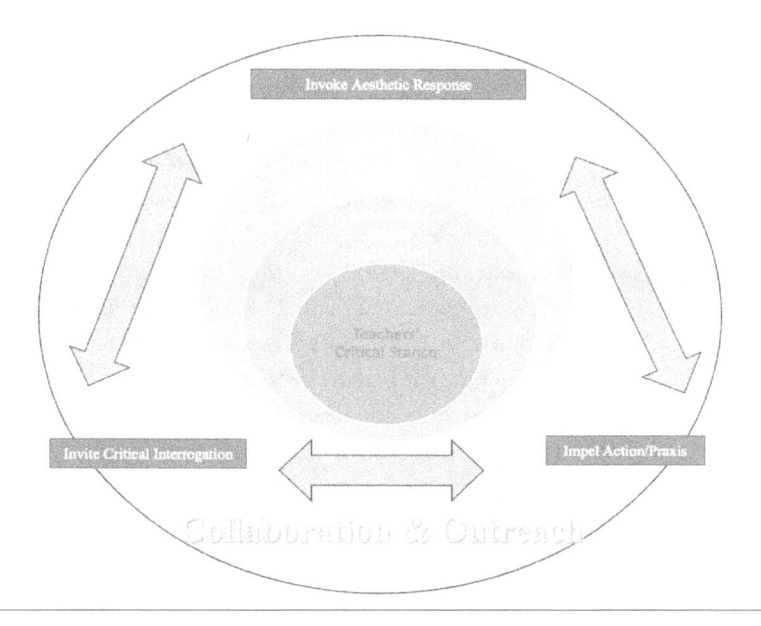

Launching a Critical Literature Response Framework in Your Classroom   141

FIGURE 6.1. I represent this final component of collaboration and outreach as the larger circle within which the classroom conditions and teacher commitments reside, thus intentionally reminding us that we don't have to do this work alone.

[Figure: A diagram showing a large oval labeled "Collaboration & Outreach" containing a smaller circle labeled "Teacher's Critical Stance" in the center. Three labeled boxes with double-headed arrows surround the center: "Invoke Aesthetic Response" (top), "Invite Critical Interrogation" (bottom left), and "Impel Action/Praxis" (bottom right).]

Collaboration and Outreach: Building Your Critical Literature Response Collaborative

In Figure 6.1, I represent this final component of collaboration and outreach as the larger circle within which the classroom conditions and teacher commitments reside, thus intentionally reminding us that we don't have to do this work alone.

Although this book focuses primarily on classroom practice, I would be remiss to not also take a moment to speak to the importance of educator collaboration and outreach. I point you to this short list that you can layer into your lively constellation of commitments and conditions that together produce an ideal landscape in which to live out your classroom practices:

👥 Collaboration and Outreach for Enacting a Critical Literature Response Framework

- Identify your immediate collaborators.

- Seek new voices and new perspectives through established groups and other outreach teacher-led initiatives. Particularly seek out those with diverse racial, linguistic, ethnic, economic, and marginalized voices and experiences.
- Read, make, talk, and listen to your own and others' stories.

As a classroom teacher, I had the pleasure of having an outstanding teaching partner in elementary teacher Monica Gonzalez in Austin, Texas. Later, as a doctoral student, I learned from the classrooms of bilingual teacher Nancy Valdez-Gainer and ESL teacher Corinna Bliss Haworth and their beautiful and brilliant students. These women were not only my colleagues but also my friends, and it was easy to make space for one another as we valued similar classroom teaching approaches and commitments. My professional network soon extended beyond my immediate peers as I became part of the Heart of Texas Writing Project (HTWP), a local chapter of the National Writing Project, with Randy Bomer and Deb Kelt. I was introduced to fellow teachers and experienced consultants who brought perspectives and teaching approaches that were different from my own. My teaching and research were deeply enhanced by my interactions with HTWP, and I am forever thankful for the deep learning from others that enriched my practice and my students' reading and writing lives. I similarly found that through my membership in the National Council of Teachers of English I was able to connect with other Black, Latinx, and Indigenous enthusiasts of picturebooks, which was essential to my professional identity as well as my continued learning. Today, as a researcher and faculty member, I am surrounded by colleagues and students (whom I see as colleagues as well) who teach me and push me to not remain complacent in my own learning and journey as a critical social educator. Media specialist Misha Fugit, AVID 12 teacher Daryl Moss, and Professor Selena Van Horn were tremendous partners when I first arrived in the Midwest. I am currently invigorated by the picturebook collective of teachers, first-generation preservice Teachers of Color, and doctoral students who together gather with me much like a think tank experience. I briefly hold up these friends and professional collaborators and organizations to emphasize the importance of identifying both an immediate group of peers to lean on *and* a group that introduces you to new ideas and voices different from your own. What can crystallize among a diverse group of thinkers is far more substantive than replicating a status quo context of professional learning.

Finding your people and building your teacher squad often unfolds naturally among educators sharing a workspace or serving on the same grade-level team. We all need those partners in crime who are going to both encourage us and keep us honest about our teaching. Our teaching also benefits from professional and civic engagement with people and communities outside of our everyday encounters. In sum, in addition to identifying your immediate collaborators, pursue outreach opportunities to grow and be challenged, and specifically seek out diverse voices and experiences to become an ally and a learner. Currently, a number of professional organizations offer insightful, research-based language arts learning for teachers, organizations that are also guided by ethical, justice- and equity-oriented, antiracist, and anti-oppressive teaching for children and youth (see the list of relevant organizations at the end of Chapter 2). Chances are high that in your immediate area you will also find a number of local outreach initiatives, entities, and resources that would pair perfectly with your efforts to enact a Critical Literature Response Framework with others. Those might include local community libraries, bookshops, and family and community literacy groups, as well as other justice-oriented initiatives.

The luxury of today's social media also provides an invaluable link to children's literature-focused webinars, slow chats on social networks, and relevant hashtags and resources, particularly in the wake of COVID-19, when face-to-face gatherings are often uncertain. I think the incredible team at #DisruptTexts is doing a fantastic job of bringing folks together in conversation from all over the country through both face-to-face and virtual invitations. I highly encourage you to follow and participate in their professional learning opportunities to grow both personally and professionally as a children's literature educator. I also find that the work on everyday advocacy by Cathy Fleischer and Antero Garcia (2020) provides incredible guidance on how to begin to reclaim our individual and collective identities as teacher professionals oriented toward making for a better world. They invite us to see how the day-to-day actions we engage in as teachers can be valuable evidence in our efforts to change the narrow public narratives surrounding schools, teachers, and learning. As educators trying to advocate for a Critical Literature Response Framework in the classroom, identifying our everyday advocacy is essential.

As a last word on the issue of collaboration and outreach, I want to invite you to remember that we are each on a critical social educator journey, a sojourn toward powerful classroom practices with diverse children's picturebooks. Some of us are just beginning and others of us have been doing this for a while. Either way, we are all entering this work with things to learn and reaching for the same outcome. Taking time to read, make, talk, and listen with one another's journeys in mind will be essential to forming the relationships of mutual respect and trust needed to do this work together. I have been humbled again and again and repeatedly improved

Inviting Teacher Reflection

- Who are your current professional collaborators?

- In what ways do you explore professional learning together? How often?

- Do you all ever read, review, or try out materials beyond those resources available in your curriculum bookroom?

- How often do you seek materials that challenge, push, or grow your thinking about equity and diversity in schools? In children's literature?

- What professional education networks do you pursue outside of your immediate community?

- What diverse voices and stories do you seek out as part of your professional learning? Whose stories are present? Whose are missing?

- Where will you go next to grow your network of collaborators and outreach?

my partnerships when I take time to receive my partners where they are. I have experienced how sharing my experiences has nudged someone forward in their journey. This is truly work from the heart and soul, so we need to make sure we are mindful of how to care for and welcome one another where we are as we collaborate to develop better representation in our text collections and instruction.

Questions Revealed

As you continue on your journey as a critical social educator and develop your literature instruction toward a Critical Literature Response Framework, questions may reveal themselves as they relate to a wide array of issues. Below, I explore some of the relevant issues that emerged in my partnerships with teachers like you and share some of the ways we approached the work.

1. Many of the white children in my class feel left out when I read a book that highlights the brilliance of racially, linguistically, and ethnically diverse communities.

When I was told this recently, I asked for time to reflect on the comment. I concluded after being in conversation with others that if the curriculum and materials consistently center white, middle-class, Standardized English experiences, what does it mean for Children of Color or impoverished families or children from different Tribal Nations to finally have their experiences reflected in the pages of a book their teacher is reading aloud to the class? If we truly value diverse representation in children's picturebooks, then we understand that all children have the capacity to learn to listen and to appreciate worlds and experiences that are different from their own, and to understand that many children spend their entire schooling experience feeling left out. We can remedy feelings of exclusion for all children by taking a more inclusive approach through a Critical Literature Response Framework.

2. How do I assess students' learning when enacting a Critical Literature Response Framework in my classroom?

As with so many opportunities when teaching and assessment unfold in the language arts classroom, we've found that approaching young children's literature discussions as an opportunity to engage in formative assessment can be highly effective. Informed by Maria Nichols's guidance in *Comprehension through Conversation* (2006) as well as by the critical literary arrows that emerge as part of our literature explorations, we have found that we are able to document students' growing understandings of the themes explored through their talk. For example, how are children building text-to-text connections across the themes explored over time? How are children using visual thinking strategies to interrogate representations of power in illustration (think beginning- and end-of-unit data collection)? A closer look at the charts and reader-response documents students produce provides such evidence. In addition to children's talk, you can look at any compositions they've crafted during the literature exploration, including notebooks, literature response invitations, and other multimodal text invitations. Certainly, culminating projects are telling summative assessment data to be interpreted and directly inform your instruction.

Guiding questions to help you interpret the data produced in the classroom can be informed by the objectives and state standards you are addressing. What evidence of inferring from image or print did you observe among the students in Lottie's classroom? What evidence of vocabulary development did you observe among Kara's students? What evidence of grammar learning did the children in Whitney's classroom display? You can begin to put such questions to work by pairing reading skills focused objectives with additional questions such as, "What talk or writing or drawing or play demonstrates students' initial understandings of power? Equity? Border crossing? Civil rights?" These are broad topics that can become more detailed as informed by the focused literature discussion you design and implement in your classroom.

3. I don't have time to do this work because my schedule is mandated by my administration.

There are so many tensions surrounding time and scheduling as an early childhood and elementary teacher in today's classrooms. This was and continues to be an ongoing discussion for so many of us, particularly in the wake of increased scripted curricula that have dictated literacy schedules and Response to Intervention time. How do you make time for this work when your schedule is dictated for you? The classroom teachers I have observed best navigate this constraint in small ways, looking for critical openings to substitute diverse titles in the curriculum while still meeting the curriculum objectives. After doing this successfully and with growing confidence after building partnerships with one another, the teachers have moved forward with their efforts to speak with their district administration about making more decisions in their language arts instruction. In sum, we have found that working within or around the limitations as a launching point, a first small step, can still lead to significant change. For example, I have observed how teachers have substituted texts listed in their district curriculum with picturebooks that better reflect the children and families in their classrooms. They still meet the course objectives, follow the curriculum, *and* nurture a Critical Literature Response Framework. These teachers have essentially revised the district curriculum and are now sharing their revised materials with the district leadership to promote more culturally responsive teaching within the district. Starting small with your collaborators goes a long way!

4. I don't know whether I will always know what to say or do when students say something uncomfortable.

In moments when we feel on the spot and unsure how to respond, pausing to take a moment to consider ways to respond helps. I've found that young children are okay when we say:

- You know, I need to think more about that.
- Let's talk more about this when I've had some time to think.
- I don't know enough yet to feel good about answering that, but I will go read to learn more.
- I don't know, but I will ask someone who I think can help me learn.

The significance of these interactions is not so much in how we respond in the moment, but in the follow-through to continue the discussion. It's easy to let the conversation drop, and there may even be moments when you have to choose which line of topics to pursue. Only you know your students and your readiness level and what would be productive. However, challenge yourself to take on and explore topics rather than avoid them altogether. If young children are bringing us the issues and questions, they should not be denied the space to dig deeper because of our own fear or uncertainty.

In the classroom chapters, the critical encounters reflect moments I've held still on paper for you to analyze and consider. In reality, these moments unfolded quickly, leaving the teachers just moments to decide how to proceed. Sometimes we get it right and sometimes we reflect and determine we might approach the topic differently the next time. We've learned that the best way to respond is honestly and thoughtfully, informed by what we know and believe through a Critical Literature Response Framework.

5. How do I build my library on a shoestring budget?

When I am asked this question, I always feel as though I must acknowledge the tension in the question—why should teachers have to seek funding to grow their classroom libraries and other materials? I am familiar with the additional labor we teachers face as we dig into our own pockets to provide additional resources for our classrooms. It's a comment on the value our nation places on education that so many of us find ourselves building our collections of diverse picturebooks on our own dime. If you are still at the beginning of this work, only now building your team of partners, and find yourself with no budget for a book flood, start small. Find a handful of favorite titles each year and launch your discussions through whole-class read-alouds. Over time, I've also come to believe that the daily work of building better picturebook collections for our children is everyday advocacy (Fleischer & Garcia, 2020), specifically, the way we establish allies for this work through *collaboration*. As a team of partnering colleagues, approach libraries and librarians (both public and in school) to invest in picturebooks with better representation. Contact your school and district administrators to emphasize the importance and possibilities of these picturebooks for children's self-efficacy as readers and writers, as well as for their broader language and literacy learning. How can we invite bigger systems of education and literacy to support the building of these collections for children to read and discuss? For example, teacher groups I have partnered with have identified outside collaborators such as bookshops, book festivals, and local community businesses that share the same goal of growing students' reading lives through picturebooks. I share this collaborative approach to emphasize that the onus is not on you alone to do the work, relying on "go fund me" and "wish list" efforts that suck up your time and energy. Together, we can do more and better to impact change that puts great books in children's hands.

Let's Do This!

How we share these books with young readers is at the heart of a transformative reading experience. As the stories are changing in our classroom literature collections, so we must change the way we teach with them. Carefully selecting and embracing these books with tremendous humility as a learner and confronting our own discomfort with an anti-oppressive approach remains essential. Always be aware that we can benevolently do more harm than good, possibly even replicate the same injustices we are aiming to deconstruct, if we are not fully present when we sit side by side with children as they read.

Thank you for allowing me to share a Critical Literature Response Framework with you and for letting this work live alongside you and your students as you all read, critically interrogate, collaborate, discuss, question, write, think, learn, and embody meaning in response to picturebooks with diverse representation. Children *can* engage in critical discussions of picturebooks and *can* handle anti-oppressive education and *can* embrace the joy and beauty of their own and others' worlds. As a matter of fact, they run circles around us daily when they have the freedom to do so. We still have so much to learn from our students and their families and our fellow teachers who don't always find themselves reflected in the stories on our bookshelves. It's time to do right by our students and by ourselves as caring teachers. Like you, I'm ready for the work.

Annotated Bibliography

Thank you to Mary Adu-Gyamfi and Adrianna Ybarra González, who helped me to annotate the books featured below. I have gathered them in smaller collections so that you and your colleagues can read them with focus and care. Each subheading will resonate with you depending on where you are on your critical social educator journey and where you are in your knowledge of picturebooks and picturebook pedagogy.

Launching Your Critical Literacy Journey

Ahmed, Sara K.
Being the Change: Lessons and Strategies to Teach Social Comprehension
Heinemann, 2018

> Ahmed's book focuses on the skills and habits of social comprehension that can help students navigate honest and sometimes uncomfortable conversations. Teachers can integrate the lessons and activities provided within each chapter to help students develop clearer understandings of relevant topics such as race, sexuality, gender, religion, and politics while also addressing concepts such as bias, identity, and discrimination.

Dunbar-Ortiz, Roxanne, adapted by Jean Mendoza and Debbie Reese
An Indigenous Peoples' History of the United States for Young People
Beacon Press, 2019

> Drawing from the work of Dunbar-Ortiz, this adapted text for young people offers a different perspective on colonization and the settlement of Indigenous lands through the insights, stories and experiences of Indigenous peoples. The book includes discussion topics, original maps, and archival images to encourage young readers to think critically about the historical and the current roles of settler colonialism, American Indian genocide, and their impacts on shaping what came to be the United States.

España, Carla, and Luz Yadira Herrera
En Comunidad: Lessons for Centering the Voices and Experiences of Bilingual Latinx Students
Heineman, 2020

> España and Herrera draw from their schooling and teaching experiences to reveal the powerful ways classrooms can become liberating by centering the stories, voices, languages, and experiences of bilingual Latinx students. Offering culturally and linguistically classroom-ready lessons, the authors argue that through amplifying the varied stories and identities of Latinx children, teachers and children can think about their ideas of language and learn to advocate for their languages and lives.

Espinosa, Cecilia M., and Laura Ascenzi-Moreno
Rooted in Strength: Using Translanguaging to Grow Multilingual Readers and Writers
Scholastic, 2021

> The authors emphasize the importance of upholding and embracing emergent bilingual students' linguistic and cultural resources and consider these resources as strengths from which the rest of the class can learn. The authors note translanguaging as a practice that taps into emergent bilingual students' linguistic and sociocultural knowledge and capital. Throughout the book, Espinosa and Ascenzi-Moreno offer additional strategies and literacy practices specifically designed to successfully develop emergent bilingual students' writing and reading skills.

Fleischer, Cathy, and Antero Garcia
Everyday Advocacy: Teachers Who Change the Literacy Narrative
Norton & Company, 2020

> Literacy educators Fleischer and Garcia argue that "everyday advocacy" offers ways to reframe the public narrative about schools, teaching, teachers, and learning. They invite teacher leaders and educators to conceptualize an advocacy approach by seeking to define what we mean by everyday advocacy, unveiling how advocacy is shaping secondary ELA instruction,

and examining how this approach can be used in English teacher education. When advocacy becomes part of everyday life, teachers and educators are empowered to see teachers and teaching differently.

Kinloch, Valerie, Emily A. Nemeth, Tamara T. Butler, and Grace D. Player
Where Is the Justice? Engaged Pedagogies in Schools and Communities
Teachers College Press and National Council of Teachers of English, 2021

> This book offers practical and theoretical resources for educators interested in engaged pedagogies that situate justice at the center of the classroom. Focusing on collaborative work that extends beyond the classroom, the authors share their stories working with and alongside students, teachers, teacher educators, families, and community leaders to demonstrate classroom possibilities focused on equity, justice, and love.

Muhammad, Gholdy
Cultivating Genius: An Equity Framework for Culturally and Historically Responsive Literacy
Scholastic, 2020

> Muhammad's book presents an equity framework called Historically Responsive Literacy, with specific attention to empowering historically marginalized students. This framework presents four main learning goals: identity development, skill development, intellectual development, and criticality. Muhammad guides readers through the use of reflective questions while offering additional resources such as sample lessons and exemplary texts.

Pandya, Jessica Zacher
Exploring Critical Digital Literacy Practices: Everyday Video in a Dual Language Context
Routledge, 2019

> This text focuses on digital literacies developed and enacted through students' digital video production in a dual language school with few resources. With specific attention to English language learners, immigrant students, and students with special needs, Pandya examines the role of critical digital literacy

in developing students' agency and language toward social justice.

Wynter-Hoyte, Kamania, Eliza Braden, Michele Myers, Sanjuana C. Rodriguez, and Natasha Thornton
Revolutionary Love: Creating a Culturally Inclusive Literacy Classroom
Scholastic, 2022

> The authors challenge readers to move from deficit views of racism on children's learning toward an antiracist stance with a focus on "revolutionary love." In sharing their own personal and professional experiences teaching as a means of showing how to disrupt and unpack unconscious biases, they offer practices and guides on how to select diverse children's books and create meaningful reading and writing lessons for a classroom community that seeks to honor the knowledges, identities, and cultures that students and their families bring to school.

Developing Expertise in Children's Literature

Ada, Alma Flor
A Magical Encounter: Latino Children's Literature in the Classroom
Allyn & Bacon, 2003 (2nd ed.)

> Ada focuses on bringing attention to the ways in which literature can develop students' language(s), higher-level thinking, and creativity in the classroom, specifically highlighting classroom examples that utilize texts written by Latinx authors to empower Latinx children and expand the cultural understandings of non-Latinx children. Ada also provides extensive annotations of children's literature and young adult books by Latinx authors.

Crisp, Thomas, Suzanne M. Knezek, and Roberta Price Gardner, editors
Reading and Teaching with Diverse Nonfiction Children's Books: Representations and Possibilities
National Council of Teachers of English, 2021

> This edited collection features important contemporary conversations regarding diverse

children's books in K–8 classrooms, calling for teachers to step away from the traditional literary canon toward authentic representations of students' lives. By centering the experiences, histories, and cultures of historically marginalized populations, this book pushes toward new pedagogical possibilities. The collection also features practical tips, relevant texts, and other resources.

Dahlen, Sarah Park, and Paul Lai
Asian Americans in Story: Context, Collections, and Community Engagement with Children's and Young Adult Literature
ALA Editions, 2022

> Writing for a variety of readers, from scholars to librarians to teachers, the authors emphasize the value inherent in Asian American children's and young adult literature, specifically texts that celebrate Asian American heritage and inclusivity. First exploring the political and social histories of Asian Americans, the authors then dive into key themes and genres in Asian American literature. Included is a survey of authors and titles suitable for a variety of grade levels, including interviews with editors, librarians, and others.

Dahlen, Sarah Park, and Ebony Elizabeth Thomas, editors
Harry Potter and the Other: Race, Justice, and Difference in the Wizarding World
University Press of Mississippi, 2022

> This collection focuses on problematizing the representations of diverse and multicultural identities and communities in J. K. Rowling's *Harry Potter* series. Contributors examine and interrogate these representations across media forums, books, films, and the classroom, challenging readers to question how race and difference have shaped the world of wizardry, its justice system, and a generation of readers.

García, Marilisa Jiménez
Side by Side: US Empire, Puerto Rico, and the Roots of American Youth Literature and Culture
University Press of Mississippi, 2021

> In her comprehensive analysis of literary materials such as young adult literature, textbooks, comics, music, and more, García presents the contributions of Puerto Ricans to the literature and culture of American youth. In light of recent debates on diversity in children's and youth literature, as well as the stressed relationship between Puerto Rico and the United States, García pushes the reader to first problematize who is considered an expert and to resist essentializing narratives.

Sipe, Lawrence R.
Storytime: Young Children's Literary Understanding in the Classroom
Teachers College Press, 2008

> *Storytime* illustrates picturebook art as aesthetic object. Through his research and analysis of classroom conversations, Sipe presents a grounded theoretical model of young children's understanding of picturebooks, suggesting that children respond to picture storybook read-alouds in five different ways. Organized into three sections, the book takes readers on a journey to consider how picturebooks offer opportunities for literacy meaning making and offers implications for teaching and future research.

Thomas, Ebony Elizabeth
The Dark Fantastic: Race and the Imagination from Harry Potter to the Hunger Games
New York University Press, 2019

> In her book, Thomas presents readers with the concept of the "dark fantastic" to help us understand the role racial difference plays in shaping young adult and broader societal imagination. Thomas's book explores representations of race in four popular works of young adult fiction, offering analyses of the experiences of four Black girl characters within their respective stories. Thomas responds to problematic and essentialist representations by highlighting the worlds of fantasy that Youth of Color have imagined for themselves and offers new ways to examine and rethink literature collections.

Wolf, Shelby A., Karen Coats, Patricia Enciso, and Christine A. Jenkins, editors
Handbook of Research on Children's and Young Adult Literature
Routledge, 2010

> This collection brings together leading scholarship from the disciplines of education, English, and library and information sciences to examine children's and young adult literature. Through these varying lenses, this handbook illuminates different aspects of literacy, reading, texts, and contexts, offering perspectives on readers and reading literature in different contexts and introducing analytic frames for studying texts and the social contexts of literary study.

Enhancing Your Picturebook Pedagogy

Laminack, Lester L., and Kelly Stover
Reading to Make a Difference: Using Literature to Help Students Speak Freely, Think Deeply, and Take Action
Heinemann, 2019

> This book illuminates how educators can develop their teaching practices with diverse literature through more than simple exposure, providing examples of classroom practices, questions for reflection, and powerful literacy resources that teachers and educators can incorporate alongside purposeful teaching practices, from elementary to college-level classrooms.

Leland, Christine H., Mitzi Lewison, and Jerome C. Harste
Teaching Children's Literature: It's Critical!
Routledge, 2023 (3rd ed.)

> Intended for students, teachers, and teacher educators, this book offers numerous strategies for integrating children's literature across the curriculum and features examples of teachers implementing such critical literacy practices in their classrooms. In bridging the gap between theory and practice, this book directs the reader to a wealth of resources in the following forms: text sets, specific classroom invitations, professional development, and links to online resources.

López-Robertson, Julia
Celebrating Our Cuentos: Choosing and Using Latinx Literature in Elementary Classrooms
Scholastic, 2021

> López-Robertson calls for infusing literature by Latinx authors and illustrators in classrooms as a means to reflect the voices and experiences of students and as a window of insight into peoples from Spanish-speaking countries and communities. The book provides educators and families with tools and information to engage in and identify literature that illuminates cultural and linguistic authenticity and diversity. It also provides examples of how educators can engage in the literature through read-alouds, group discussion, reading and writing projects, and class lessons.

Ray, Katie Wood
In Pictures and in Words: Teaching the Qualities of Good Writing through Illustration Study
Heinemann, 2010

> *In Pictures and in Words* argues for providing students the information and tools they need to practice ownership and become decision makers in their writing. Through students' sample work, Ray documents how childrens' thinking and understanding are fostered as they engage in and explore illustrations. Her philosophies of composing and illustration further shape the suggestions she provides that encourage educators to think about how illustration offers ways for students to conceptualize and internalize aspects of craft, thinking, and meaning making through picture books.

Ryan, Caitlin L., and Jill M. Hermann-Wilmarth
Reading the Rainbow: LGBTQ-inclusive Literacy Instruction in the Elementary Classroom
Teachers College Press, 2018

> Ryan and Hermann-Wilmarth argue for LGBTQ-inclusive literacy teaching and meaningful learning in elementary school classrooms. Examining three

approaches, the book offers specific strategies, classroom examples, and recommended literature for engaging with LGBTQ-inclusive texts and teaching practices. Part 3 combines the first two approaches and challenges educators to move beyond monolithic stories of representation by incorporating intersectionality as a lens to further create inclusive classroom spaces. Designed to be interactive, the text also addresses potential challenges, pressures, and possibilities that teachers may face in varying contexts around these topics.

Sanden, Sherry, Cassandra Mattoon, and Sandra L. Osorio
Book Talk: Growing into Early Literacy through Read-Aloud Conversations
Teachers College Press, 2021

Book Talk brings together theories about literacy learning with the current contexts and realities of reading and talking with culturally and linguistically diverse young children, providing a practical guide for educators interested in engaging in book discussions that promote read-aloud experiences reflective of students' lives and the development of literacy skills. The authors also provide recommendations for designing a classroom reading environment, selecting books, and developing discussion materials and goals alongside curricular demands.

Serafini, Frank
Reading the Visual: An Introduction to Teaching Multimodal Literacy
Teachers College Press, 2013

This book provides an introduction to multimodality and visual literacy that includes tips on how to teach multimodal literacy. While presenting a range of texts from picturebooks to news reports, Serafini provides not only the theoretical foundations for such work but also the curricular and pedagogical frames. Included are multiple resources such as text sets, lesson plans, and analysis guides to aid teachers in engaging with multimodal literacies in their classrooms.

Notes

1. I use the term *People of Color* to reference interracial solidarity without centering the idea of interracial or ethnic conflict.

2. To (re)claim literature as sociopolitical art, I refrain from speaking of literature as something we use but instead as art to share, experience, respond to, discuss, make meaning of, critique, connect with, explore, ponder, interrogate, etc.

3. You'll notice that I reference the teaching as "our" or "we" at times. I do so to acknowledge the collaboration at work in both the teaching and the reflection. I found I as the researcher was learning through reflection during critical encounters with as much frequency as the classroom teachers.

4. Data and analysis also in part featured in Adu-Gyamfi et al. (2021), https://www.iastate digitalpress.com/tcse/article/id/11531/.

5. By Standardized English Print, I'm referring to the systematized and regularized variety of printed (and spoken) English that is privileged in most academic settings.

6. Data and analysis featured in "'It Might Be Different from What We Think': Critical Encounters with Linguistically Diverse Picturebooks in an Elementary Classroom" by Reid et al. (2022).

References

Ada, A. F. (2003). *A magical encounter: Latino children's literature in the classroom* (2nd ed.). Allyn & Bacon.

Adu-Gyamfi, M., Zapata, A., & Reid, S. (2021). "Who was scared?" Entering into reflection toward change as critical social educators. *The Critical Social Educator 1*(1). https://doi.org/10.31274/tcse.11531

Anzaldúa, G. (1987). How to tame a wild tongue. *Borderlands/La Frontera: The new mestiza*.

Ascenzi-Moreno, L. (2018). Translanguaging and responsive assessment adaptations: Emergent bilingual readers through the lens of possibility. *Language Arts, 95*(6), 355–69.

Baker, J. A. (2006). Contributions of teacher–child relationships to positive school adjustment during elementary school. *Journal of School Psychology, 44*(3), 211–29.

Baumann, J. F. (2014). Vocabulary and reading comprehension: The nexus of meaning. In S. E. Israel & G. G. Duffy (Eds.), *Handbook of research on reading comprehension* (pp. 347–70). Taylor & Francis.

Baumann, J. F., Ware, D., & Edwards, E. C. (2007). "Bumping into spicy, tasty words that catch your tongue": A formative experiment on vocabulary instruction. *The Reading Teacher, 61*(2), 108–22.

Bishop, R. S. (1990). Mirrors, windows, and sliding glass doors. *Perspectives: Choosing and Using Books for the Classroom, 6*(3), ix–xi.

Bomer, K. (2021). Leaving behind the "learning loss": Loving and learning from the ways students talk, write, and draw right now. *Language Arts, 98*(6), 352–59.

Bomer, R., & Bomer, K. (2001). *For a better world: Reading and writing for social Action*. Heinemann.

Britton, J. (1970). *Language and learning*. Penguin.

Brown, S., & Hao, L. (Eds.). (2022). *Multimodal literacies in young emergent bilinguals: Beyond print-centric practices*. Multilingual Matters.

Callow, J. (2008). Show me: Principles for assessing students' visual literacy. *The Reading Teacher, 61*(8), 616–26.

Canagarajah, S. (2012). *Translingual practice: Global Englishes and cosmopolitan relations*. Routledge.

Cappello, M., & Walker, N. T. (2016). Visual thinking strategies: Teachers' reflections on closely reading complex visual texts within the disciplines. *The Reading Teacher, 70*(3), 317–25.

Cowan, K., & Albers, P. (2006). Semiotic representations: Building complex literacy practices through the arts. *The Reading Teacher, 60*(2), 124–37.

De Los Ríos, C. V., Seltzer, K., & Molina, A. (2021). "Juntos somos fuertes": Writing participatory corridos of solidarity through a critical translingual approach. *Applied Linguistics, 42*(6), 1070–82.

DeNicolo, C. P., & Fránquiz, M. E. (2006). "Do I have to say it?": Critical encounters with multicultural children's literature. *Language Arts, 84*(2), 157–70.

Duke, N. K. (2000). For the rich it's richer: Print experiences and environments offered to children in very low- and very high-socioeconomic status first-grade classrooms. *American Educational Research Journal, 37*(2), 441–78.

Duncan-Andrade, J. (2009). Note to educators: Hope required when growing roses in concrete. *Harvard Educational Review, 79*(2), 181–94.

Eeds, M., & Peterson, R. (1991). Teacher as curator: Learning to talk about literature. *The Reading Teacher, 45*(2), 118–26.

Elliot, Z. (2016). Inclusivity and indie authors: The case for community-based publishing. *Urban Library Journal, 22*(2), art. 4.

Espinosa, C. M., & Ascenzi-Moreno, L. (2021). *Rooted in strength: Using translanguaging to grow multilingual readers and writers*. Scholastic.

Fleischer, C., & Garcia, A. (2020). *Everyday advocacy: Teachers who change the literacy narrative*. Norton.fo

Flores, N., & Rosa, J. (2015). Undoing appropriateness: Raciolinguistic ideologies and language diversity in education. *Harvard Educational Review*, 85(2), 149–71.

Fontanella-Nothom, O. (2019). "Why do we have different skins anyway?" Exploring race in literature with preschool children. *Multicultural Perspectives*, 21(1), 11–18.

Fox, D. L., & Short, K. G. (2003). *Stories matter: The complexity of cultural authenticity in children's literature*. National Council of Teachers of English.

García, O., & Kleifgen, J. A. (2020). Translanguaging and literacies. *Reading Research Quarterly*, 55(4), 553–71.

Heath, S. B. (1983). *Ways with words: Language, life, and work in communities and classrooms*. Cambridge University Press.

Hill, J. H. (2009). *The everyday language of white racism*. Wiley.

Huyck, D., & Dahlen, S. P. (2019, June 19). Diversity in children's books 2018. *sarahpark.com* blog. Created in consultation with Edith Campbell, Molly Beth Griffin, K. T. Horning, Debbie Reese, Ebony Elizabeth Thomas, and Madeline Tyner, with statistics compiled by the Cooperative Children's Book Center, School of Education, University of Wisconsin-Madison: https://ccbc.education.wisc.edu/literature-resources/ccbc-diversity-statistics/books-by-about-poc-fnn/. Retrieved from https://readingspark.wordpress.com/2019/06/19/picture-this-diversity-in-childrens-books-2018-infographic/

Jones, S. P. (2020). Ending curriculum violence. *Teaching Tolerance*, 64(1), 47–50. https://static1.squarespace.com/static/5c8734287eb88c4d76aef6cc/t/5f8de7230c18e7474d4b52bc/160313 5273863/Ending+Curriculum+Violence+Teaching+Tolerance.pdf

Kissel, B. (2023). Struggles that should never be normalized: Politics, policy, and the prohibition of thought. *Language Arts*, 100(5), 408–15.

Langer, J. A. (1990). The process of understanding: Reading for literary and informative purposes. *Research in the Teaching of English*, 24(3), 229–60.

Langer, J. A. (1994). Focus on research: A response-based approach to reading literature. *Language Arts*, 71(3), 203–11.

Larrick, N. (1965, September 11). The all-white world of children's books. *Saturday Review*, 48(11), 63–65.

Leander, K., & Boldt, G. (2013). Rereading "A pedagogy of multiliteracies": Bodies, texts, and emergence. *Journal of Literacy Research*, 45(1), 22–46.

Leland, C. H., & Lewison, M. (with Harste, J. C.). (2017). *Teaching children's literature: It's critical!* (2nd ed.) Routledge.

Lifshitz, J. (2016, July 7). Part 1: Having students analyze our classroom libraries to see how diverse it is. *The Open Book Blog,* Lee & Low Books. https://blog.leeandlow.com/2016/07/07/part-1-having-students-analyze-our-classroom-library-to-see-how-diverse-it-is/

Luke, A. (2013). Defining critical literacy. In J. Pandya & J. Ávila (Eds.), *Moving critical literacies forward: A new look at praxis across contexts* (pp. 19–31). Routledge.

MacKay, S. H. (with Salazar, K.). (2021). *Story workshop: New possibilities for young writers*. Heinemann.

Martínez, R. A. (2010). "Spanglish" as literacy tool: Toward an understanding of the potential role of Spanish-English code-switching in the development of academic literacy. *Research in the Teaching of English*, 45(2), 124–49.

Muhammad, G. (2020). *Cultivating genius: An equity framework for culturally and historically responsive literacy*. Scholastic.

Muhammad, G., (2023). *Unearthing joy: A guide to culturally and historically responsive teaching and learning.* Scholastic.

Myers, C. (2014, March 16). The apartheid of children's literature. *The New York Times.* www.nytimes.com/2014/03/16/opinion/sunday/the-apartheid-of-childrens-literature.html

Myers, W. D. (1986, November 9). Children's books: I actually thought we would revolutionize the industry. *New York Times Book Review*, Sec. 7, p. 50.

Myers, W. D. (2014, March 15). Where are the people of color in children's books? *The New York Times.* www.nytimes.com/2014/03/16/opinion/sunday/where-are-the-people-of-color-in-childrens-books.html

Nichols, M. (2006). *Comprehension through conversation: The power of purposeful talk in the reading workshop.* Heinemann.

Pantaleo, S. (2013). Revisiting Rosenblatt's aesthetic response through *The Arrival. The Australian Journal of Language and Literacy, 36*(3), 125–34.

Ray, K. W. (2010). *In pictures and in words: Teaching the qualities of good writing through illustration study.* Heinemann.

Reese, D. (2007). Proceed with caution: Using Native American folktales in the classroom. *Language Arts, 84*(3), 245–56.

Reese, D. (2018). Critical Indigenous literacies: Selecting and using children's books about Indigenous peoples. *Language Arts, 95*(6), 389–93.

Reid, S. D., Zapata, A., Adu-Gyamfi, M., & Hoffmann, W. (2022). "It might be different from what we think": Critical encounters with linguistically diverse picturebooks in an elementary classroom. *Language Arts, 100*(2), 122–34.

Rodríguez, N. N., & Swalwell, K. (2021). *Social studies for a better world: An anti-oppressive approach for elementary educators.* Norton.

Rosenblatt, L. (1995). *Literature as exploration.* 1938. Modern Language Association.

Roser, N. L., Hoffman, J. V., Labbo, L. D., & Farest, C. (1992). Language charts: A record of story time talk. *Language Arts, 69*(1), 44–52.

Roser, N. L., & Martinez, M. G. (with Yokota, J., & O'Neal, S.) (Eds.). (2005). *What a character! Character study as a guide to literary meaning making in grades K–8.* International Reading Association.

Ryan, C. L., & Hermann-Wilmarth, J. M. (2018). *Reading the rainbow: LGBTQ-inclusive literacy instruction in the elementary classroom.* Teachers College Press.

Serafini, F. (2015). Multimodal literacy: From theories to practices. *Language Arts, 92*(6), 412–23.

Short, K. G. (2011). *Strategies for reading and discussing paired books.* World of Words, The University of Arizona. https://wowlit.org/blog/2011/02/28/strategies-for-reading-and-discussing-paired-books/

Sipe, L. R. (2011). The art of the picturebook. In S. A. Wolf (Ed.), *Handbook of research on children's and young adult literature* (pp 238–52). Routledge.

Thomas, E. E. (2016). Stories still matter: Rethinking the role of diverse children's literature today. *Language Arts, 94*(2), 112–19.

Thomas, E. E. (2019). *The dark fantastic: Race and the imagination from Harry Potter to the Hunger Games.* New York University Press.

Turner, B. (2019). Teaching kindness isn't enough. *Learning for Justice, 63.* https://www.learningforjustice.org/magazine/fall-2019/teaching-kindness-isnt-enough

Vasquez, V. M., Janks, H., & Comber, B. (2019). Critical literacy as a way of being and doing. *Language Arts, 96*(5), 300–311.

Veronica. (2017, May 22). Classroom library assessment: How culturally responsive is your library? *The Open Book Blog,* Lee & Low Books. https://blog.leeandlow.com/2017/05/22/

classroom-library-assessment-how-culturally-responsive-is-your-classroom-library/

Yenawine, P. (2013). *Visual thinking strategies: Using art to deepen learning across school disciplines.* Harvard Education Press.

Yoon, B., Simpson, A., & Haag, C. (2010). Assimilation ideology: Critically examining underlying messages in multicultural literature. *Journal of Adolescent & Adult Literacy, 54*(2), 109–18.

Yoon, H. S., & Templeton, T. N. (2022). Reflecting, representing, and expanding the narrative(s) in early childhood curriculum. *Urban Education*, 1–31. https://doi.org/10.1177/00420859221097893

Young, V. A., & Martinez, A. (Eds.). (2011). *Code-meshing as world English: Pedagogy, policy, performance.* National Council of Teachers of English.

Zapata, A. (2020). Cultivating a critical translingual landscape in the elementary language arts classroom. *Language Arts, 97*(6), 384–90.

Zapata, A. (2022). (Re)animating children's aesthetic experiences with/through literature: Critically curating picturebooks as sociopolitical art. *The Reading Teacher, 76*(1), 84–91.

Zapata, A., Fugit, M., & Moss, D. (2017). Awakening socially just mindsets through visual thinking strategies and diverse picturebooks. *Journal of Children's Literature, 43*(2), 62–69.

Zapata, A., King, C., King, L., & Kleekamp, M. (2019). Thinking with race-conscious perspectives: Critically selecting children's picture books depicting slavery. *Multicultural Perspectives, 21*(1), 25–32.

Zapata, A., Kleekamp, M. C., & King, C. (2018, December). Expanding the canon: How diverse literature can transform literacy learning. *Literacy Leadership Brief.* International Literacy Association.

Zentella, A. C. (1998). *Growing up bilingual: Puerto Rican children in New York.* Blackwell.

Index

The letter *f* following a page locator denotes a figure, and the letters QR indicate a QR code will be found in the text.

Abran paso a los patitos [Make Way for Ducklings] (McClosky), 1–2
activism, transformative, 18, 21
Ada, Alma Flor, 3–4
Adu-Gyamfi, Mary, 47, 149
aesthetic responses
    book floods in centering, 35
    evoking, 15–16
    visual thinking strategies (VTS), 43*t*
Alko, Selina, 57–59, 61, 74–78
Amini, Mehrdokht, 132
anti-Blackness, challenging, 17–18
anti-oppressive philosophy, 17
Anzaldúa, Gloria, 94–95, 102–105
Arroz con Leche: Popular Songs and Rhymes from Latin America (Delacre), 2
art, picturebook as sociopolitical, 15–16, 16QR
arts-based integration, 32, 32QR
Askar, S., 84–85
assessment, 144–145
assumptions, deconstructing with critical encounters, 131–132

Bang, Molly, 41
Baumann, Jim, 90
bilingual picturebook authors and illustrators, 2–5
Bishop, Rudine Sims, 5
Black Indigenous People of Color (BIPOC), 108QR
blackness, challenging misconceptions of, 107–108
blogs, resources to support CLRF, 48
Bomer, Randy, 142
book awards
    bilingual picturebook authors and illustrators, 4
    resources to support CLRF, 54
book floods

    aesthetic responses, 69
    classroom practice of, 34–36
    conferring with readers during, 67–68
    critical noticings, 69
    example, 36
    family study, 65–70
    focused or closed, 36, 37
    immigration and border-crossings, 37, 92
    launching, 65–70
    literary arrows, 66–67
    open-ended, 36
    whole-group share, 68–70
Britton, James, 44
Brown, Monica, 4
Brownie Book magazine, 10
Build Your Stack (NCTE), 12
Buitrago, Jairo, 37
Bunting, Eve, 95

The Case for Loving: The Fight for Interracial Marriage (Alko), 57–59, 61, 74–78
Cepeda, Joe, 111
children
    exclusion, remedying feelings of, 144
    practices supporting critical encounters, 80–81, 109, 134–135
    they're not to young to talk about race, 61QR, 62*f*
    valuing as knowing and capable, 61–62
children's literature, diversity in. *See also* picturebooks, diverse
    absence of, 10–11
    bilingual picturebook authors and illustrators, 2–5
    history of calls for inclusion of, 10–13
    movement for, 12–13
classroom libraries, 38, 146–147
classroom practices for enacting a CLRF
    arts-based integration approaches, 32
    book floods, 34–36
    early reading, support an expansive view of, 63–64

elicit in-depth talk from readers, 88–90
foundational, 32
grow vocabulary for complex issue discussion, 90–92
language and identity relationships, explore, 119–121
language charts, 32
multilingual and multimodal literature response, 43–46
reader-response notebooks, 32
scaffold picture reading, 40–43
summary, 140
support an expansive view of language, 118–119
value young children as knowing and capable, 61–62
wide and varied collections, 36–40
Colón, Raúl, 4, 41
color blindness, language of, 59QR
commitments for enacting a CLRF
　critical encounters with text, 20–21
　literature-based instruction, 18–20
　overview, 22*f*
　summary, 140
　teachers' critical stance, 17–18
Comprehension through Conversation (Nichols), 143
conditions for enacting a CLRF
　evoke aesthetic response, 15–16
　invite critical interrogation, 16
　overview, 22*f*
　summary, 140
Cooke, Trish, 68
Cooperative Children's Book Center (CCBC), 10–11
critical encounters
　assumptions, deconstructing, 131–132
　inferring critical meaning from illustrations, 74–78
　interrogating skin shade through visual thinking, 70–73
　language and identity, making claims into, 132–134
　language differences, rethinking reading of, 128–131
　learning from, 80, 108–109, 134
　misconceptions of blackness, 107–108
　power in illustration, 105–107
　questioning themes of meritocracy, 102–105
　valuing, 20–21
　with young children, practices supporting, 80–81, 109, 134–135
Critical Literature Response Framework (CLRF)
　components of the, 14
　described, 14
　foundational beliefs and practices, 46
　the heart of, 20

Mariposa Street School, 29–30
purpose of, 22, 138–139
teachers featured in the text, 25–29
Critical Literature Response Framework (CLRF), enacting a
　assessment, 144–145
　challenges of, 138–139
　classroom practices for, 32–46, 140
　collaboration and outreach for, 141–144, 141*f*
　commitments for, 17–22, 22*f*, 140
　conditions for, 15–17, 15*f*, 22*f*, 140
　to effect change, 139
　questions about, answered, 144–147
　time requirements, 145
　uncomfortable comments, responding to, 146
Cultivating Genius (Muhammed), 37
curriculum violence, 8–9

Dahlen, Sarah Park, 11
Dear Primo: A Letter to My Cousin (Tonatiuh), 4, 84
De Colores and Other Latin-American Folk Songs for Children (Orozco), 2
Delacre, Lulu, 2
Diversity Jedi, 13
Draw (Colón), 41
Drawn Together (Lê), 57
Dreamers (Morales), 37, 83, 88–89, 94–97, 99, 105–107
Dubois, W. E. B., 10

Ebarvia, Tricia, 12
Elliot, Zetta, 39
equity, multilingual and multimodal literature invitations for, 45
exclusion, remedying feelings of, 144

Family Pictures / Cuadros de familia (Garza), 3
family study in a first grade classroom, CLRF and
　book flood, 65–70
　classroom atmosphere, 59–60
　focused literature exploration, 64–65
　picturebooks for family study, 81–82
　picture reading example, 57–58
family study in a first grade classroom, CLRF classroom practices
　early reading, support an expansive view of, 63–64
　value young children as knowing and capable, 61–62
family study in a first grade classroom, CLRF critical encounters

inferring critical meaning from illustration, 74–78
interrogating skin shade through visual thinking, 70–73
From Far Away (Munsch & Askar), 84–85
feedback, 32
Fleischer, Cathy, 143
Flores, N., 124
Friends from the Other Side / Amigos del Otro Lado (Anzaldúa), 94–95, 102–105
Front Desk (Yang), 86, 99, 104
Fugit, Misha, 142

Garcia, Antero, 143
Garza, Carmen Lomas, 3
Germán, Lorena, 12
Golden Domes and Silver Lanterns: A Muslim Book of Colors (Khan), 132
Goldstein, Marva Cappello, 43
González, Adrianna Ybarra, 149
Gonzalez, Monica, 142
grammar elements, teaching, 36

Hadestown, 97–98
Harrison, Vashti, 70
#DisruptTexts, 12, 143
#OwnVoices, 6, 37, 39
hashtags professional resources, 49
Haworth, Corinna Bliss, 142
Hermann-Wilmarth, Jill M., 65QR
Hey You! C;mere! A Poetry Slam (Swados & Cepeda), 111–113, 115–116, 120, 128–130
Higuera, D. B., 94
Humanizing Stories, 5
Huyck, David, 11

identities, reading, 122–124
identity, language, and power relationships, 112–113
identity and language
  exploring relationships, 119–124
  making claims into, 132–134
  self-portraits, 126–128, 127*f*
illustrations. *See also* picture reading
  inferring critical meaning from, 74–78
  motifs and symbols in, 96–97
  reading power in, 105–107
imagination gap, 69
immigration and border-crossings in a fourth grade classroom, CLRF and

book floods, 37, 92
classroom atmosphere, 86–88
focused literature exploration, 83, 92–102
identifying relevant connections across texts, 83–85
literary arrows, 93
motifs and symbols in illustrations, 96–97
musical pairings, 97–98
picturebooks exploring immigration, 109–110
theme generation, 84–85
immigration and border-crossings in a fourth grade classroom, CLRF classroom practices
  elicit in-depth talk from readers, 88–90
  grow vocabulary for complex issue discussion, 90–92
immigration and border-crossings in a fourth grade classroom, CLRF connections
  current events, 100–102
  independent and shared reading, 99
  known concepts, 99–100
  students' lives, 100–102
immigration and border-crossings in a fourth grade classroom, CLRF critical encounters
  challenging misconceptions of blackness, 107–108
  learning from, 108–109
  questioning themes of meritocracy, 102–105
  reading power in illustration, 105–107
in-depth talk, eliciting from readers, 88–90
The International Literacy Association (ILA), 13
internet feeds, resources to support CLRF, 48–49
interrogation, inviting critical, 16
invitations, literary, 34–35, 45
Isadora, Rachel, 68, 118–120

Jaleel, Aaliya, 67
Jimenez, Laura, 5
Jones, Stephanie P., 8
The Journey (Sanna), 83, 106

Kahn, Hena, 67–68
Keats, Ezra Jack, 2
Kelt, Deb, 142
Khan, Hena, 132
King, LaGarrett, 10
Kleven, Elisa, 2

Lai, Remi, 99
Laínez, René Colato, 37, 85
Lánger, Judith, 86
language, identity, and power relationships, 112–113

language, supporting an expansive view of, 118–119
language and identity
    exploring relationships, 119–121
    making claims into, 132–134
    self-portraits, 126–128, 127f
language charts, 32
language differences, rethinking reading of, 128–131
language maps and lists, 124–125, 125f
Larrick, Nancy, 10
The Last Cuentista (Higuera), 94
Lê, Minh, 57
LGBTQ+ people, 65QR
libraries, classroom, 38, 146–147
Lifshitz, Jessica, 38
linguistic toolkits, documenting, 124–125
literacy
    impelling action through, 16–17
    multilingual and multimodal, 43–46
    visual, 42
literary arrows, 34–35, 66–67, 93
literature
    basic principles as teachers of, 46
    multilingual and multimodal response to, 43–46
    valuing critical encounters with, 20–21
literature exploration in a fifth grade classroom, CLRF and
    assumptions, interrogating, 113
    classroom atmosphere, 114–117
    identities, reading, 122–124
    initial literature response discussions, 112–113
    language, identity, and power relationships, 112–113
    language and identity assumptions, resisting, 122–124
    language and identity self-portraits, 126–128, 127f
    language maps and lists, 124–125, 125f
    linguistically diverse picturebooks as mentor texts, 121–122
    linguistic toolkits, documenting, 124–125
    multimodal and multilingual features of picturebooks, 112–113
    multimodal and multilingual literature response, 122–128
    picturebooks for language study, 135–136
    poetry, listening to and visualizing, 111–113
    positioning students as writers and illustrators, 117
    race, imagining, 122–123
    voices, reading, 122–124
literature exploration in a fifth grade classroom, CLRF classroom practices

expansive view of language, support an, 118–119
language and identity relationships, explore, 119–121
literature exploration in a fifth grade classroom, CLRF critical encounters
    assumptions, deconstructing, 131–132
    language and identity, making claims into, 132–134
    language differences, rethinking reading of, 128–131
    learning from, 134
Little Night (Morales), 4

A Magical Encounter (Ada), 3–4
Make Way for Ducklings (McClosky), 1–2
maps and lists, language, 124–125, 125f
Mariposa Street School, 29–30
Marisol McDonald Doesn't Match (Brown), 4
Martínez, Ramón, 44
McClosky, Robert, 1–2
McNair, Jonda, 10
Méndez, Consuelo, 102
mentoring, transformative act of, 132–133
mentor texts, 35
meritocracy, questioning themes of, 102–105
mirrors, windows, and sliding glass doors, 5, 34
mock languaging, 129–131
moral and ethical imperative
    for sharing diverse picturebooks, 138
    for teachers, 17
Morales, Magaly, 4
Morales, Yuyi, 4, 37, 41, 83, 88–89, 94–97, 99, 105–107
Moss, Daryl, 142
Muhammed, Gholdy, 37, 138
multilingual, term use, 44
multilingual and multimodal literacies, 43–46
Munsch, R. N., 84–85
musical pairings, 97–98
Myers, Christopher, 12
Myers, Walter Dean, 10, 12
In My Family / En mi familia (Garza), 3
Under My Hijab (Kahn), 67–68
My Shoes and I (Laínez), 37

Nichols, Maria, 143
From North to South (Laínez), 85
notebooks, reader-response, 32
Nyong'o, Lupita, 70–73

One Green Apple (Bunting), 95
Orozco, José-Luis, 2

Oxenbury, Helen, 68

Pancho Rabbit and the Coyote: A Migrant's Tale (Tonatiuh), 37
Parker, Kimberly N., 12
People of Color (POC), 108QR
picturebook collections
    building wide and varied, 36–40
    on family study, 81–82
    focused, 94
    on immigration, 109–110
    on language study, 135–136
    text selection process, 93–96
picturebook pedagogy, 152–153
picturebooks, diverse. *See also* children's literature, diversity in
    critical work of advocating for, 7
    curtain metaphor, 5–6
    impel action/praxis, 16–17
    invite critical interrogation, 16
    limitations of status quo Eurocentric texts, 6, 9
    as mentor texts, 121–122
    as mirrors, windows, and sliding glass doors, 5, 34
    moral and ethical imperative for sharing, 138
    multimodal and multilingual features of, 112–113
    selecting, 36–40
    as sociopolitical art, 15–16, 16QR
    transformative nature of, 6–7, 8
picture reading
    deconstructing assumptions when, 131–132
    example, 63, 88–89, 96–97, 112–113, 115–116
    inferring critical meaning from, 74–78
    motifs and symbols in, 96–97
    multimodal, 63
    reading power in, 105–107
    scaffolding, 40–43
    tell me more approach, 88–89
In Pictures and in Words (Ray), 41
Picture This: How Pictures Work (Bang), 41
Pie in the Sky (Lai), 99
pleasure, reading for, 15
poetry, listening to and visualizing, 111–113
power, identity, and language relationships, 112–113
power, reading in illustrations, 105–107
Preparing Teachers with Knowledge of Children's and Young Adult Literature (NCTE), xv–xviii, 7, 9, 14, 17–21, 46

professional resources, favorite picturebooks for
    family study, 81–82
    immigration, 109–110
    language study, 135–136
professional resources for learning more about
    #OwnVoices, 39QR
    arts integration resources, 32QR
    BIPOC (Black Indigenous People of Color), 108QR
    Brownie Book magazine, 10
    The Case for Loving: The Fight for Interracial Marriage, 59QR
    developing expertise in children's literature, 150–152
    elements of visual design, 42
    ending racism, 61QR
    enhancing picturebook pedagogy, 152–153
    imagination gap, 69QR
    language of color blindness, 59QR
    launching your critical literacy journey, 149–150
    LGBTQ+ people, 65QR
    literature response, 31
    multilingual and multimodal literacy, 45
    POC (People of Color), 108QR
    racial politics, 59QR
    "Your Kids Aren't Too Young to Talk about Race: Resource Roundup," 61QR
professional resources to support CLRF
    blogs, 48
    feeds, 48–49
    hashtags, 49
    national book awards, 54
    professional reading, books and research, 52–54
    publishing houses, 50–52
    social media, 48–50
    text selection, 52
    websites, 49–50
publishers, expanding representation by, 38
publishing houses, resources to support CLRF, 50–52

Qualls, Sean, 57

race, imagining, 122–123
race, they're not to young to talk about, 61QR, 62*f*
racial politics, 59QR
racial sterotyping, childrens literature furthering, 10–12
racism
    blackness, challenging misconceptions of, 107–108
    challenging, 17–18

ending, 61QR
skin shade, interrogating through visual thinking, 70–73
Ray, Katie Wood, 41
reader-response notebooks, 32
readers, adult, 36
reading
    aesthetic, 15–16
    early, multimedia in, 63–64
    for pleasure, 15
    repeated, 35
    supporting an expansive view of early, 63–64
Reading the Rainbow (Ryan & Hermann-Wilmarth), 65QR
Reese, Debbie, 5–6, 11
Reid, Sarah, 47
Rodríguez, N. N., 17
Rosa, J., 124
Roser, Nancy, 34
Ryan, Caitlin L., 65QR

Sanna, Francesca, 83, 106
Santat, Dan, 63
self-portraits, language and identity, 126–128, 127*f*
Short, Kathy, 36
Sipe, Larry, 40
Sis, P., 83
skin shade, interrogating through visual thinking, 70–73
social justice, 16–18
social media
    bilingual picturebook authors and illustrators, 5
    focus on literature for children, 5, 143
    movement for better representation in literature, 12–13
    resources to support CLRF, 48–50
So Much! (Cooke), 68
storyworlds, immersive experiences in, 86–87
Sulwe (Nyong'o), 70–73
Swados, Elizabeth, 111
Swados & Cepeda, 111–113, 115–116, 120, 128–130
Swalwell, K., 17

teachers
    courage to step into discomfort, 20–21
    decentering as expert and authority, 20–21
    developing a critical stance, 17–18
    humility, benefits of, 21
    of literature, basic principles for, 46
    moral and ethical imperative, 17
    transformative activist stance, 18, 21
teaching
    grammar elements, 36
    literature-based instruction, 18–20
    picturebook pedagogy, resources on, 152–153
    social justice-oriented approaches to, 17–18
Teaching Tolerance (Jones), 8
text selection, resources to support CLRF, 52
Thomas, Ebony Elizabeth, 5, 11, 69
Tonatiuh, Duncan, 4, 37, 84, 104
Torres, Julia E., 12
translanguaging, 44
Two White Rabbits (Buitrago & Yockteng), 37

Un día de nieve [Snowy Day] (Keats), 2
Undocumented: A Worker's Fight (Tonatiuh), 104
Unearthing Joy (Muhammed), 37

Valdez-Gainer, Nancy, 142
Van Horn, Selena, 142
Velasquez, Eric, 4
visual design, 42
visual literacy, 42
visual thinking strategies (VTS), 42–43, 70–73
Visual Thinking Strategies Protocol, Adapted, 43*t*
vocabulary, growing for complex issue discussion, 90–92
voices, reading, 122–124

The Wall (Sis), 83
website resources to support CLRF, 49–50
whole-group share, book floods, 68–70
writers
    positioning students as, 117
    transformative act of mentoring, 132–133

Yang, Kelly, 86, 99, 104
Yo, Jo! (Isadora), 68, 118–120
Yockteng, Rafael, 37
Yoon, B., 96

Author

Angie Zapata, associate professor of language and literacies education at the University of Missouri, is a longtime teacher, teacher educator, and researcher. Through collaborative inquiry partnerships with practicing and inservice preK–12 teachers, her research and teaching highlight classroom experiences featuring picturebooks with diverse representation, and how and what translingual and transmodal literacies are produced in these moments. Zapata's work is guided by her experiences growing up bilingual in Texas as a daughter of immigrant parents from Perú, as well as by deep commitments to centering anti-oppressive and justice-oriented language and literacies experiences in the classroom that nurture more inclusive schooling experiences for racialized bi/multilingual/multidialectal children and youth. In addition to being a picturebook enthusiast and researcher, Zapata can be described as a pug lady and gardener.

This book was typeset in Adobe Caslon Pro and PT Serif by Barbara Frazier.

Typefaces used on the cover include
Avenir Next Medium, Avenir LT Com 65 Medium,
Chronicle Display, and Norwester.

The book was printed on 50-lb., white offset paper.

Printed in the USA
CPSIA information can be obtained
at www.ICGtesting.com
JSHW060603040124
54750JS00004B/4

9 780814 101612